The Schema of the Theory of Reification

Historical Materialism Book Series

The Historical Materialism Book Series is a major publishing initiative of the radical left. The capitalist crisis of the twenty-first century has been met by a resurgence of interest in critical Marxist theory. At the same time, the publishing institutions committed to Marxism have contracted markedly since the high point of the 1970s. The Historical Materialism Book Series is dedicated to addressing this situation by making available important works of Marxist theory. The aim of the series is to publish important theoretical contributions as the basis for vigorous intellectual debate and exchange on the left.

The peer-reviewed series publishes original monographs, translated texts, and reprints of classics across the bounds of academic disciplinary agendas and across the divisions of the left. The series is particularly concerned to encourage the internationalization of Marxist debate and aims to translate significant studies from beyond the English-speaking world.

For a full list of titles in the Historical Materialism Book Series available in paperback from Haymarket Books, visit: www.haymarketbooks.org/series_collections/1-historical-materialism.

The Schema of the Theory of Reification

Wataru Hiromatsu

Translated by
John Hocking

with an introduction by
Makoto Katsumori

Haymarket Books
Chicago, IL

First published in 2022 by Brill Academic Publishers, The Netherlands
© 2022 Koninklijke Brill NV, Leiden, The Netherlands

Published in paperback in 2025 by
Haymarket Books
P.O. Box 180165
Chicago, IL 60618
773-583-7884
www.haymarketbooks.org

ISBN: 978-1-64259-923-7

Distributed to the trade in the US through Consortium Book Sales and
Distribution (www.cbsd.com) and internationally through Ingram
Publisher Services International (www.ingramcontent.com).

This book was published with the generous support of Lannan
Foundation, Wallace Action Fund, and the Marguerite Casey Foundation.

Special discounts are available for bulk purchases by organizations and
institutions. Please call 773-583-7884 or email info@haymarketbooks.org
for more information.

Cover art and design by David Mabb. Cover art is a detail from *Construct
13, William Morris, Willow Boughs / Lyubov Popova, Untitled Textile Design*,
paint and wallpaper mounted on linen (2006). Collection of Barts Health
NHS Trust.

Printed in the United States.

Library of Congress Cataloging-in-Publication data is available.

Contents

Translator's Preface

With the exception of the book cover, the title page and this preface, Japanese names are given in the Japanese order i.e. with the surname first.

In the original, Chapters I and II have endnotes, Chapter III and the Epilogue have footnotes, Chapter IV has both in-text notes and footnotes, and Chapter V has no notes. In the translation, I have decided, for convenience and consistency, to use footnotes throughout, except for Chapter IV where I have maintained the in-text references and footnotes.

The expressions 唯物史観／唯物史論 (materialist history) and 史的唯物論 (historical materialism), are both used. Although they refer to the same thing I have strictly translated each expression according to this differentiation i.e. 唯物史観／唯物史論 as "materialist history" and 史的唯物論 as "historical materialism".

As is evident from the text, I have followed a close style of translation. This provides, I believe, the best reproduction of the writer's "voice" and of her or his particular literary style. I have not used the standard English translations of Marx and Engels, Heidegger etc. preferring to translate directly from the Japanese in order to maintain the Japanese perspective and style.

Material contained within double square brackets (i.e. ⟦ ⟧) is material inserted by the translator. Similarly, material prefaced by the abbreviation Tr. is material inserted by the translator. Material contained within single square brackets (i.e. [ ]) and single brackets (i.e. ( )) is material parenthesised by Hiromatsu.

For those unfamiliar with German, in the footnotes Bd. stands for Vol. (i.e. volume), S. stands for p. (i.e. page) Aufl stands for Ed. (i.e. Edition), and vgl stands for cf.

The translation of the German on page 162 was provided by Evi Ruhle. Ray Hocking provided assistance with the diagram on page 204.

A number of people have been of help and support during this project. First and foremost I wish to thank Dr. Yasuhiko Watanabe. He carefully read the entire manuscript, and his knowledge and meticulousness were of great help. I would also like to thank Professor Raj Pandey for support and deep friendship; amongst other things, she introduced me to Professor Harry Harootunian. I wish to thank Professor Harootunian for reading a first draft of the epilogue and for his encouragement to continue on with the project. I wish also to thank him for introducing me to Sebastian Budgen at *Historical Materialism* who read the first draft translation of the epilogue as part of the vetting process for publication of the book as part of the *Historical Materialism* series with Brill.

Professor Harootunian also introduced me to Dr. Elena Lange and Professor Raji Steineck at the University of Zurich. Professor Steineck kindly provided comments on part of the epilogue translation. In addition, he introduced me to Professor Makoto Katsumori. I wish to thank Professor Katsumori for providing comments on the first draft of the epilogue translation and for writing the introduction to the book, and for his general encouragement of the project as a whole. He is the leading authority on Hiromatsu. He also introduced me to Dr. Watanabe, for which I am extremely grateful.

I am extremely grateful to those who have read all or parts of the translation. It goes without saying, however, that the final responsibility for errors or infelicities rests with me.

I wish to thank Jennifer Obdam at Brill. She cheerfully and expertly brought the project to fruition. I also wish to thank Danny Hayward at *Historical Materialism*. He was always efficient, prompt, and a pleasure to deal with; he also did the Index for me. Thanks are also due to Noortje Maranus who guided me through the process of proofreading. I also wish to thank Sebastian Budgen, Dr Watanabe and Professor Gavin Walker at McGill University for clearing the way with the Japanese publisher; a critical task.

Lastly, I would like to express my thanks to friends who have provided friendship and encouragement during the project. I wish to thank Raj Pandey, Elizabeth Day, Jonathan Mark Hall, Paul Daniels, Anne Hocking, and Ray and Joan Hocking. In particular, I would like to thank Paul for his weekly encouragement.

John Hocking
June, 2022
Spring Gully, Victoria

Introduction

The present volume, *The Schema of the Theory of Reification*, is a translation of Hiromatsu Wataru's (廣松渉 1933–1994) book 『物象化論の構図』, which was published by Iwanami Shoten in 1983 and later included in 『廣松渉著作集』 [Collected works of Hiromatsu Wataru], Vol. 13 (HWC 13:9–268). The book consists of five chapters and an epilogue, and those chapters, except for the third section of the first chapter, were originally published as discrete essays in journals between 1969 and 1983. The third section of Chapter 1 and the epilogue were newly written for the book publication. While a number of Hiromatsu's major books, including the present one, have been translated into Chinese, translations into European languages have to date been limited to some individual essays and excerpts from books.[1] The present publication is indeed the first ever English translation of an entire book by the author.

Undoubtedly one of the most important philosophers in twentieth-century Japan, Hiromatsu has so far been relatively little known abroad, not least in Europe and North America, among other regions.[2] As his German translator Raji Steineck rightly suggests, this hitherto limited attention to Hiromatsu's work may be attributed to the fact that his thought does not fit into the widespread preconception of "Japanese philosophy" as essentially tied to or rooted in the East-Asian cultural traditions.[3] While such culturally essentialist notions of Japanese philosophy could be questioned even with regard to its supposed representative figures, such as Nishida Kitarō or some other largely prewar philosophers, their inadequacy becomes all the more apparent with reference to Hiromatsu. His work may be characterized as a rigorous and critical engage-

---

1   The epilogue to the present work has been translated into German by Raji Steineck as Hiromatsu 2018. Other translations of his writings include "La Philosophie de Marx (pour nous)," translated by Minatomichi Takashi, in *Actuel Marx*, 2: *Le Marxisme au Japon* (Paris: L'Harmattan, 1987), 72–84, whose Japanese original is included in *Hegel and then Marx* 『ヘーゲルそしてマルクス』 (HWC 7:223–36); an English translation by Viren Murthy of a section of *The Intersubjective Being-Structure of the World* 『世界の共同主観的存在構造』 (HWC 1:38–44) as Hiromatsu 2011; a French translation by Diego Company and Naitō Nobuo of "Some Remarks on the Theory of Meaning" 「意味論研究覚書」 (HWC 1:471–91) as "Quelques remarques sur la théorie de la signification," in *Philosophie*, No. 117 (2013), 79–95; an English translation by John W.M. Krummel of a section of *Being and Meaning* 『存在と意味』, Vol. 1 (HWC 15:381–95) as Hiromatsu 2019a; and an English translation by Michael Santone of the essay 「記号論の哲学的次元」 (HWC 1:492–523) as Hiromatsu 2019b.

2   For recent English-language surveys of Hiromatsu's philosophy, see Uehara 2019 and Katsumori 2019. For a German-language overview of his work, see Ishizuka 2004.

3   See the translator's introduction to Hiromatsu 2018, 314.

ment with modern philosophy whose scope and context are by no means restricted to, or centered on, the cultural or geopolitical entity of Japan or East Asia. In this introductory essay, I wish to situate in an appropriate context the author Hiromatsu, his philosophical thought, and specifically the present work *The Schema of the Theory of Reification*.[4]

Born in Yamaguchi Prefecture in 1933, Hiromatsu grew up mainly in Fukuoka Prefecture, southwestern Japan. Immediately after the end of World War II in 1945, Hiromatsu as a schoolboy took a keen interest in Marxism and started extensively reading left-wing literature, notably the Japanese edition of *The Collected Works of Marx and Engels*. While in junior high school, he joined Communist-led political activities, and a few years later, he was expelled from high school for distributing fliers protesting the then raging Red purge. After passing the high-school equivalency examination, Hiromatsu entered the University of Tokyo in 1954, and studied philosophy while at the same time further engaging in political activities. During this process, he became increasingly at odds with the orthodox or "Russian" school of Marxism over a series of theoretical and practical issues, and consequently parted company with the Japan Communist Party. Shifting toward what was then taking form as the New Left, he helped develop a new orientation of the revolutionary movement, and this effort was, on the basic theoretical level, bound up with his seminal project of exploring and reinterpreting Karl Marx's thought.

During the 1960s, the young Hiromatsu emerged first of all as a new leading theorist of Marxism. Starting with his 1963 essay "Marxism and the Theory of Self-Alienation," he presented a novel interpretation of Marx's thought that differed from orthodox Marxism as well as from the "humanist" version of Marxism based on the notion of "alienation." As is well known, Marx's early critique of alienation, as developed in his *Economic and Philosophical Manuscripts*, revolves around the idea that the human subject externalizes itself into an alien object and yet eventually overcomes this alienation, turning back to itself. In Hiromatsu's reading, this idea of alienation is "inseparable from a specific concept of the subject" as represented by Hegel's concept of "spirit" – which was subsequently recast by the Young Hegelians into various notions such as "humanity," "self-consciousness," or "species-being" – and it was within such a conceptual framework that the early Marx set forth his critique of alienation (HWC 8:347). In due course, however, according to Hiromatsu,

---

4 The content of the present essay has been partly derived from material in Katsumori 2019. For a biographical survey of Hiromatsu's early life, see Part 1 of Kumano 2004. An outline of Hiromatsu's life and work is also presented in Kumano 2009.

Marx's thought underwent a radical change. In the middle of the 1840s, starting in his unfinished joint work with Friedrich Engels, *The German Ideology*, Marx developed a renewed critique of society no longer based on the abstract notion of the subject, but rather on his new conception of the human being as "the ensemble of social relations." This new orientation of Marx's thought had hitherto been obscured, however, by the then standard edition of *The German Ideology*, Part I, which, in Hiromatsu's view, was seriously flawed by an arbitrary compilation of the authors' manuscripts. Hiromatsu accordingly proceeded through a detailed textual criticism of *The German Ideology*, which eventually resulted in the publication of his own edition of the text (Marx and Engels 1974).

In his 1969 book *The Horizon of Marxism*『マルクス主義の地平』and other writings, Hiromatsu characterized the development of Marx's thought as the transition from "the theory of alienation" to "the theory of reification." The mature Marx's critique of "reification" (*Versachlichung*) is no longer aimed at the subject turning into an alien object, but at the "fixation of social activity" arising from the naturally evolved cooperative relations between individuals. As succinctly summed up by Hiromatsu, 'reification' for Marx refers to the circumstance that "the relation between persons appears as a relation between things, as a thing-like substance, or as a thing-like attribute" (HWC 7:233). Analyzing this idea of reification as it was introduced in *The German Ideology* and further developed in Marx's later work, particularly in *Capital*, Hiromatsu sought to show how this conceptual innovation implies surpassing the framework of modern philosophy marked by the subject/object schema. His new interpretive approach to Marx's thought as just outlined was received with fervor by a wide range of readers, especially among young students involved in the rising campus struggles during the late 1960s. Then teaching at Nagoya University, Hiromatsu himself acted in solidarity with the student revolt, and in 1970 resigned from the university in support of the movement. He remained outside academia until 1976, when he became assistant professor of philosophy at the University of Tokyo.

Notwithstanding its great intellectual impact, Hiromatsu's work in Marxism and Marx studies by no means covered the whole of his scholarship. As can also be perceived from his analysis of Marx's thought, he was deeply grounded in a broad range of Western philosophy, notably German idealism, neo-Kantianism, and phenomenology, as well as the thought of physicist-philosopher Ernst Mach. More importantly, however, unlike many other contemporary researchers in the field, Hiromatsu engaged above all in *philosophizing* with remarkable originality and systematic coherence. He developed his own philosophical project in his 1972 book *The Intersubjective Being-Structure of the World*『世界の

共同主観的存在構造』 and subsequent works, most elaborately in his masterpiece *Being and Meaning* 『存在と意味』, vol. 1 (1982) and vol. 2 (1993). The basic motif of his philosophy was a systematic critique of the "modern worldview," which he characterized as substantialist and bound by the subject/object schema. He sought to overcome this modern world-view by extending Marx's innovative ideas, particularly his critique of reification, to the general philosophical dimension.

The starting point of Hiromatsu's analysis is that all phenomena in the world bear "meaning" or "value," or, in other words, that they appear *as* something. The phenomenon always appears as something more or something other than the phenomenal or real given. For instance, "[t]he sound that is just heard appears intuitively *as* a car horn; what is seen outside the window appears *as* a pine tree" (HWC 1:33). Any phenomenon thus consists of two factors, the given and the meaning/value, which are inseparably linked in such a way that the former appears *as* the latter. Further, Hiromatsu continues, the phenomenon is every time a phenomenon "for someone," and this someone is also of twofold character. For example, a hammer has an instrumental value for someone insofar as he/she "plays the role of striking a nail" with it. In this way, something appears to someone *as* a general "role-taking Someone." It is important to note that the formation of a meaning or value is correlative with the process through which different subjects make themselves "intersubjectively isomorphic" to become a general Someone. In this way, "intersubjectivity" serves as an essential link between meaning/value and Someone.

The above twofold structures of both subject-side and object-side are combined to form what Hiromatsu calls the "fourfold structure" (四肢構造): "A given presents itself as something to someone as Someone" (HCW 15:199). For instance, the sound *dog* bears the meaning of 'dog' for someone as an English speaker. It is also in terms of the fourfold structure that Hiromatsu analyzes Marx's account of the commodity: A product of labor appears as a value to someone as a subject of abstract human labor. As Hiromatsu stresses, the above four moments of the phenomenon are not independent elements, but exist only as terms of the fourfold functional relationship. This relational character of phenomena has been missed, however, in the substantialist philosophical tradition, and Hiromatsu critically designates this tendency as "reification" (物象化).

Broadening Marx's concept of reification into a general philosophical concept, Hiromatsu redefines reification as the hypostatizing misconception of what is actually a functional relation. While, for Marx, reification is limited to the hypostatization of *social* relations, what may be reified in Hiromatsu's sense covers relations in general, including natural and nonhuman relations. He specifically focuses on the reification of meaning and value, extended from the Marxian reification of the economic value of commodities. He also critically analyzes the reification of role action, in which roles are misconceived as fixed and ready-made positions and statuses. By thus uncovering and overcoming various forms of reification, Hiromatsu seeks to replace the modern world-view with a new philosophical orientation marked by the primacy of relation and the intersubjective fourfold structure.

Among Hiromatsu's numerous works, the present book is the only one that centrally thematizes the idea and theory of reification. To be sure, as he himself admits, the book may, in a sense, appear to be a kind of "patchwork" of essays originally written independently (p. 12). Far from being just one topic among others, however, the concept of reification plays a key unifying role in Hiromatsu's work: It runs through his overall scholarly project covering both his interpretive approach to Marx's thought and his systematic effort in general philosophical reasoning. On the one hand, as we have seen, Hiromatsu's reading of Marx revolves around the thematic of reification as distinct from that of alienation. In the first essay of this volume, he outlines his basic views of Marx's transition from his earlier theory of alienation to his later theory of reification, and in the second essay, presents an in-depth analysis of this Marxian idea of reification. On the other hand, as noted above, he reformulates the idea of reification in the general philosophical dimension in such a way that the critique of reification serves as the leading motif in his endeavor to develop a new philosophical world-view. Steps in this conceptual extension is first taken in the third essay on the reification of the historical world, which also contains a fourfold-structural analysis of Marx's theory of the commodity. The fourth essay on Marx and Engels' conception of nature is also highly relevant to Hiromatsu's extension of the idea of reification, notably to his critical approach to "the historical reification of nature" as exemplified by the modern mechanical view of nature. It is above all in the long "epilogue," however, that he thematically discusses his project of expanding the theory of reification, which is to include the reification of norms, institutions, and social power, among other constructs in the practical dimension. Thus, it is no wonder that he characterizes the epilogue as, "along with the second essay, the central part of this book" (p. 12).

In this way, the present book provides the reader with a vantage point for viewing Hiromatsu's overall scholarly enterprise, where the thematic of reification constitutes a pivotal link connecting his major fields of inquiry. The reader who has completed reading this book will be able, without too much difficulty, to proceed to other works by Hiromatsu, whether his more detailed accounts of Marx's thought, his general theory of the fourfold structure, or his philosophical

analysis of natural science, particularly relativity theory, among other themes.[5]
It is all the more hoped that translations of his other books will also be available
soon.

June 2022,
Katsumori Makoto

Abbreviation

HWC   『廣松渉著作集』 [Collected Works of Hiromatsu Wataru] (Tokyo: Iwanami
Shoten, 1996–1997).

References

Hiromatsu Wataru 廣松渉. 2011. "The Subjective Duality of Phenomena," trans.
by Viren Murthy. In Thomas P. Kasulis, and John C. Maraldo, eds., *Japanese
Philosophy: A Sourcebook* (Honolulu: University of Hawaii Press), pp. 973–8.

Hiromatsu Wataru 廣松渉. 2018. "Entwurf einer Theorie der Versachlichung:
Epilog," trans. by Raji Steineck, *European Journal of Japanese Philosophy* 3:303–
36.

Hiromatsu Wataru 廣松渉. 2019a. "Articulation Forms of the World of Fact-
Things," trans. by John W.M. Krummel. In Krummel 2019, 157–70.

Hiromatsu Wataru 廣松渉. 2019b. "The Philosophical Dimension of Semi-
otics: The Subsistence Mechanism of Signification," trans. by Michael Santone,
European Journal of Japanese Philosophy 4:235–270.

Ishizuka Ryōji 石塚良次. 2004. "Hiromatsu-Schule," in *Historisch-kritisches
Wörterbuch des Marxismus* (Hamburg: Argument Verlag).

Katsumori Makoto 勝守真. 2016a. "Hiromatsu on Mach's Philosophy and
Relativity Theory," *European Journal of Japanese Philosophy* 1:149–88.

Katsumori Makoto 勝守真. 2016b. "Hiromatsu on Marx's Theory of the
Commodity," in Morisato Takeshi, ed., *Critical Perspectives on Japanese Philosophy*, *Frontiers of Japanese Philosophy* 8 (Nagoya: Chisokudō Publications),
170–92.

Katsumori Makoto 勝守真. 2017. "Reading Hiromatsu's Theory of the Fourfold Structure," *European Journal of Japanese Philosophy* 2:229–62.

---

5   For studies on these different branches of Hiromatsu's work, see Katsumori 2016a, 2016b, 2017.

Katsumori Makoto 勝守真. 2019. "Hiromatsu's Philosophy: An Introductory Survey," *European Journal of Japanese Philosophy* 4:271–91.

Krummel, John W.M., ed. 2019. *Contemporary Japanese Philosophy: A Reader* (London: Rowman & Littlefield International).

Kumano Sumihiko 熊野純彦. 2004. 『戦後思想の一断面: 哲学者廣松渉の軌跡』 [A cross-section of postwar thought: Traces of the philosopher Hiromatsu Wataru] (Tokyo: Nakanishiya Shuppan).

Kumano Sumihiko 熊野純彦. 2009. 「解説」 [Commentary], in Kumano Sumihiko, ed., 『廣松渉哲学論集』 [Hiromatsu Wataru: Collection of philosophical essays] (Tokyo: Heibonsha), 525–82.

Marx, Karl, and Friedrich Engels. 1974. *Die deutsche Ideologie*. Neuveröffentlichung des Abschnittes 1 des Bandes 1, ed. by Hiromatsu Wataru (Tokyo: Kawade Shobō Shinsha).

Uehara Mayuko 上原麻有子. 2019. "Trends and Prospects in Japanese Philosophy after 1945: The Contemporary Philosophy of Hiromatsu Wataru from Marxist Philosophy to the Theory of Facial Expression," in Krummel 2019, 249–74.

Prologue

"The composition of the theory of reification" serves as an important key for understanding the later thought of Marx for me, and, also, serves as the methodological foundation for my own conception of the philosophy of society, the philosophy of history and the philosophy of culture. Whilst I have expressed this occasionally over the last ten or more years I have hesitated for a long while to discuss as the main theme the "logical composition of the theory of reification" itself. This is because, on the one hand I had left a slight degree of impasse in the work of interpreting comprehensively in line with the composition of the theory of reification Marx's system of "critique of (the study of) political economy" which encompasses the complete three volumes of *Capital*, but mainly because, on the other hand, in the matter of the influential determinant in my philosophy of praxis, especially in the arrangement of role action, it was difficult to see through to a necessary and sufficient methodological deployment. However, in the last year or two, in regard to the former, having gained as co-author the specialist Mr Yoshida Norio, I have come to be likely to achieve a revision and expansion of my old work *The Philosophy of* Capital and consequently a restructuring of interpretation containing the whole of the system of "Marx's critique of (the study of) political economy." In regard to the latter, too, as the draft of *Being and Meaning* Volume II "The Being-Structure of the World of Praxis" has gradually come together I have reached the point where my conception has more or less firmed. This is the reason that I am here putting forward this book which takes as its thematic content the "composition and range of the theory of reification" for public examination and am seeking correction from the well-informed reader.

This book is not, however, something which discusses abstractly and generally the composition of the theory of reification in the form simply of methodology. Moreover, this book is a collection of essays, and it contains an old essay published in an academic society journal more than ten years ago. In addition, although it takes the general title of *The Schema of the Theory of Reification*, the main *body* of the book is limited to the theory of reification of Marx and Engels, and my own conception is only revealed in the form of an epilogue.—Though by nature I am slothful, it's not that I didn't have in mind to write a "newly written text." Also, once I had decided on the form of a collection of essays I did, temporarily, draft a long introduction. However, after careful consideration, I decided on the current form, having a particular thing in mind.

I personally desire in mind that to more easily gain the understanding of the reader regarding the composition and range of the theory of reification, taking the form, as in this book, of restricting the ridge of the theory of reification in Marx and Engels to the primary "backbone" of discussion and fleshing things out in my description of such first, and then having done that stating in an abbreviated form my conception as a continuation and development of such would—rather than the normal forms of resolving to be too accurate and tending to stray into byways, or reducing complexity and describing things comprehensively—rather be more suitable. I sincerely pray that such thinking of mine is not complacent.

To the extent that they were written independently of each other, the five essays contained within the book should be comprehensible even if perused in a random order, but in order to ascertain the schema of the theory of reification it would be best to read them through in the order in which they are arranged. However, for a certain kind of reader, the first essay may be seen as an unnecessary preamble, and I fear that it may be felt to be boring. At such a time, I would ask that the second essay and the epilogue be read, and that the first essay be bypassed for the time being.

The first essay, "For an Extolling of Materialist History", whilst rejecting crude understandings of the image of historical materialism, extols the perspective of materialist history as world-view and its composition, but in the context of this book, it, in particular, is such that it should perform the function of an introduction in regard to Marx's theory of reification with discussion, in particular, of the continuous discontinuity = discontinuous continuity of the so-called "theory of alienation" in the "early Marx" and the "theory of reification" in the "later Marx." Furthermore, section 3 of this essay, "The Sublation of the Theory of Alienation, and The Theory of Reification", is newly written, and with this addition I have also done some revision of the text and notes (the notes are provided together at the end of the chapter)[1] of the preceding sections 1 and 2.—In this book I do not go into the specific content of materialist history itself, and I would be grateful if this lack can be made up for through the easily obtainable separate work, *The Original Image of Materialist History* (San'ichi shobō, Shinsho Edition). In this separate work, whilst dismissing crude forms of materialist history, I discuss as main themes the view of society, the view of the state and the view of history of Marx and Engels, and I engage in an explicatory investigation of the fundamental concepts of materialist history. Also, regarding the features of Marx and Engels' discussion of human being, I ask that you see chapters 3 and 4 of the separate work, *The Horizon of Marxism* (Keisō shobō).

---

1 〖Tr. For convenience and consistency notes have been provided throughout as footnotes on each page, rather than end notes.〗

The second essay, "The Composition and Scope of the Theory of Reification", has the feature of originally being a rewriting in the form of an independent essay of the incomplete "Section 3" of the first essay, but, putting aside the circumstances of its formation, regarded just in the context of this book, it forms the central trunk of such. In including it in this book expansion and revision was undertaken, primarily in the notes.—No matter how much this essay has the features and the position of being a continuation of the first essay, it was published in the form of an independent essay and it includes points which to some degree duplicate those in the first essay, but, fearing causing jumps in the gist of the argument, I deliberately didn't undertake a large-scale cutting of material.

The third essay, "The Theory of Reification of the Historical World", is the manuscript for an academic society special lecture written in the late autumn of 1968 (it was published in the academic society journal *beforehand*, with corrections made in January 1969), fifteen years previous to now, and it discussed the proposal to extend the composition of the theory of the "world of the commodity" in *Capital* into the reificatory being-structure in the "historical world" in general. This old essay is worth commemorating for me as the essay in which I first state my interpretation of Marx's theory of the world of the commodity, and it is also, at the same time, the essay in which I first state publicly my "role theory composition", but I have until now refrained from including it in an essay collection. The reason for this is *not* because it contained points I wished to withdraw, but because, later, I published section 2 of this essay in an elaborated and developed form as "The Being-Structure of the Linguistic World" and "The Co-operative Being-Structure of the Historical World", (both are contained in my work *The Intersubjective Being-Structure of the World* published by Keisō shobō), and also, I published "Heidegger and Reificatory Misapprehension" (republished in my work *An Outpost Towards a Koto-Centred View of the World* published by Keisō shobō) which develops as the main theme points of critique from this essay, and further, I published as an independent book, *The Philosophy of* Capital (published by Gendai hyōron sha), the reading of *Capital* which supports section 1 of the essay, and so in this way, I developed as main themes foundational statements from this essay = academic society lecture in a variety of directions, and therefore published the essay in a different form. In this way, I abandoned the essay to an academic society journal which would never be read at all by anyone apart from the typesetter, but this old essay, no matter how much of a rough sketch it is, indeed, because it is a foundational rough sketch, can be seen as convenient in bringing into relief the main line of argument in the context of this book. This is the reason I have dusted it off and republished it.—Because the idea is to republish my first statements regarding the various aforementioned themes, I have stopped at correcting of misprints and have taken the expedient of inserting somewhat explanatory "translations" (within square brackets) of European words. I hope that I might be somehow forgiven for duplication with other essays. For this academic society lecture, taking into consideration the circumstance that the audience was a school of philosophers with little connection with Marx but with a close affinity with Heideggerian terminology, I make frequent use of Heideggerian jargon. Whilst I fear that I will invite the displeasure of a certain kind of reader I can only ask that attention to and distinction of Heideggerian terminology be made.—Although the fact that the essay is not on the whole sufficiently developed was beyond my control, for me the major dissatisfaction is the fact that I completely omitted relating discussion to Marx's "theory of value form." Of course, human relations in the "theory of value form" only fully applies to "the simple commodity producer model." It was having carefully considered this that I omitted relating discussion to the theory of value form. Even so, it can't be denied that this lack is a cause of pushing the discussion into an abstract realm, and to you readers who are economists it is likely that you will have the impression that "with this kind of discussion in the end a consistent reading of the complete three volumes of *Capital* using the composition of the theory of reification can't possibly be believed." Certainly, in extolling, not only in this essay but in the book as a whole, the theory of reification which runs through the complete three volumes of *Capital*, I have left a large amount of work undone. To fulfil this work, however, concrete discussion focused along the lines of *Capital*, such as the "problem of transformation" etc, is necessary and would easily necessitate a book with this as its main theme. For this reason, I have deliberately refrained in this book from incomplete discussion of related, non-central matters. For the time being, regarding the "theory of value form" and the "theory of fetishism", I would be grateful if the lack in this book is supplemented through my previously published, separate book *The Philosophy of* Capital (incidentally, this existing work of mine is scheduled to be newly published by Keisō shobō next spring, having undergone expansion and correction).

The fourth essay, "The Historical Reification of the Natural World", is once again a republication of an old essay written for an academic society journal, and apart from a condensing of the notes at the end of the essay, and the supplementation of material in square brackets I have stopped at only correcting misprints. The points of argument and the quotations in this essay are almost all duplications with those in the first essay, the second essay and the epilogue, and it wasn't that I didn't hesitate to republish it, but this short essay is the only essay for me where I discussed as the main theme Marx and Engels' concept of nature, and recently, for reasons of its rarity, I have frequently been asked about it, so I chose to publish it here as an "addendum in a different place", refraining from altering the duplication of points of argument. I'd like to beg forgiveness.

The fifth essay, "Philosophy in Marx", is the record of a speech given under the auspices of "Terakoya",[2] and it is not an essay which takes the theory of reification as a direct topic, but deals with the matters of the composition of "systematic description = systematic critique" mentioned in the second essay and the "realising sublation = sublating realisation of philosophy" in the place of practice, and in general it also has an aspect of generalising motifs (though from a particular vantage point) contained in this book, so this too has been included as an "addendum." Apart from omitting part of the preamble and addendum notes it is a mostly faithful republication.

The epilogue, "Expanding the Theory of Reification", is an outline of my own thoughts and proposals as to how I wish to continue and develop, on the basis of what kind of direction and with what kind of deployment, Marx and Engels' theory of reification. Even though, formally, it is an "epilogue", this long, new essay can be seen as, along with the second essay, the central part of this book. In the context of it as a continuation of the main text I haven't refrained from re-declaring points of discussion and reinserting quotations.

Reading the printer's proofs it is difficult not to feel embarrassed. Even though it was put together in accordance with a pre-established line, I am extremely ashamed of the duplication arising from the republication of material, especially the duplication of quotations. For example, a certain section of *The German Ideology* is not only quoted in every chapter but has ended up being used twice within the same essay, making things extremely unattractive. Also, from a different perspective, this book presents such a patchwork appearance, and in contrast to the more than ten essay collections I have previously sent out into the world being a unity furnished with an internal arrangement in their own way, in the case of this book, it is simply a completely distorted five-pointed star. In the group of my works this book is bound to be judged the most unattractive.

Rethinking things, however, being published in advance of the revised, new edition of *The Philosophy of* Capital and the volumes to follow it, and alongside *Being and Meaning* Volume ii, in the case of this book which promotes the composition of Marx's theory of reification and which ought to present my own composition of the theory of reification, this clumsiness may perhaps be

---

2   ⟦Tr. Terakoya dates from the Edo period (1603–1868). It refers to private provision of education to commoners.⟧

on the contrary well equal to its task. The essays contained in it have, for me, each been accompanied by catharsis, and all I can do now is hope for good luck.

In the forming of this book, I have been grateful for the good wishes of many people. With first and foremost Mr Urabe Saburō who gave me encouragement, and Mr Aiba Atsushi who kindly took charge of the project for me, this book was able to come into being through the kindness of the various people involved at Iwanami Shoten. At the proofreading stage I unavoidably had to go into hospital and undergo an operation, and as a result I caused a great deal of trouble for those involved. I wish to add a word of gratitude and apology.

21 October, 1983
Hiromatsu Wataru

For an Extolling of Materialist History

If we speak of materialist history or historical materialism, in textbooks and the like, it is often, based on the words of Lenin, regarded as "something which is an application and expansion of dialectical materialism into the areas of society and history". In such a case, a schema in the style of modern philosophy which distinguishes the world into the two hemispheres of the world of "nature" and the world of "history" is established, and a composition can be seen in which the "primary philosophy" of "dialectical materialism" seems to precede in regard to the two major areas of the "dialectic of nature" and "historical materialism" which correspond to the two hemispheres in question.—This formula may be convenient as one which provides a formulaic description in a textbook-like style, aligning the system of Marxist philosophy with the systems of pre-existing philosophies, but there is a fear that it already leads to a misunderstanding of the composition of Marxist philosophy.[1] When the "application

---

1   Such an understanding even came to be seen in a part of the world of philosophy in East Germany in conjunction with the publication of the new edition of *The German Ideology*. I would like, for example, to refer you to Helmut Seidel: "Vom praktischen und theoretischen Verhältnis der Menschen zur Wirklichkeit. Zur Neuherausgabe des Kapitels I des I. Bandes der 'Deutschen Ideologie'", *Deutsche Zeitschrift für philosophie*, 1966, Heft 10. There is an essay of mine regarding this essay of Seidel's, 「『ドイツ・イデオロギー』新版が投じた東ドイツ哲学界の新しい波紋」 [["New Repercussions in the East German World of Philosophy Thrown up by the New Edition of *The German Ideology*"]] (『日本読書新聞』[[*The Japan Reading Newspaper*]], 27 February 1967) [reprinted in my collection of essays 『マルクス主義の成立過程』 [[*The Process of Coming into Existence of Marxism*]], Shiseidō, published in 1968], and as a Japanese translation of the debate surrounding the Seidel essay there is the Shibata Shingo edited 『現代のマルクス主義哲学論争』 [[*Debates in Contemporary Marxist Philosophy*]] (Aoki Shoten, 1970). In addition, as one would expect, *Marxistische Philosophie, Lehrbuch*, 2. Aufl., 1967 (the Japanese translation of this by both Fujino Watari and Akima Minoru is Ōtsuki Shoten's 『マルクス主義哲学』 [[*Marxist Philosophy*]]), which came out under the editorial supervision of Alfred Kosing, who was a critic of Seidel but who also showed a certain understanding of his posing of the issues, and which differed in direction from the Soviet style textbooks which had solidified during the Stalin era. However, unfortunately, these East German new textbooks soon became "proscribed" and ended up once again becoming nationally prescribed in, rather than a Soviet style, what ought to be called "translated editions of Soviet textbooks". As an essay of mine regarding this matter please see 「マルクス主義の哲学と『実践』の概念－東独哲学界の椿事－」 [["Marxist Philosophy and the Concept of 'Praxis' – Strange Developments in the World of Philosophy in East Germany –"]] (『東風』[[*East Wind*]], May 1974).

and expansion of dialectical materialism" is spoken of, this doesn't necessarily mean that a process of theory formation, in the sense of dialectical materialism being applied and expanded after having first been established, is proclaimed; rather, it seems as if the structural arrangement of the system has simply been cited. Nonetheless, it cannot be denied that "application and expansion" are frequently understood as corresponding to the process of the history of the formation of the theory, and this distorts materialist history in a tragicomical way. Fortunately, amongst Marx scholars in our country, even if we leave out earlier traces in Miki Kiyoshi and others from before the war, Mr Tanaka Kichiroku's argument from soon after the war of the *chronological* preceding of materialist history in comparison to dialectical materialism has become established and there is little tendency to take literally the matter of "application and expansion". Nevertheless, for us, we need to extol the composition of the world-view of materialist history with, as a conduit, the question of whether, even from the composition of the system, materialist history is really the "application – expansion" of the "primary philosophy" of dialectical materialism.

In the semi-clean manuscript[2] of Part 1 "Feuerbach—Opposition of the Materialist and Idealist Outlooks" of the co-written manuscript by Marx and Engels, *The German Ideology*, regarded as the classic text announcing the birth of materialist history, is stated the following:

> We know only a single science (*Wissenschaft* = systematic knowledge), the science of history (*Geschichte*). History can be considered from two sides, can be divided into the history of nature and the history of humankind. The two sides, however, cannot be separated. For as long as human beings live, the history of nature and the history of society condition each other. We will not go into the history of nature, the so-called natural sciences, here. But regarding the history of humankind, however, we will have to do so. This is because if reduced to its origin almost all of that which we call ideology amounts to either being something which has understood the history of humankind in a distorted manner, or being something which has completely abstracted human history.[3]

---

2   In a series of articles, with 「『ドイツ・イデオロギー』編輯の問題点」 ["Problems in the Editing of *The German Ideology*"] (Spring 1965) [reprinted in ibid. 『成立過程』 [*The Process of Coming into Existence*]] first and foremost, I have discussed the different layers of basic manuscript – revised different manuscript – semi-clean manuscript – clean manuscript in the extant manuscripts of *The German Ideology*, and I would be grateful if, relying on the book noted in the next footnote, you would check in detail the actual state of the manuscripts and the internal connections.

3   手稿復元・新編輯版『ドイツ・イデオロギー』 [*The German Ideology* Restored

I wish to focus on the span of the concept of "history" to be seen here. It is a unitary – unified "history", having the "two sides (*Seite*)" of the "history of nature" and the "history of society". Furthermore, in this case, that which is called the "history of nature" is not the history of the natural world in the dimension of the evolutionary history of the universe or the evolutionary history of the Earth, it is specified as the "history (*Geschichte*) of nature" = "the so-called natural sciences".—Marx and Engels from the beginning do not take the understanding of being of the style of modern philosophy which bifurcates the natural world and the human world (the natural world and the historical world).[4]

If "history" when we speak of materialist *history* (the materialist understanding of "history") is, as we see here, a special sense of "history" encompassing the "history of nature" and the "history of society", and if materialist history (*materialistische Auffassung der Geschichte*) is none other than the unitary – unified "systematic knowledge of history" when it is said that "we know only a single science, the science of history", then materialist history without a doubt has to be said to be a comprehensive world-view, and not the *usual* view of history concerned with the hemisphere of the historical world lined up next to the natural world.

There is likely to be a sceptical tendency amongst readers regarding taking as a basis for argument a "fragmentary few words" from *The German Ideology*. Also, we ourselves bear the responsibility of determining the systematic relationship amongst dialectical materialism, materialist history and the dia-

---

Manuscript – Newly Edited Edition]] (Kawade shobō shinsha, 1974). The original text S. 23., the Japanese translated text p. 23.

   In addition, the entire text of this paragraph is erased in the manuscript (and for that reason it isn't printed in the former popular edition), but the crossing out, it seems, is not due to the content of the text being invalid, but rather was a rethinking that it was unsuitable *as the opening* of the "chapter" which they had begun with this paragraph. I won't go into, here, investigation regarding this assumption of the reason for erasure, but will simply note the fact that not only is the text in question not in contradiction with the argument in other parts of the manuscript, it is in conformity with such.

4 As essays dealing with this point, I would like to refer you to my 「歴史化された自然と自然化された歴史」 [["Historicised Nature and Naturalised History"]] (published in 『自然について』 [[*On Nature*]] edited by the Philosophical Association, Yūhikaku, 1974) [reprinted as IV in this book], and 「マルクス主義の哲学」 [["The Philosophy of Marxism"]] (published in the joint work with Sakamoto Hyakudai et al 『現代哲学を考える』 [[*Considering Contemporary Philosophy*]] Yūhikaku, 1978). Further, although it's not the case that he has the same viewpoint as myself, Alfred Schmidt: *Der Begriff der Natur in der Lehre von Marx* (『マルクスの自然概念』 [[*The Concept of Nature in Marx*]], Hōsei University Press (trans. Motohama Seikai)) is of great interest.

lectic of nature. However, here, putting aside until the main part of the essay the clearing up of probable doubts, for the time being, that materialist history is not simply a part of the Marxist theoretical system, that it is the composition of the world-view itself of Marxism, I conjecture as a preparatory point.

In addition, it is my intention to put forward several new points below in this essay, but I fear that some degree of duplication might occur with points I have occasionally made over the last ten or more years. Allowing for the fact that this essay is for me *my own summarising* regarding *the theme of the horizon of materialist history*, if there are to be seen here and there sections which appear to be condensed restatements of my previously published material, I most sincerely beg forgiveness.

1   The Dialectical Sublation of Classical Philosophy

Engels, recollecting the period of formation of materialist history, writes, in the manuscript from his later years *Ludwig Feuerbach and the End of German Classical Philosophy*, commonly known as *On Feuerbach*, in the following way.

> The Hegelian School had already broken up, but Hegel's philosophy had not been critically overcome. Strauss and Bauer each took one aspect of Hegel's philosophy and positioned it in opposition to the other aspect. Feuerbach broke through the system of Hegel's philosophy and simply threw it aside. However simply declaring that a certain philosophy is in error doesn't mean that one has dealt with that philosophy. Casually ignoring vast work such as Hegel's, which had, in reality, exerted a huge influence on the spiritual development of the nation, didn't deal with things. Hegel's philosophy had to be "sublated" in the particular sense this has in this philosophy.[5]

---

5   *Karl Marx-Friedrich Engels, Werke*, Institut für Marxismus-Leninismus beim ZK der SED, Dietz Verlag, Bd.21, S.273. Below, this collected works is abbreviated to MEW. As a Japanese translation of this MEW, there is Ōtsuki Shoten's 『マルクス・エンゲルス全集』 [*The Complete Works of Marx-Engels*]. The page of the original MEW is printed in the margin of this *Complete Works*, so I won't provide the page number of the Japanese translation on each occasion. In addition, in choosing the translation for quoted material I made liberal reference to the Ōtsuki *Complete Works* edition and to other Japanese translations. Taking advantage of this opportunity, I express my thanks, and I apologise for the discourteousness of not providing names on each occasion.

—That which realised the internal "sublation" of Hegel's philosophy, which stood at the pinnacle of German classical philosophy, this is in other words Marxism.

Viewed too from the position of we as a third party, this self-confidence can be recognised as having sufficient cause. In sublating Hegel's philosophy, which stood as the final effort of modern philosophy, Marx and Engels went beyond the horizon itself of modern philosophy. Materialist history is none other than that which corresponds to a new world-view horizon opened up here.

1.1

In the present day, in discussing the overcoming of the philosophical, world-view horizon of modernity (= the capitalist epoch as an historical stage), it is the convention that people make the overcoming of the schema of the so-called "subjective – objective"[6] the *Merkmal* 〚Tr. characteristic〛 of this, and for us too we can, as has been done up until now, make this the distinguishing feature.

German classical philosophy, in particular Hegel's philosophy, in a sense, is the pinnacle of philosophies based on the "subjective – objective" schema. Even so, in a sense, as is so already with the philosophy of Fichte and Schelling, Hegel's philosophy, even though it lies within the schema of "subject – object", was something which aimed at overcoming the dichotomy of "subjective – objective".—That Marx and Engels were able to overcome the "subject – object" schema is largely due to the fact that they saw the tracks of the precursor to this in Hegel.

In what can be called his debut work, *The Difference Between Fichte's and Schelling's Systems of Philosophy*, from the earliest Hegel states in the following way. Incidentally, the same thought can also be seen, amongst other places, in *Introduction on The Essence of Philosophical Criticism Generally, and its Relationship to the Present State of Philosophy in Particular*[7] and in the so-called *Jena Real Philosophy I*,[8] and we can see that this was an unshakeable position for Hegel.

---

6   I discussed this characteristic in Chapter 1 of my 『世界の共同主観的存在構造』〚*The Intersubjective Being-Structure of the World*〛 (Keisō shobō, 1972).

7   Hegel: Über das Wesen der philosophischen Kritik überhaupt und ihr Verhältnis zum gegenwärtigen Zustand der Philosophie insbesondere, *Hegel Werke in zwanzig Bänden*, Suhrkamp Verlag, Bd. 2, S. 171 ff. In particular S. 184 f.

8   Hegel: *Gesammelte Werke*, hrsg. v. Rheinisch-Westfälische Akademie der Wissenschaften mit der Deutschen Forschungsgemeinschaft, Bd. 6, S. 290 ff. In this new complete works edition it isn't called *Jena Real Philosophy*, but here I follow the common name.

Oppositions in the form of spirit and matter, mind and body, faith and understanding, freedom and necessity etc. etc ... shifted to the form of an opposition of an absolute *subjectivity* and an absolute *objectivity*. The sublation of this fixed kind of opposition, this indeed is the only matter of concern for reason.[9]

Dogmatic idealism from the beginning denies objectivity and determines, in its own fashion, the subjectivity which is one of the items of the dichotomous suppositions as an absolute (thing) ... but, this is the same as dogmatism (in its purest form materialism) denying the subjective.—If one item of the dichotomous supposition is denied and the homogeneity brought about by absolute abstraction, the desire single-mindedly seeking this kind of homogeneity, is seen to be placed at the foundation of philosophical thought, no matter which of the subjective and the objective is denied the outcome is the same. Both of the dichotomous assumptions lie within consciousness, and the existentiality of both are founded on consciousness. When it comes to the fact that both [the] pure consciousness [of the idealist] and the thing-(in)-itself of the dogmatist are not proven in experience, they are the same. Neither the subjective nor the objective on its own completes consciousness. Insofar as the purely subjective is an abstraction it is the same as the purely objective. Dogmatic idealism locates the subjective as the real basis of the objective and dogmatic realism locates the objective as the real basis of the subjective etc.[10]

Hegel, on the basis of this understanding, established a position "overcoming" the dichotomy of subjective and objective, the dichotomy of subjectivism and objectivism, of "dogmatic idealism" and "dogmatic realism", a position of "absolute idealism" which makes absolute spirit the real = the subject.— Hegel's absolute idealism, although viewed from the standpoint of a third-party observer an idealism, takes itself to have "sublated" the dichotomous nature of the subjective and the objective, the "dichotomy of idealism and realism".

Marx and Engels, at least in the process of the formation of their thought, inherited Hegel's motif of attempting to overcome not only the dichotomous opposition of subjectivity and objectivity, of spirit and matter, but the opposition of the individual and the universal, the existent and essence, form and

---

9   Hegel: *Differenz des Fichteschen und Schellingschen Systems der Philosophie*. Bd. 2, S. 21 of
     the Suhrkamp edition *Works* of footnote 7 above.
10   ibid., S. 61f.

matter, the limited and the infinite, freedom and necessity etc. etc., and further, the opposition between idealism and realism. And, eventually, they came to be able to discern the reason that Hegel was unable to achieve this, and from a new perspective they came to plan to achieve it. It was on the lines of continuing development of the Hegelian motif that Marx and Engels opened up a new world-view horizon inseparable from materialist history; though that process wasn't linear, having considerable distortion, and showing leaps as well.

This essay is not a tracing as a main theme of the process of formation of materialist history, but as a tool for rendering for-itself the perspective and composition of materialist history let us, bearing in mind how Hegel's philosophy was sublated, look at several aspects of the process of formation.

1.2

Marx, when he was twenty-six years old, writes in the following way in *The Holy Family* (written in 1844), jointly written with Engels, two and a half years younger than him, as if supporting the first half of Engels' recollection from *On Feuerbach* quoted above.

> In Hegel's philosophy there are three elements. Namely, firstly Spinoza's matter, secondly Fichte's self-consciousness, and thirdly Hegel's unity of both, absolute spirit. The first element is *nature* separated off from human beings and metaphysically re-formed, the second is *spirit* separated off from nature and metaphysically re-formed, and the third is the unity of these two metaphysically re-formed, real *Man*, real human beings.[11]
>
> Strauss from Spinoza's position, and Bauer from Fichte's position, each, from beginning to end, developed Hegel in the field of theology ... With the appearance of Feuerbach, he, through a dissolving of the metaphysical absolute spirit into 'the real human being standing on the foundation of nature', for the first time completed Hegel standing in Hegel's position, and critiqued hi.[12]
>
> The existing opposition between spiritualism and materialism was thoroughly vanquished, and was finally conquered by Feuerbach.[13]

At this point in time, the autumn of 1844, Marx was at the level of giving high praise[14] to Feuerbach, and he planned to sublate Hegel's philosophy along the

---

11 MEW, Bd. 2, S. 147.
12 ibid., S. 147.
13 ibid., S. 99.
14 In the *Economic and Philosophic Manuscripts* Marx wrote that "Feuerbach took a seri-

lines of Feuerbach. Marx concluded that the Hegelian "absolute spirit", the union of the dichotomy of objectivity and subjectivity, of the duality of nature and spirit, was none other than the metaphysical re-forming of the "human being", and he settles his position on the Feuerbachian "human being".[15] The true union of nature and spirit is not the metaphysical "absolute spirit", it is simply the "human being". Marx at the time, through taking as the principle the real union of subjectivity and objectivity, of spirit and matter, that is the "real human being", thought that for the first time the Hegelian motif of sublating the opposition of dogmatic idealism and realism could be truly achieved.

What I want to focus on here is that Marx at the time, though praising Feuerbach, without advocating the position of Feuerbach's "materialism",[16] deliberately forcibly reads the "overcoming of the opposition of spiritualism and materialism" into Feuerbach, and that he takes such a position.—It goes without saying, both Marx and Engels, as Hegelians, at the beginning took a position of idealism; though they came to receive a strong impact[17] from Feuerbach's materialism they did not immediately accept the position of materialism, and from 1843 to 1844 they were persistently exploring for a "position to sublate the opposition between idealism and materialism".

---

ous, critical stance regarding the Hegelian dialectic and he is the only one who has made real discoveries in this area, and generally speaking he is the person who truly overcame the old philosophy" (MEW, *Ergänzungsband*, 1. Teil, S. 569. Translated by Messrs. Shirotsuka Noboru and Tanaka Kichiroku, Iwanami Bunko edition, p. 191), and in a letter dated 11 August 1844 addressed to Feuerbach he wrote that "I regard your *Principles of the Philosophy of the Future* and *The Essence of Faith According to Luther* as works possessing an importance greater than the sum of the totality of today's German literature. ... You give a philosophical foundation to socialism in these treatises. ... The unity of human being and human being with its foundation in the real differentiation of human beings, the concept of a human species brought down from an abstract heaven to the real earth, this is the very thing which is nothing but the concept of society!" (MEW, Bd. 27, S.426).

15   Though, when viewed from a third party viewpoint, Marx took into more specific account than Feuerbach, and from an early stage, the sociality of human beings. Before others, he writes in *Introduction to a Contribution to the Critique of Hegel's Philosophy of Right* published in the *Franco-German Yearbook* "human being, such means the human world, such means the State, society (*Sozietät*)" (MEW, Bd. 1, S. 378).

16   However, Feuerbach himself said that "materialism is the foundation of the building of human knowledge but it is not the building itself" and he described himself as "looking backwards I agree with the materialists, but looking forwards I do not", so I think that we probably shouldn't emphasise this point too much.

17   I would like to refer you to the relevant places in my 『青年マルクス論』 [*On the Young Marx*] (Heibonsha, 1971) and 『エンゲルス論』 [*On Engels*] (Morita shoten, 1968) regarding just how extreme this was.

That in the *Economic and Philosophic Manuscripts* written ahead of *The Holy Family* also in 1844[18] Marx advocated "humanism = naturalism, naturalism = humanism" as a position to sublate the opposition of "subjectivism and object-ivism", "spiritualism and materialism", and that he was advocating[19] a position that was "different to both idealism and materialism, and which, at the same time, was a true position unifying both", is well known, and, therefore, surely doesn't need to be proven through quotations in detail here.—Engels too in a series of journal essays published in 1844 stated that:

> "materialism, without attacking the contempt for the human of Chris-tianity, in place of the God of Christianity simply made nature absolute and placed it in opposition to the human". "The battle against the abstract subjectivism of Christianity drove eighteenth century philosophy into a one sidedness opposite it. *Objectivism* was placed in opposition to *sub-jectivism*, nature to spirit, *materialism* to *spiritualism* ... The eighteenth century didn't solve the opposition of the substance and the subject, of nature and spirit, of necessity and freedom. But the eighteenth century did develop and place in opposition in an extremely sharp and complete manner the two sides of these oppositions, and, as a result, made the sub-lation of these oppositions a necessity",

---

18   Regarding the chronological relation between the time the *Economic and Philosophic Manuscripts* were written and the five *Economic Notes* of Marx's Paris years there was a view that Lapin's explanation was accepted as the standard. In recent years, however, a differing view came to be put forward. (The Lapin explanation is Nikolai I. Lapin: "Vergleichende Analyse der drei Quellen des Einkommens in den 'Ökonomisch-philo-sophischen Manuskripten' von Marx", *Deutsche Zeitschrift für Philosophie*, 1969, Heft 2. A Hosomi Suguru translation was published in 『思想』 [[*Thought*]], March 1971). Marx's situation during this time is conveyed by Hattori Fumio (「『経済学・哲学手稿』所見」 [["Remarks on the *Economic and Philosophic Manuscripts*"]] Tōhoku University 『経済学』 [[*Economics*]], Vol. 40 No. 2, 1978, and 「『経済学・哲学手稿』研究の新段階」 [["A New Stage in Studies of the *Economic and Philosophic Manuscripts*"]], 『現代と思想』 [[*Modernity and Thought*]] December 1979). Inge Taubert's problematic essay of this period "Probleme und Fragen zur Datierung der 'Ökonomisch-philosophischen Manuskripte' von Karl Marx" is contained in *Beiträge zur Marx-Engels - Forschung*, 3, 1978, S.17–35. [—In addition, as recent research, there is "Problems of the So-Called *Economic and Philosophic Manuscripts of 1844*—Report of the Linz Conference Commemorating One Hundred Years since the Death of Marx—" published in translation by Yamanaka Ryūji in 『思想』 [[*Thought*]], Vol. 8, 1983].

19   MEW, Ergänzungsband, 1. Teil, S.577. The aforementioned Iwanami bunko edition Japan-ese translation, p. 205.

and made clear his intention of overcoming the contradictory opposition of "idealism and realism".[20]

Marx and Engels eventually come to take the position of materialism and cease referring to the sublation of the opposition of spiritualism and materialism, of idealism and realism; however, this doesn't mean that they chose the "materialism" they had previously themselves attacked the one sidedness of. Although materialist history is certainly a materialist view of history, materialism here is not a simple, plain "materialism"; it contained the previous motif of aiming at the sublated unity of idealism and realism, of spiritualism and materialism, and in it the previous motif (this thought itself is something which can be said to exist since German romanticism) of a true union of subjectivity and objectivity, of spirit and nature ... is maintained.

To see the circumstances of this matter let us cast a glance at their thought in 1844 when they positioned themselves at the "human being" as the "true state of absolute spirit".

1.3

Even though Marx at the time of the *Economic and Philosophical Manuscripts* and *The Holy Family* planned an internal sublation of Hegel's philosophy with Feuerbach as a model, this doesn't mean that he was positioned within the philosophy of Feuerbach, but rather he displays his own particular thought. In it can be seen a substantial germination of the thought of his later years. However, what I want to focus on as the current matter of discussion is the idea that "absolute spirit" in Hegel is positively placed in its "true state" of the "human being", and through this, the real union of nature and spirit is posited.

Hegel, as is well known, makes, in *The Phenomenology of Spirit*, absolute spirit the substance = subject,[21] and views the world as the complete process of the self-alienation and self-acquisition of this substance = subject, presenting a majestic system composition. In the *Economic and Philosophical Manuscripts*, in particular the third manuscript where he discusses as the main theme Hegel's philosophy, Marx presents a stance of continuing this schema of Hegel's, recasting it and critiquing it.[22]

---

20   The source of the series of three quotes here is MEW, Bd. 1, S. 500, S. 551f., S. 553.

21   In addition to the well-known place of Hegel: *Phänomenologie des Geistes*, Vorrede (*Werke* [Suhrkamp], Bd.3, S. 22f.), I would like this implication and composition to be understood through such as a place in his [Über] *Friedrich Heinrich Jacobis Werke* (*Werke* [Suhrkamp], Bd. 4, S. 432ff.), and, further, a place in the so-called *Real Philosophy I*, the *Jenaer Systementwürfe I* referred to in the new complete works edition of footnote 8 above (Bd.6, S. 315).

22   As a thematic analysis of the circumstances here, I would like you to refer to Chapter 8 of

Marx at the time regards Hegel's schema itself of the self-alienation and self-acquisition of the substance = subject as the "discovered" "expression of historical movement", positively evaluating it.[23] But he sees a fatal difficulty in Hegel's making this "substance = subject" "absolute spirit".

"The process of movement of [alienation and acquisition] as the dialectic has to have a bearer, a subject. However, the subject comes into being for the first time as a result. It is the case that this result, that is to say, the subject knowing itself as absolute self-consciousness, is [in the case of Hegel] *God*, is *absolute spirit ...*".[24] For this reason, in Hegel "subject and predicate" have fallen into "a relation of absolute reversal".[25]

According to Marx at the time, what Hegel calls "absolute spirit" is none other than a metaphysically re-formed "human being", and what Hegel calls the self-alienation and self-acquisition of absolute spirit is none other than the process of self-alienation and self-acquisition in human "labour", the metaphysical re-forming of this "historical process", its speculative reflection.

The above way of putting things is a formulaic conclusion, and for Marx, although Hegel has a variety of limitations, he in any case provisionally interprets him as "understanding the essence of labour ... grasping conceptually the true human being as the *result of the labour* of human beings themselves",[26] and as "grasping *labour* as the essence of human beings, as the essence of human beings providing positive proof of themselves".[27] And he reveals a stance of developing and continuing Hegel's philosophy following this line.

Through a focusing along the lines of the *historical process* of self-alienation and self-acquisition in the labour of "human beings", in the thinking of Marx at the time the union of nature and spirit aimed at by Hegel is for the first time truly completed.

my 『青年マルクス論』 [[*On the Young Marx*]] (Heibonsha, 1971). In addition, in the three chapters of Chapter 6, Chapter 7 and Chapter 8 of this book I focus on investigation of the *Economic and Philosophic Manuscripts*, and the complete second half of this book has, therefore, the characteristic of being such that it should be called my *On the Economic and Philosophic Manuscripts*. Such being the case, I would like to trouble you to give it your consideration.

23   Incidentally, in the *Economic and Philosophic Manuscripts* it is even written that "what is great in Hegel's *Phenomenology of Spirit* and its final result ... is ... the fact that Hegel grasps the self-production of human beings as a process, the fact that he grasps thing-ification as de-thing-ification, as externalisation, and as sublation of this externalisation" (MEW, Ergänzungsband, 1. Teil, S.574. p. 199 of the aforementioned Japanese translation).

24   ibid., S. 584. p. 218 of the Japanese translation.
25   ibid., S. 584. p. 218 of the Japanese translation.
26   ibid., S. 574. p. 199 of the Japanese translation.
27   ibid., S. 574. p. 200 of the Japanese translation.

> The so-called totality of world history is none other than the creation of human beings through human labour, the transformation of nature for human beings ... human beings transform as the *Dasein* of nature for human beings, and nature transforms for human beings as the *Dasein* of human beings.[28] Human history, that is to say, nature as it transforms within the act of creation of human society, is the actual nature of human beings, and for that reason, even if it transforms in an alienated form it is true anthropological nature.[29] History itself is an actual part of natural history, in other words, it is an actual part of the transformation of nature of human beings (*Werden der Natur des Menschen*)[30] and in the same way that all natural things have to be created, human beings too have their act of creation, their history. This history is, for human beings, ... an act of creation which sublates itself as an act of creation accompanying consciousness.[31]

"History" is the process of self-alienation and self-acquisition of "human beings", is none other than the process of the manifesting in an in-and-for-itself form of "human beings".

The Marx of the *Economic and Philosophical Manuscripts* not only develops what can be called an "ontology of labour", he is already undertaking discussion of a specific economic concreteness, and, if we quote in regard to later discussion, he even makes the following argument. "*Industry* is the actual historical relation towards the natural human being. ... if industry is grasped as the exposure of the essential forces of human beings, the natural human essence or the natural essence of human beings is also understood. ... nature created through industry is true anthropological nature" etc. etc.[32]

To the extent that we speak in regard to a schema, however, Marx at this time takes a composition which "legitimises" the "human being" as the "true state" of the Hegelian absolute spirit, as the substance = subject of the dialectical historical total process unifying nature and spirit, objectivity and subjectivity, and to that extent, what is being called "human being" isn't *simply* the actually existing individuals but is "the human being" (*der Mensch*) as that which Feuerbach calls "species essence – species being" (*Gattungswesen*). Although, it is neither simply essence nor simply an existential, and it remains within the model of

---

28   ibid., S. 546. p. 147 of the Japanese translation.
29   ibid., S. 543. p. 143 of the Japanese translation.
30   ibid., S. 544. p. 143 of the Japanese translation.
31   ibid., S. 579. p. 208 of the Japanese translation.
32   ibid., S. 543. p. 143 of the Japanese translation.

a "shared understanding" in the Hegelians regarding the substance = subject, subject = substance, in in-and-for-itself form it was understood as the actual union of essence and existential, species and individual. Incidentally, Marx in the *Economic and Philosophic Manuscripts* goes so far as to write that "we must firmly grasp the path of movement which is the *human being (der Mensch)* continuing endlessly to be the subject",[33] and "*death* appears as the pitiless triumph of species over the specific individual, and seems as if it contradicts the unity of individual and species, but, however, a specific individual is simply a specific species existent, and as such a specific it is mortal".[34]

In this way, in the Marx of the point in time of 1844, the idea of a "sublating union" was put forward locating the oppositions of nature and spirit, objectivity and subjectivity ... not in the Hegelian metaphysical absolute spirit, but in the substance = subject which is "human being", and, what's more, locating it in the actual historical process which is human labour.

But does this consequently mean that the formula of "subjective – objective (subject – object)" has really been overcome through this composition? Certainly, a union of the dichotomous nature of subject – object is aimed at. Nevertheless, however, as long as a schema of the Hegelian so-called "dialectic of subject – object", a schema of the thing-ification and re-subjectification of substance = subject, is maintained is it not the case that this remains within the formula of "subject – object?"

In actual fact, Marx, as early as in the following year, self-sublates this provisional proposal from the point of time of 1844. With an attention fixed on the perspective of the historical process of human labour first and foremost, he maintains many points, yet he also comes to overcome the composition of the Hegelian school self-alienation and self-acquisition of the substance = subject, and, consequently, the schema itself of "subjective – objective". Through this, Marx goes beyond the horizon of modern philosophy in general and opens up the horizon of a new world-view. This is none other than the horizon within which "materialist history" is based.

---

33   ibid., S. 545. p. 146 of the Japanese translation.
34   ibid., S. 539. p. 135 of the Japanese translation.

2   The Overcoming of Humanism and a New Horizon

In Marx sublating the temporary proposal of the point in time of 1844 and the opening up of a new horizon, together with an internal maturing a particular external shock is received. This was the "internally violent" debate[35] within the Left Hegelians which at that very time had become fierce, in particular the shocking internal critique of Left Hegelian-ism as a whole Max Stirner put forward in his *The Unique One and His Property* [Tr. *The Ego and Its Own*].

Tracing the debate internal to the Left Hegelians, and analysing in detail the "Stirner shock",[36] lies outside our topic here, but through casting a glance at part of the "debate", and through Marx and Engels making their way through the maelstrom of the debate, let us turn our attention as we go to how they overcame the level of the Left Hegelians, in particular the level of the "human"-ism, and to how they came to open up new ground through this.

In addition to each publishing two essays in the *Franco-German Yearbook* at the beginning of 1844 ("On The Jewish Question", "Introduction to a Critique of Hegel's Philosophy of Right", and "Outlines of a Critique of Political Economics", and "On Carlyle"), at the beginning of 1845 they published the joint work *The Holy Family*, but it didn't bring forth much of a response.[37] Although there

---

35   Regarding this situation, see my essay-in-installments 「『ドイツ・イデオロギー』と その背景 – 文献学的研究から内容的討究への架橋のために①」 [*"The German Ideology* and Its Background – For a Bridge from Philological Studies to Content Studies (1)"] (『知の考古学』 [*The Archaeology of Knowledge*] First Issue, March 1975, published by Shakai shisō sha). The majority of the group of debate essays here are planned to be published in 『ヘーゲル左派論叢・第一巻』 [*Collected Essays of the Left Hegelians – Volume I*] to be co-compiled – supervised by myself and Rachi Chikara (Ochanomizu shobō, to be published in the spring of 1984).

36   This shock also had a strong influence on Feuerbach and B Bauer. Regarding the fact that even they were forced to make a "trajectory correction" I'd like you to see my comments in the three-way discussion with Shirotsuka Noboru and Shimizu Takichi, 「マルクス主義 の思想的核心」 [*"The Thought at the Core of Marxism"*] (『理想』 [*Ideal*] September 1977). As an essay which has dealt with this problem, there is Kokubun Kō's 「ヘー ゲル学派における人間主義の顛末」 [*"The Details of Humanism in the Hegelians"*] (名古屋人文科学研究会『年報』 1981 [The Nagoya Society for Humanities Research *Yearbook* 1981]). I ask that it be read alongside this essay as a supplement to it.

37   McLellan's identification of this matter is on p. 131 of 『マルクス伝』 [*Karl Marx: A Biography*] (jointly translated by Sugihara Shirō, Shigeta Kōichi, Matsuoka Tamotsu and Hosomi Hide), Mineruva shobō. Cornu's is in August Cornu: *Karl Marx und Friedrich Engels*, Bd. 2, 1962, S. 349 f. In addition, I hear, according to information presented by Rachi Chikara, that such as K Heinzen (he was the next editor-in-chief after Marx of the *Rhenish Newspaper*) even writes in *Die Helden des deutschen Kommunismus*, Bern, 1848, S.60. that the publisher of *The Holy Family* had more copies returned than had been shipped; in

was reference made in mutual critiquing within the Left Hegelians, it was only at the level of lightly dismissing Marx and Engels as imitators of Feuerbach.[38] Although to our eyes today it can be seen that already at that time they had everywhere gone beyond the confines of Feuerbach, to the extent that they are regarded as being located at the time within the broad frame of a Feuerbachian "human (human as a species being)"-ism their being regarded as imitators is not without justification.—If in response to the criticism of a "human"-ism of (the nature of) imitators of Feuerbach they had changed their position to a "human"-ism things would have been simple. However, their intellectual development no longer allowed a resting in a "human"-ism. They required a self-critiquing going beyond agreement with a Feuerbachian "human"-ism. Even so, this was not a matter of a simple yielding to their critics. At the same time as they overcame "human"-ism they also overcame the level of their critics, and, in general, transcending in total the paradigm on which the ideology of the Left Hegelians was based, they stood within a new horizon.

2.1

Stirner only mentions Marx once in his major work, *The Ego and Its Own*, and that, what's more, is in the form of a footnote, and it is in the following kind of context.

> The task for Christianity was in fact none other than from the very beginning the realisation of "what is human", "the true human". Although Christianity, as is to be seen in immortal doctrines and the salvation of the soul, at first glance appears to place limitless value on the *self* [Ich = I], this is a misconception. Christianity places value on nothing but *that which is human*, and only *that which is human* is immortal, and I am also immortal only to the extent that I am human. In actual fact Christianity certainly taught that the soul is not lost. In the same way, liberalism equates all people as human beings. But this eternal life and this equality are both concerned with *that which is human* within me, and is not about me. As the bearer of that which is human, as the one who provides a dwelling to that which is human, to that extent alone am I immortal. It is the same set up as 'the King doesn't die'. Even if Rudolf dies that which is the

---

other words, that even the authors' complimentary copies were sent back. (『マルク ス・コメンタール』 [*A Marx Commentary*] Gendai no riron sha, Vol. II, p. 200).

38   Regarding the response of Bruno Bauer himself, I would like you to see my presentation of this material in my essay of the above footnote 35. In addition, I have presented material regarding reviews of *The Holy Family* in Issue 3 of the same periodical.

King remains. Even if I die ... that which is human remains. Whereupon, people, believing that that which is human and I have to be treated as exactly the same, come up with the following demand and have come to propound it as a thesis. That is to say, that I have to be a 'real species being', etc. (For example, see Marx on p. 197 of *The Franco-German Yearbook*)[39]

—The sentence within brackets at the end is a footnote. Further, the expression I have obstinately translated as "the human" is "human" with the definite article attached, *der Mensch*. Because in the case of the Japanese word "人間 (*ningen*)" differentiation with simply individuals is unclear, I have deliberately translated it 〚Tr. *der Mensch*〛 as "that which is human", so that it expresses the "human being as essential being", in the sense of being differentiated from existential selves. In this essay I take this rule of thumb of translation as necessary below, but in places where the nuance is clear from context I leave things at translating it as simply "human beings/humans". I would like this point to be borne in mind.

Stirner places the existentially unique person (the "ego" as such a thing) in opposition to the essential species human being ("that which is human"). – *The Ego and Its Own* is made up of two parts, part one being titled *On the "Human"* and part two *On the "Ego"*, with the discussion in part one bringing together discussion towards a critique of the "human"-ism of Feuerbach and his imitators.—Stirner has in mind the traces of his predecessors, wherein the Christian "God", in Hegelian terms "absolute spirit", is re-conceived in the process of development of the Left Hegelians as "'God' is in fact the 'human being'", in the manner of its true state being "human being" (Strauss), its true state being "the self-consciousness of humankind" (B. Bauer[40]), and its true state being "that which is human" (Feuerbach).

---

39 Max Stirner: *Der Einzige und sein Eigentum*. [Der wörtliche Abdruck der ersten Auflage, hrsg. v. P. Lauterbach, 1892, S. 205].—In the book easily obtainable in the present day, the Reclam Library edition of A. Meyer, S. 192 (for convenience, page numbers will be given for this henceforth). However, footnotes in this publication of Meyer's have been supplemented in the detailed form of Z.B. Karl Marx: Zur Judenfrage. In: Deutsch-französische Jahrbücher, Hrsg. von Arnold Ruge. 1. u. 2. Lfg. Paris, 1844. S. 197. In the Japanese translation by Kataoka Keiji (Gendai shichō sha), p. 35 of the final volume.

40 Regarding the gist of the argument of Strauss and Bauer, I would like, for the moment, to refer you to my 『エンゲルス論』 [*On Engels*] p. 87 f., and my joint work with Inoue Gorō, 『マルクスの思想圏』 [*Marx's World of Thought*] (Asahi shuppansha, 1980) p. 168 f. – As research essays which have come to my attention Murakami Shunsuke 「ブルーノ・バウアーにおける自己意識の哲学」 [*"The Philosophy of*

As is well known, Feuerbach propounds that "the secret of theology is the study of the human" and says that in the thesis that "God alienated himself and became human for us" (the incarnation of Jesus Christ) "subject and predicate are reversed", going so far as to assert that the correct understanding is that "human beings alienate their own essence and put forth God".[41] When it is said that "God is humankind", naturally "humankind" is not the living individual human beings. It is not the case that living individual human beings take straightforwardly predicates such as omniscient or omnipotent. That which is titled "human being" is not the existential individuals but is "that which is human" as species being – essence (*Wesen*) being.

Stirner attacks here in the following way. The followers of Feuerbach declare that human being, indeed, is the highest existence and proclaim the positioning of human being as a principle, but this "human being" is not the existential, real human being it is "that which is human" as essence being, and as is appositely declared in "God = human being", "human being" is simply another name for "God". Although the point has been reached where worship of "God as God" has been rejected, we have the composition where the living human being of existential individuals is still worshipped as "that which is human" (= "the true state of God"!) Now the Feuerbachian composition itself of regarding "that which is human" as the highest existence and taking "human being" as species essence, as substance = subject, has to be sublated.[42]

According to Stirner, "that which is human" is, in the same way as is the case with "God", no more than an *Idee* (idea)". Such a thing doesn't actually exist. What actually exists is only existential egos.

From our present time, Stirner is to be counted along with Kierkegaard as an originator of "existentialism"[43] but he neither proclaimed existentialism

Self-Consciousness in Bruno Bauer"] (Senshū daigaku daigakuin *Keizai to hō* [Senshū University Graduate School of *Economics and Law*] Vol. 8, March 1977), Ōba Ken 「ヘーゲル宗教哲学のバウアー的転覆」["The Bauerian Overturning of Hegel's Philosophy of Religion"] (『現代思想』[*Modern Thought*], December 1978, Special Expanded Issue), and a section of D. Hertz-Eichenrode: *Der Junghegelianer Bruno Bauer im Vormärz*, Phil. Diss. FU., Berlin, 1959, S. 42 ff. are of particular value.

41   Vgl. Feuerbach: *Das Wesen des Christentums*, 1. Aufl., 1841, 2. Aufl., 1843; *Vorläufige Thesen zur Reform der Philosophie*, 1843; *Grundsätze der Philosophie der Zukunft*, 1843 – Further, there is succinct discussion on p. 131 f. of Shirotsuka Noboru's authoritative, great work 『フォイエルバッハ－人間疎外の究明－』[*Feuerbach – Investigating Human Alienation*] (Keisō shobō).

42   Max Stirner: *Der Einzige und sein Eigentum*, hrsg. v. A. Meyer, S. 33 ff., S. 84 f., S. 191 f., S. 194 f., S. 201, etc.

43   For example, Hans G. Helms: *Die Ideologie der anonymen Gesellschaft. Max Stirners "Einziger" und der Fortschritt des demokratischen Selbstbewußtseins vom Vormärz bis zur Bundes-*

abstractly nor did he develop his discussion within the field of religious philosophy. – He states that Hegel and his school

> "introduced the idea into all things, into the world, and 'proved' that 'in all things is the idea, is reason' ... In today's culture 'that which is human' corresponds to this",[44] and he points out that "when emphasis comes to be placed on *that which is* human such is once again an idea, ... and it means that 'that which is human is immortal!' ... People think that it is that which is human which is the very self of history, the subject of world history, and it ends up being the case that people are convinced that this ideal being (idea based being) which is that which is human, that this [as substance = subject] in reality develops itself, that, in other words, it *proceeds to realise* itself",[45]

and, thereupon, severely criticising the view of history which has the composition of seeing "world history as the history of 'that which is human'", he places his own particular view of history in opposition to it.[46]

Here, however, we won't go as far as going into Stirner's view of history. He is a person who also attempted a German translation of Adam Smith and others, but at this point in time his theory of history lacks a social science concreteness. It will be sufficient for us to ascertain the details of what kind of new sphere Marx and Engels opened up stimulated by his strong criticism of the "human"-ism of Feuerbach and his "imitators".

2.2

Immediately after reading *The Ego and Its Own*, Engels wrote briefly, to Marx, in November 1844, in the following way.

> In the point of rejecting Feuerbach's 'human being', at least the 'human being' in the essence of Christianity, Stirner is correct. ... The 'human being', to the extent that it does not have its base in the human being of

---

republik, 1966. The like of Löwith counts Kierkegaard too as a left Hegelian. Vgl. Karl Löwith: *Die Hegelsche Linke*, 1962, Einleitung.—It is an eccentric way of putting things, but in the internal debates of the Left Hegelians the debate of "substance and self-consciousness" between Strauss and Bauer can be said to form the first round, with the debate of "human being and the only one" (the essential human being and the existential human being) between Feuerbach and Stirner forming the second round.

44   Stirner: *Der Einzige und sein Eigentum*, S. 408.
45   ibid., S. 410.
46   ibid., S. 410 f.

experience, is a ghost. In short, to the extent that we attempt to assert our thought, in particular what we call 'human being', as true we must begin from empiricism – materialism. We must extract the universal from the particular, and we must not extract it from itself, nor, in Hegelian fashion from empty space (*Luft*).[47]

Marx's letter of reply in response to this letter from Engels has not, unfortunately, survived,[48] but we can tell that Marx was unable to ignore Stirner's argument from such things as the fact that in Paris where he was living at the time he promises the editor of *Vorwärts*, Börnstein, to contribute an essay critiquing Stirner.[49]—Although this promise was not fulfilled. The thematic appearance in writing of Marx's critique – anti-critique of Stirner occurs in Part 3, "Saint Max", of *The German Ideology* written more than a year later.[50] However, it can be surmised that receiving Stirner's critique of "human"-ism, during this year and more, Marx would have come through a psychological – intellectual process of considerable contortion.[51]

---

47 MEW, Bd. 27, S. 11 f.
48 That a responding letter existed can be ascertained from the next letter of Engels' (vgl. MEW, Bd.27, S. 14). In my 『 エンゲルス論 』 [*On Engels*], p. 259 f., I conjectured, on the basis of Engels' second letter and a letter from Moses Hess addressed to Marx as well as Hess's *Die letzten Philosophen* etc., on the outline of Marx's discussion of Stirner in his letter of reply. I would like to have you refer to such.
49 Vgl. Marx, Brief an H. Börnstein, MEW, Bd.27, S. 432. In a newly discovered letter addressed to Börnstein (dated the 2nd of December 1844) contained in *Marx-Engels-Jahrbuch*, Bd.3, 1980, S. 299, Marx apologises that he will be one week late, but that he promises again that he will definitely send the manuscript next week.
50 This part, which takes up more than half the pages of this vast manuscript, a manuscript requiring two volumes, is "relentless", being what could be called a point by point critique of *The Ego and Its Own*, and we can see that Marx-Engels at that time recognised important meaning in critique of Stirner. It is difficult to agree with the explanation of Mönke et al (Bert Andréas u. Wolfgang Mönke: Neue Daten zur "Deutschen Ideologie", *Archiv für Sozialgeschichte*. Bd.8, 1968, S. 25 f.) regarding the drafting and the planned publication of *The German Ideology*. In connection with this matter, see also Galina Golowina: Das Projekt der Vierteljahrsschrift von 1845/1846. Zu den ursprünglichen Publikationsplänen der Manuskripte der "Deutschen Ideologie", *Marx-Engels-Jahrbuch*, Bd. 3, 1980, S. 260 ff.
51 I won't go into analysis of that process here, but I would like you to bring to mind that Marx promised in February 1845 the Darmstadt publisher, Leske, a two-volume book titled *A Critique of Politics and National Economics*, and that, although he even received an advance payment, he was in the end unable to finish writing the work—it seems that this book aligns with the *Economic and Philosophic Manuscripts*. Incidentally, in a letter to Leske dated the 1st of August 1846, Marx confesses that he had put aside the promised book half a year earlier, and in defence of the reason for doing so he writes: "in other words, before affirmatively unfolding my own theory, it seems extremely important to put forward ahead

In order to ascertain on what points and in what areas of thought Marx made leaps with the "Stirner shock" as his point of stimulation, let us for the moment analyse from the position of a third-party observer how Stirner's critique of the "human being" found its mark in Marx.

Stirner differentiates between the existential and essence, and says that "that which is human" as essence being is not an independently existential existent, and that it is at best no more than an "ideal (idea)".[52] Yet neither Feuerbach nor Marx, of course, considered such a thing as that "that which is human" as essence-being self-exists independently separate from the existential individuals. So, then, does Stirner's criticism of the Feuerbachian "human being" not strike a blow against Feuerbach or Marx at all? No. In a certain sense, it was of such a degree that it was substantially sobering for Marx.

When Feuerbach and Marx talk of "human being" as species being – species essence, that they understood such in close relation to human being as individual being – individual existential, to the extent that they were aiming at positioning things in "sensual – concrete" reality, this is of course obvious. Even if we put aside this obviousness, a unifying grasping of existential and essence was already a major problem in Hegel's philosophy, and when in 1840 the Prussian authorities switched from the protection of Hegel's philosophy they had given up until then to suppression of the Hegelians,[53] that which the elderly Schelling, who had been invited to Berlin as the advance guard, presented as

of this a book arguing against German philosophy and previous German socialism" (MEW, Bd.27, S. 448f.). It is to be surmised that, for Marx, realising that without first carrying out what he calls in later years "a settling of accounts of my philosophical conscience (*Gewissen*) up until then" (MEW, Bd. 13, S. 10) he would be unable to take a step forward, that he was now unable to unfold his own theory along the lines of his previous conscience, and so from the beginning of 1846 that he devoted himself to completion of *The German Ideology*, and in particular the Stirner critique section.

52   We have looked at this matter above so I will not provide citation for it again, but matters are understood from this kind of perspective in B. Bauer's essay, "Description of the Characteristics of Ludwig Feuerbach", which has been investigated to have acted as a direct causal link for the writing of *The German Ideology* (see Bagatulia "A Re-composition of *The German Ideology* Part 1", translated by Sakama Masato, 『情況』 [*The State of Affairs*] January 1974). Vgl. Bauer: Charakteristik *Ludwig Feuerbachs, Wigand's Vierteljahrsschrift*, 1845, Bd. 3, S. 105.—A Japanese translation of this essay of Bauer's is planned to be included in volume 1 of the essay collection of footnote 35 above. Concerning the issues surrounding the period when *The German Ideology* was written, I would like to refer you to Hayashi Masaji's time-laden work 「『ドイツ・イデオロギー』の世界観」 [*"The World-view of The German Ideology"*] (Part Two of Three) (contained in the bimonthly 『インパクション』 [*Impakushon*] Issue 25, Izara shobō, September 1983).

53   Regarding this matter, I would like to refer you to the relevant places in the aforementioned joint work with Inoue Gorō 『マルクスの思想圏 – 本邦未紹介資料を中

the pivotal point in his criticism of Hegel was none other than the problem of the existential and essence,[54] and from the circumstance that meeting this challenge was a major issue for the Hegelians,[55] Feuerbach and Marx paid particular attention to the union of the existential and essence. And, to tell the truth, Stirner's proposition of criticism directed at Marx by name, the thesis that "I have to become [through a "human liberation"] a real species being", also comes from the motif of a self-aware unity of the existential and essence.

In general, essence and existential, universal and particular, species and individual ... do not unify. It is for this very reason that that major philosophical debate since the Middle Ages, the so-called "universals debate", occurs. In regard to this, Hegel put forward the standard of essence and existential unifying in a privileged way in God = the absolute.[56] Incidentally, even if we put aside the criticism of the elderly Schelling, in the Left Hegelians there is a *re*-interpretation of "God" as his "true state", "the human being", and we cannot argue simply that there is a "privileged unifying of essence and existential". Thereupon, Feuerbach establishes the schema of "existential and essence unifying" in the situation where human beings have regained "God" (the state of alienation of the essence of human beings) within themselves, in the situation of the way of being of self-recovery from alienation.[57] Marx, going beyond the area of a dissolution of simply religious alienation, expressed an in-and-for-itself agreement of existential and essence in the self-recovery from the alienation of human beings in the unique "democratic system" of the State at the point of time of 1843, the time of *A Critique of Hegel's Theory of the State*,[58] in "human emancipation" in *On the Jewish Question*,[59] and in "communist" society

---

心に－』 〚*Marx's World of Thought—With a Focus on Previously Unpresented Material in This Country*—〛, and to 『エンゲルス論』 〚*On Engels*〛, p. 85 f.

54   Schelling: *Sämmtliche Werke*, Bd. 13, S. 57 f.

55   Engels himself, from 1841 into 1842, responded to the attack with the so-called "Anti-Schelling" trilogy of essays (MEW, Ergänzungsband, 2. Teil, S. 163–170, S. 173–221, S. 225–246). Incidentally, launching the *Franco-German Yearbook* in co-operation with Ruge, Marx sends a letter, dated the 3rd of October 1843, to Feuerbach asking that he contribute an essay, and what it was that Marx wanted from Feuerbach was an essay critiquing Schelling.

56   Hegel: *Werke* [Suhrkamp], Bd. 8, S. 135, etc.

57   Feuerbach: *Sämmtliche Werke*, hrsg. v. Bolin u. Jodl, Bd. 2, S. 316, etc. In relation of this to Marx, I would like you to see ibid., S. 244, etc. Vgl. auch Bd. 6, S. 38 f. etc.

58   MEW, Bd. 1, S. 231 f. "Here [in democratic government] species itself appears as an existential" etc. etc.

59   ibid., S. 370. "When the real individual human being ... has ..., whilst being an individual human being, ... become a species being ... at such a time human liberation is accomplished etc etc".

in the *Economic and Philosophic Manuscripts*.[60] In both Feuerbach and in Marx the *true* unity of existential and essence was realised not in the normal state of human existence, but in an in-and-for-itself state.

So then, in the situation before the realising of the state of in-and-for-itself, the situation of a state of alienation, are on the one hand the existential and on the other hand essence separated in a disconnected way, and do they coexist in such a state? Naturally, no. According to the understanding of being of the Hegelians, the existential particular and the essential universal are certainly not things which each self-exist independently. The existential particular exists in reality in the way of being of always "carrying" the essence universal, and the essence universal exists in reality in the way of being of always "inhering" in the existential particular, on each occasion the particular and the universal always existing in reality in a unified way of being. In this case, to the extent that the "carrying" substance and the "inhering" substance exist in the form of a dichotomous separateness it is not the case that the two are in actuality unified (as stated above, an actual unity is limited to the state of in-and-for-itself); however, the existential particular and the essence universal are always in their own way unified. (As I discuss later, this unification isn't static, within the framework of a unity carrying this separateness a *small* path of movement of alienation – recovery which is a bi-polarisation – re-unification proceeds sequentially in a spiral-like way). This matter can be said to be the consensus of the academic schools of thought since Hegel put forward his understanding of the "concrete universal" in a form in line, as it were, with Thomas Aquinas' *universalia in rebus* (the universal within the thing) in regard to the debate over the universals concerning the relationship between the particular and the universal, the first substance and the second substance, individual and species. And, to that extent, it is not possible to say which of universal and particular (essence and existential) is placed in a predominant position.—Nevertheless, however, when we place our focus on the composition of the dialectical *large* path of movement of substance = subject, on the total process of self-alienation and self-recovery of absolute spirit, or on the historical total process of the self-alienation and self-recovery of human being, we face the situation of having to say that what bears self-identity as a coherent substance = subject is under no circumstance the moment of the existential particular as particular substance, it is the moment of the essential universal as universal substance.

---

60   MEW, Ergänzungsband, 1. Teil, S. 536. p. 131 of the previously cited Japanese translation. "This communism ... is the true solution to the oppositions of existential and essence, ... of freedom and necessity, of individual and species".

What Stirner attacks is precisely the composition of this large path of movement.—Let us turn our gaze, here, to "human being" when we speak of the
historical total process of the self-alienation and self-recovery of human being.
The "human being" in the case of the history of human beings, of human history, is clearly not simply individuals, but rather has the meaning of species
being. Indeed, even though it is not the case that "human being" exists independently, separated from individuals, simply gathering together biographies
of individuals doesn't lead to the "history of human being", a history which has
a particular history of development. When we speak of the "history of human
being", we speak of a composition in which it is as if there were a single –
particular subject, and as if there were a describing of the continuous development form of this single grammatical subject.—Even though individuals are
from the beginning a union of existential particular and essential universal,
and even though they are, for example, the subjects of the "self-alienation and
self-recovery" in the *small path of movement* of thing-ification – externalisation through personal production and de-thing-ification and internalisation
through personal consumption, they are not the "substance = subject" of the
large path of movement of the human history self-alienation of the historical
establishment of the system of private ownership and the human history self-
recovery of the establishment of communist society. The "substance = subject"
of the large path of movement is a "subject in a species universal form", a subject of a separate dimension to individuals.—In actuality, on the whole, when
history as human history is the matter under discussion, the dichotomy of the
subject of the operation of history in the dimension of individuals and the subject of history in the dimension of "human being" always arises as a problem,
and the determining of a relation between the two becomes an issue.[61]

Here, if people take the nominalistic viewpoint of seeing the subject which
is the "human being" etc. as simply a logical invention, with the subject of
history being only the existential individuals, this is, in this, one position.
(Isn't it the case that "people of the modern era" tend to lean towards this
viewpoint, a viewpoint which only recognises realness in the existential individuals? Indeed, though it is uncertain whether "the history of human being"
is really fully grasped with this viewpoint, nonetheless, if questioned as to
whether then it is the case that the "subject of history" of "human being" exists
in reality separate to individuals, isn't it the case that it is usual to reluctantly

---

61   I would like you to see my 『事的世界観への前哨』 [[*An Advance Post for a Koto-
      Centred World View*]] (Keisō shobō, 1975) p. 285f. regarding the circumstances and the
      composition of this matter.

acknowledge the "nominalistic viewpoint", "the viewpoint that only the individual exists in reality?") In reality, Stirner takes this viewpoint and dismisses "human being".

However, at the least, Marx up until the *Economic and Philosophic Manuscripts*, to the extent that he was within the *general framework* of the Left Hegelians, though it be entirely natural, held to a composition which establishes "human being" in a dimension where such cannot be reduced into individuals. And it's not as if it is a negative residue. Marx at the time, as we saw in the previous section, "replaced" Hegel's "absolute spirit", the "substance = subject" of the large path of movement, with "human being", the "true state" of absolute spirit, and positively held to the grand conception of his grasping (*begreifen*) of human history as the large path of the movement process of the self-alienation and self-recovery of "human being". To that extent, as the historical subject, it is then the case that "human being" as species essence being, distinguished from individual existential being, was, in terms of logical composition, affirmatively assumed. Stirner, naturally, couldn't possibly have known of the unpublished *Economic and Philosophic Manuscripts*. (If he had perused these manuscripts and had known the thinking included therein he would have leapt for joy and made of them a perfect target!) However, he interpreted the composition of the problem we are focusing on at the moment from Marx's published essays in the *Franco-German Yearbook* and directed the knife of his criticism towards it.— As long as one attempts to grasp human history as the large path of movement process of the self-alienation and self-recovery of "human being", a coherent "human being", which is "grammatical subject = substance = subject", has to be "human being" as species being, distinguished dimensionally from simply individuals. When putting forward *simply* individuals as the subject of history, "history" breaks with the death of individuals. (Although, a nominalistic viewpoint which sees a comprehensive describing of the *discontinuous* succession of the birth and death of individuals as human history is also possible, but this is not the position Marx took). So, Marx up until the time of the *Economic and Philosophic Manuscripts* declares, as I have also quoted above, that "we have to firmly grasp that path of movement in which human being is continuously the subject [*human being* as species being]", that "*death* appears as the harsh victory of the species in regard to the particular individual, and appears as if in contradiction to the unity of individual and species, yet, the particular individual is simply a specific species being, and is mortal as such a particular individual".[62] If we proceed to follow through with the logic here, the large path

---

62   The same as note 33 and note 34 above.

of movement of "substance = subject" in the Hegelians doesn't escape in general the model of being such a composition, and this is the reason for the fact that the situation is a schema where species being as the universal, different to the mortal particular, is immortal, and that as such the being "human being" continues to be held to be the coherent subject of this path of movement.

What Stirner criticises is the "human being" as the "subject of history" assumed as coherent "substance = subject" in precisely this kind of composition. He sneers that with this kind of composition it is the same mechanism as "Rudolph dies but the King lives". He, if we quote without begrudging repetition, ridicules that "the matter is that 'human being doesn't die!' ... people think that human being is the very thing which is the subject of world history, and they end up believing that human being ... that this in reality unfolds itself, that, in other words, it proceeds to enact itself",[63] and he astutely criticises the fact that in the Hegelians, in particular Feuerbach and his "imitators", we have a composition which makes "world history the history of 'human being'".

When we examine things in this way, although it's certainly not the case that Marx himself literally thought that "human being doesn't die" or "world history is the history of 'human being,'" when we render for-itself the Hegelian composition of logic which he took at the time of the *Economic and Philosophic Manuscripts* we see that Stirner's criticism regrettably does hit the mark.

Hereupon, Marx, reflecting on the level of his own thought, a level where he was in agreement with Feuerbach*ian* "human"-ism, radically re-examined the "history of human being", particularly the "subject of history", and came to the stage of carrying out a reconstruction of theory based on a new standpoint and composition.—We can verify the achievement of this by means of a series of texts which take the following year, 1845, as the turning point.

2.3

Marx, just before he encountered Stirner's criticism of "human"-ism, and taking a debate with the Bruno Bauer faction as his opportunity, from within himself had partly come to a realisation of the problems contained within the composition of logic of the Hegelian-style large path of movement of the self-externalisation and self-acquisition of the substance = subject. This can be easily recognised if we analyse the famous passages of *The Holy Family*, which indicted the "secret of the speculative composition" of the Hegelians. However, I will leave this matter, which involves the composition of logic of the theory of alienation, to the next section, and here, focusing along the lines of the prob-

---

63   The same as note 45 above.

lem of "human being", on the problem of essence and existentiality, let us look at the new horizon opened up by Marx-Engels.

In addition, when discussing matters in the form of a focus on the history of the formation of ideas, discussing Marx and Engels from the beginning as one is not permitted, with it being necessary to go into the issue of the "share" of the two.[64] In such a case, too, one has to consider in detail the debate with the Bauer faction, the response of Stirner, and also the break with those of the so-called "true socialism", and the influence from Moses Hess, etc. However, I think it will be sufficient here, not going in depth into the issue of "share" etc., to grasp the general framework outcome.[65]

2.3.1

In the so-called *Theses on Feuerbach*, the eleven point notes determined[66] to be notes written down in 1845, Marx, in complete contrast to his high praise

64   Research which takes up this issue already exists in our country, with Mochizuki Kiyoshi's 『マルクス歴史理論の研究』 [*A Study of Marx's Theory of History*] (Iwanami shoten, 1973) in the lead. However, I have a different view in several decisive areas concerning Mochizuki's identification regarding "share". In this matter, I would like to trouble you to consider my essay 「『ドイツ・イデオロギー』研究の現段階」 [*"The Current Stage of Studies of The German Ideology"*] (『日本読書新聞』 [*The Japan Reading Newspaper*], serialised over eight occasions beginning with the 17th of June 1974 issue) and my discussion 「望月清司氏の『ドイツ・イデオロギー』論をめぐって」 [*"Concerning Mochizuki Kiyoshi's Study of The German Ideology"*] (『情況』 [*The State of Affairs*], December 1974).

65   Undertaking proper investigation of these matters it is necessary to commit to a group of studies from here and overseas. However, I would like to pledge such for another occasion. In particular, research in this direction in our country is substantially stronger compared to such overseas, and I regret that I am unable to deal with these matters here given that there are numerous outstanding works in this area, with, in the area of monographs alone, apart from Mochizuki's magnum opus mentioned in the previous footnote, such as Nakagawa Hiroshi's 『史的唯物論の形成と発展』 [*The Formation and Development of Historical Materialism*] (Aoki shoten, Shiteki yuibutsuron kouza [A Course in Historical Materialism] Vol. 2 1977), and Hosoya Takashi's 『マルクス社会理論の研究』 [*A Study of Marx's Theory of Society*] (Tōdai shuppankai, 1979). In this essay, for better or worse, I have refrained from discussing these major works as the direct discussion doesn't overlap with them, so I ask for your understanding. [Recently, Shigeta Suimio's 『資本主義の発見』 [*Discovering Capitalism*] Ochanomizu shobou, 1983, also dealing with this matter, has also appeared].

66   Although the year of 1845 is irrefutable, there is doubt about placing it, in the manner of the existing commonly held view, in the earlier half of Marx and Engels. Regarding this matter, I would like you to see footnote (1) of my 「『ドイツ・イデオロギー』とその背景—文献学的研究から内容的討究への架橋のために（完）—」 [*"The German Ideology and Its Background – For a Bridge from Philological Studies to Content Studies (Final) –"*] (『知の考古学』 [*The Archaeology of Knowledge*] published by Shakai shisō sha, 1975 Issue 3).

of Feuerbach in the two essays carried in the *Franco-German Yearbook* of the previous year and in *The Holy Family*, comes to severely criticise him. —There, as is well known, the following passage is to be seen.

> Feuerbach resolves the religious essence into the human essence. But the human essence is no abstract general inherent in each single individual. In its reality, the human essence is the whole of the social relations. Feuerbach, not entering into critique of this real essence, has the following forced upon him.
>
> 1. That he abstracts the progression of history, ... and presupposes an abstract, isolated human individual.
>
> 2. Essence, as a result, can only be grasped as "species", as an internal, mute universality naturally linking the many individuals.[67] Feuerbach doesn't see that the abstract individual he analyses belongs to a particular form of society etc. etc.[68]

The *Theses on Feuerbach* show a general closeness to the statements of the much more senior Moses Hess, who Marx at the time was in close association with,[69] with Hess having written in the following way.

> "With the phrase the 'real' human being Feuerbach anticipates, on some occasions, human being as individuated bourgeois society ... and on other occasions, human being as society, 'human being as species', 'the essence of human being', and he thinks that he has pushed this essence into the human being as individual. ... But human being as species is only real within a particular society, that is to say, a particular society where all human beings form themselves in it ... and can undertake their self-activity," and "the essence of human being is a social essence."[70]

---

67   MEW, Bd. 3, S. 6.
68   ibid., S. 7.
69   Regarding this, please see the points I make in my 「初期マルクス像の再構成」 [["A Recomposition of the Picture of the Early Marx"]] (1967) [contained in my collection of essays 『マルクス主義の成立過程』 [[*The Process of Formation of Marxism*]]]. However, in doing so, I would like to ask you to consider the points I make in conjunction with Rachi Chikara's 「ヘスは若きマルクスの座標軸たりうるか」 [["Is Hess Able to Act as the Coordinate Axis for the Young Marx?"]] [contained in his 『初期マルクス試論』 [[*Essays Concerning the Early Marx*]] Miraisha], and the 「追記」 [["Postscript"]] to my 『マルクス主義の地平』 [[*The Horizon of Marxism*]] (Keisō shobō, 1969).
70   Moses Hess: *Philosophische und sozialistische Schriften*, hrsg. v. Cornu u. Mönke, S. 384, vgl. S. 330 ff.

It is unknown how Marx's *Theses* is involved with a triggering from Stirner. That Hess attacked the dichotomous nature of "human being" in Feuerbach through a triggering from Stirner is, to begin with, certain.[71]

As the sequence of debate, it will be convenient to review how Stirner discussed not only Feuerbachian "human being" but in general the dichotomous nature of the expression "human being".—Stirner explains that, even though they are in the same way called "human being", it is necessary to clearly distinguish between essential determination wherein "he is such and such a something" is predicated and existential individual wherein "he is such and such a someone" is designated. The determinateness wherein "such and such a something" is predicated in the manner of a predicate and the individual-ness wherein a "certain someone is ..." is indicated in the manner of the grammatical subject, though in the everyday expressed by the same words, "human being", the whole of the predicative determinateness of the former indicates the essence of human being (human being as "essence"), with the grammatical subject-like individual of the latter pointing to the existentiality of human being (human being as "existential"), and they are completely separate matters.[72] With this in mind, the existential individual is an existent which exists in reality, but the "essence" is an "abstract general" wherein a "common determinateness" was extracted from the numerous existential individuals, and is "no more than" ideal being. According to Stirner, that which exists in reality is only the existential individual, and that which is "human being" as essence being doesn't exist in reality. We mustn't mix or superimpose the two. Yet Feuerbach's followers end up, with their talk of human being as species being, superimposing existential individual and essential universal!

---

71   Incidentally, the relevant text by Hess, *Die letzten Philosophen*, 1845, was originally written as a preliminary attack against Stirner. The Japanese translation of this pamphlet is planned to be included in Vol. I of the four-volume 『ヘーゲル左派論叢』 [[Collected Essays of the Left Hegelians]] cited in footnote 35 above, with a commenting essay by Yamamoto Kōichi appended.

72   This thinking originates in *The Unique One and His Property*, but Stirner's essay "Recensenten Stirners", *Wigand's Vierteljahrsschrift*, 1845, Bd. 3, which is jointly the object of critique in *The German Ideology*, is explicit in this regard. A Japanese translation of this essay of Stirner's by Hoshino Satoshi is also planned to be included in the collected essays mentioned in footnote 35 above (he also has 「シュティルナーのヘーゲル左派批判」 [["Stirner's Critique of the Left Hegelians"]] 『理想』 [[Ideal]] May 1978, and 「シュティルナーにおけるヘーゲル主義」 [["Hegelianism in Stirner"]] 『現代思想』 [[Modern Thought]] December Special Expanded Issue 1978).—If I might remark additionally, the problematics of "definite description" and "individual designation" had long been already settled by the time of Stirner.

Stirner's view, certainly, is easily accepted by the untrained ear. To the extent that within the horizon of modern views of being only recognising existence in the existential individual, and regarding the essential universal as at best only existing as an ideal, is the basic theme, I fear that his argument might easily gain the agreement of the reader. However, for Marx, whilst recognising a partial validity to Stirner's point, as a whole he rejects the paradigm itself of the view of being within which Stirner stands, opening up a new horizon.

On reflection, in the history of views of being in Europe, two types of "substance" have come to be thought of. An existential, individual, primary substance, and an essential, universal, secondary substance, are such.—The thinking that essential universals such as "that which is human" or "that which is fruit" *exist in reality* separate to the individual thing (in other words, the position of "*realism*" within the "universals debate") is unpopular, indeed, in the modern period, and is not unlikely to be regarded as recklessness, but I would like it to be called to mind that in the Middle Ages this was the mainstream.— The Hegelians, as mentioned above, didn't regard the secondary substance as independently self-existing, but they did understand the two substances in a "unifying" way, in the form of the secondary substance "inhering" in the primary substance.

Incidentally, the understanding that the secondary substance "inheres" in the primary substance, the understanding, if we restate things changing perspective, that the primary substance "carries" the secondary substance, is, without it being pointed out by Stirner, indeed, a problem. For Marx, even though from the start he didn't think that it literally "inheres", to the extent that he had to guarantee the composition of the self-alienation and self-recovery of "substance = subject", that he had to guarantee particularly a coherent self-identity of "grammatical subject = substance = subject" in the large path of movement, he, as we saw above, relied on the schema of "inheres". But, now, as if in partial acknowledgement of Stirner's point, Marx declares in the *Theses on Feuerbach* previously quoted that "the human essence is not an abstract general inherent [*inwohnen* [[sic]] = inhering!] in each single individual". The primary substance existential human being does not then "host" the secondary substance essence human being. So is human essence no more than abstract idea, and is that which exists in reality only the existential individual as the primary substance? If we were to answer yes, here, that would mean complete agreement with Stirner. However, Marx not only rejects human essence *in* the form of being of a secondary substance, he also simultaneously rejects the Stirnerian view of being where individuals self-exist in the form of being of primary substance. In Marx's way of thinking, the idea of "inheres – carries" is certainly in error, but in it a true state is reflected in distorted form.

Stirner regards essence determinateness which makes a certain person such and such a person, such and such predicative determinateness, as not being the determination of being which makes the individual in question that one and only individual, and he removes all predicative determinateness from the primary substance, the existential individual.[73] From Stirner's view of the existential, the existential individual as primary substance transcends from all predicative essence determination, and has in itself a self-identity as one and only individual. But according to Marx, that which is the existential primary substance, described as self-existing even when the "predicative" determinateness of something something is entirely removed, does not in reality exist, and that which is an existential having no essence determinateness is simply empty abstraction, simply a "nothingness". (Though, Stirner, ahead of Sartre, self-determines as "nothingness",[74] and fixes his position to such). It is then not the case that the existential primary substance separate to so-called "essence" determinateness self-exists.

We need to consider here what the "determinateness" by reason of which a someone is made a being is. In the traditional European view of being matters had come to be considered according to a schema wherein something called substance exists, and qualitative determinateness inheres in or is ancillary to that substance. However, Hegel argued in great detail that qualitative determinateness which is reflected in a self-completing form in everyday consciousness, in the manner of qualitative determinateness which inheres in or is ancillary to substance, is not in actuality something which is closed inside or on the surface of a single substance, that it exists in relation to things external to the substance in question, that qualitative determinateness is in its actuality none other than something where relation-to-other-determination has been reflectingly "attributed (to the relation item substance)."[75]—Above, I used a substance-centric way of expressing things, I used a way of expressing things as if firstly there are substances and that these substances secondarily interrelate amongst themselves. Hegel certainly hasn't managed to completely do away with not only the theory of "substance = subject", but also a substance-centred view of being. However, in concrete situations he shows knowledge of a relation-centred type, and he had come close to the view that "it is the very relation state which is primary being, and that that which is the rendered

---

73   See the essay in ibid. S.180f., etc.

74   ibid. However, I do not intend to ignore the fact that Stirner puts forth his argument in a different context to the for-itself ontology of Sartre.

75   Regarding this problem, I would like to have you see the detailed discussion in my 『弁証法の論理』 [The Logic of the Dialectic] (Seido sha, 1980).

self-existing of the nodes of relations is none other than the *so-called* primary substance, and that that which is the rendered self-existing of the totality of relations-determination is the *so-called* secondary substance". If we deliberately quote in relation to Marx's *Theses*, Hegel, in *The Philosophy of Spirit*, even writes in the following way. "In the concrete being of the individual belongs a totality of the *relations* he forms with other human beings and with the world in general. This totality is *internal* to the individual, and this totality [of relations] forms the reality of the individual" etc. etc.[76]

Keeping the above in mind, let us re-read the previously quoted famous passage from *Theses on Feuerbach*.

"The human essence (*Das menschliche Wesen*) [in other words, the determinateness which makes the existential individual a human being], is in actuality, the totality of the social relations". Due to his inability to discern this actuality of the human essence, Feuerbach on the one hand puts forward "human essence" as an "abstract general inhering in single individuals", whilst on the other hand falling into the situation of taking as "precondition an abstract, isolated human individual" in which this essence "inheres".—In the *Theses* an explicit critique – anti-critique of Stirner isn't carried out, but if we anticipate the thematic critique of Stirner in *The German Ideology*, Stirner does no more than render self-existing as the true existent only the latter moment of the twofold determination carried by Feuerbach's "human being", that is to say, the latter of the two moments of essence and existential, and what he calls "the unique" and the "existential individual" are none other than an "abstract, isolated human individual [in other words, a human individual from which all social relations have been abstracted]". Stirner "ignores the fact that the abstract individual he analyses belongs to a specific social form". Thus, critique of Stirner is, *as a matter of logic*, already contained within the critique of Feuerbach's twofold determination.

Put schematically, the understanding of being within the model of the essential, universal secondary substance "inhering" in the existential, individual primary substance, this understanding of the Hegelians up to and including Feuerbach, indeed, as Stirner points out, doesn't make sense. But it is not the case that it is sufficient to eliminate the secondary substance, and to insist on the existential individual as primary substance. The Stirnerian style "primary substance"-ism has to be rejected as well.—Although the model of the essence "inhering" in the existential doesn't hold, in it the situation of the unity of the

---

totality of the relations and the *nodes* of the relations was, in distorted form, in any case, projected. In it, simultaneous with the understanding that the universal doesn't self-exist apart from the individual, the correct understanding that apart from essence (correctly speaking the totality of the relations determination) the existential doesn't independently self-exist was hidden distortedly.[77] Now, through focusing along the lines of the actuality of the relations, overcoming[78] substance-ism itself is the required task.—Not only the Feuerbachian "human"-ism which located itself in species essence, but together with the Stirnerian humanism which locates itself in the individual, existential "humanism" in general which takes "human being" as substance = subject has to be overcome.[79]

2.3.2

Marx-Engels didn't carry out an overcoming of "humanism" in the dimension of an abstract – general theory of being, they carried it out, precisely, through concreteness, locating it in "history".—For us too, let us, now, focusing along the lines of the place of "history", look at their positive thesis.

Taking an anti-critique of Stirner as their thematic opportunity, in *The German Ideology*, which proclaims a critical overcoming of Left Hegelian ideology as a whole,[80] Marx-Engels reconstruct the debate locating their axis on the people "being-in" historical relations, on the "relations of people towards nature and mutually between themselves".[81]—In the *Theses* matters were lim-

---

77 I intend that the next section will make things clear regarding this implication, so I will leave things as conjecture here.

78 This is not something limited in any way to the place of our view of the human being or our view of society, but is something which ought to be brought as far as our view of nature. I intend to make this point in a separate essay dealing with this matter thematically, but I ask that you take note of the fact that in his later years Engels puts forward this viewpoint in *Dialectics of Nature*.

79 This can be said to mean an overcoming of the position which takes "human being" as, if we put things in the style of Heidegger, *subjectum* = *hypokeimenon*, that is to say, an overcoming of what he calls *Subjektivismus*. Vgl. Heidegger: Die Zeit des Weltbildes, *Holzwege*, 4. Aufl., S. 81f.

80 This fact can be known from the book title, *The German Ideology. A Critique of Recent German Philosophy According to Its Representatives Feuerbach, B. Bauer and Stirner, and of German Socialism According to Its Various Prophets*, which Marx announced in April 1847 in the *Trier Newspaper* and in *The German Language Brussels Newspaper*, and also from the composition and content of the manuscript.

81 The restored manuscript – newly edited edition printed in footnote 3 above, Karl Marx/ Friedrich Engels: *Die deutsche Ideologie*, Neuveröffentlichung mit text-kritischen Anmerkungen, hrsg. v. Wataru Hiromatsu, Kawade shobō shinsha Verlag, Tokio Japan, 1974. (Below, this text will be abbreviated to D.I., and the pages of the original text edition and

ited to the general expression of the "totality of the social relations", but, now, the relations spoken of are structurally re-determined with the "relations of production"[82] as the key axis.

"What [*Was* = essence] [human individuals] are coincides with their *production*. That is to say, it coincides with what and how they produce".[83] Which is to say that, "in that way that individuals express their *life* [*Leben*], in accordance with that way their being is decided",[84] and this is the reason that "the specific form in which individuals express their life", that this is none other than[85] the "mode of production".

In order that we might know what significance and range the "relations towards nature and mutually amongst people located in the place of production" have in not only the context of the theory of being of human being but also in the context of the theory of being of history, let us insert here a somewhat long quotation.

> The premises we start with are certainly not arbitrary premises nor are they dogma. They are real premises, and are of a type in which it is only possible to abstract them in delusion. They are real individuals, their activity, their material conditions—that is to say, the existing life conditions to be found in front of them, and also, the life conditions created by their own activity.
>
> The first premise of human history as a whole is, it goes without saying, the existence of living human individuals. For this reason, the matter of composition which first requires ascertaining is the *physical organisation* of these individuals, and also, the *relation between* them and the remainder of *nature*, which is given them through that. Naturally, we cannot go into ⟨in detail⟩ here the physical characteristics of human beings

---

the Japanese translation edition will be printed together). D.I. original text edition S. 50. Japanese translation edition p. 50.—In 1983, the publishing of a new impression misprint-corrected edition of this Kawade shobō shinsha edition of *The German Ideology* came to fruition.

82   In *The German Ideology* this concept is still not sufficiently fixed as a technical term, but nonetheless I take the liberty of using this expression here. In *The German Ideology* the expression is used broadly, and I wish to take note of the fact that there is even a case where matters are written about in the following manner. "The existing relations of production of individuals, again, must express themselves too as political – legal relations." (MEW, Bd. 3, S. 347).

83   D.I. original text edition S.25. Japanese translation edition p. 25.

84   ibid.

85   ibid.

themselves, nor can we go into the natural conditions human beings find before them—the geological, oreohydrographical, climactic relations and so on. ⟨But these relations, not only condition the original organisation of human beings, the organisation of natural life, and especially racial difference, they condition the evolution or non-evolution of human beings from then up until the present day.⟩ The writing of history must all begin from this natural foundation ⟨of all history⟩ and the transformation of it it receives through the activity of human beings in the midst of the progression of history.[86] (Sections contained within the symbols ⟨ ⟩ are erased sections in the handwritten manuscript)

Amongst readers, there might be a tendency no less to perceive in this declaration of the vantage point and the beginning of materialist history an area in common with the ecological stance popular in current times.[87] It was more than twenty years after this that Haeckel newly created the word "ecology (*Ökologie*)" and defined it as "the study of the *relation* of the animal to both its organic environment and its inorganic environment", and it will be sufficient for it to be borne in mind that Marx-Engels were first to understand "history" from a "human ecological" perspective.

This is something I have pointed out on a separate occasion,[88] but our attention is drawn to the fact that, in the passage quoted above, in understanding history, as the matter of composition which needs to be ascertained before everything else, the "*physical* organisation of human individuals, and also, the *relation* between them and the remainder of *nature*" is given, and to the fact that, moreover, the relation in question is understood in the form of an *interrelating* connection.—Marx-Engels don't in the end regard "the natural conditions" as a fixed given, they determine them to be a given which "undergoes

86   Original text edition S.23. Japanese translation edition p. 23.

87   In recent times, it has come about that the book, *Marx and Engels on Ecology*, edited and compiled by Howard L. Parsons, Greenwood press, Westport, Connecticut, London, 1977, has even come to appear. I imagine that researchers in our country might scorn such, but, for me, I found amongst other things the more than one hundred page, lengthy "Introduction" and the extraction of an ecological expression of view from the texts of Marx-Engels of quite considerable interest.

88   See Part 2 (Section 2 「唯物史観と生態論的視角」 [["Materialist History and the Ecological Point of View"]] carried in the May issue) of my serialised work 「生態史観と唯物史観」 [["Ecological History and Materialist History"]] (『現代の眼』 [[*Contemporary Eye*]], 7 parts in total from April 1978).—With additional work having been done on it, this serialised work is scheduled for publication next year [1984] from the Nagoya publisher Yunite sha.

transformation through the activity of human beings, in the midst of the progression of history", and they understand what they call "material life conditions" as "the existing life conditions to be found before them and those created by their own activity". This can, undoubtedly, be said to be a position which is in marked agreement with an ecological perspective. When ecology understands a particular organism and its environmental conditions as a unified "system", the main point of this certainly doesn't simply lie in giving consideration to the environment for the lifeform. As is extolled in such succession theory, the main point is the inter-determining, dynamic relation of the activity of the group of organisms in question altering the environmental conditions, of subsequently this altering change determining back the way of being of the group of organisms.[89] Precisely in understanding this point, Marx-Engels diverge[90] from the like of so-called "geographical determinism" and "climate history" (crude "material"-ist history), and ground the position of "practice"[91] as objective activity in an ecological setting.

Although it is regrettable that it is difficult from the above quoted passages alone to read the part where the human side is determined back in accordance with changes in the environment, and in the base manuscript for the same *The German Ideology* the following declaration is made:

> In history, at no matter what stage, a material result, a totality of the productive forces, an historically created relation to nature and mutually between individuals is to be found. This is something which is passed on to each generation from the preceding generation ... even though these things are, indeed, on the one side changed by the new generation, on another side they assign in regard to this generation its particular life conditions, and it also endows this generation with a specific development, and a special characteristic.—In this way, just as human beings make their environment, the environment makes human beings.[92]

---

89 I would like p. 288 of Chapter 2 「歴史法則論の問題論的構制」 [["A Problematics Composition of the Theory of the Lawfulness of History"]], Part 3 of my 『事的世界観への前哨』 [[*An Advance Post Towards a Koto-Centred World View*]] to be referred to. Also, I would like Sub-section 3 of Part 1 of the serialised work mentioned in the previous footnote to also be referred to.

90 Vgl. MEW, Bd.20, S. 498 f.

91 MEW, Bd. 3, S. 5. In addition, I would like my essay, referred to in footnote 1 above, 「マルクス主義の哲学と『実践』の概念」 [["Marxist Philosophy and the Concept of 'Praxis'"]], to also be referred to.

92 D.I. original text edition S. 50 f. Japanese translation edition p. 50.

Looking at this, it is at least clear that in looking at "history" Marx-Engels represented an ecosystem-like inter-determining state of human subjects and the natural environment, and this is something worth bearing in mind.

For us, however, let us refrain, here, from further referring to the fact itself of matters being ecological (*ökologisch*). It will be sufficient if we can render for-itself the fact that Marx-Engels for the present understand the way of being of "human beings" "being-in" the world in the dimension of the ecological "relations to nature and mutually between individuals", and the fact that the "relations of production", a key category of materialist history, is also located in this fundamental scene.

"Production" is the axis of the ecological, dynamic relation of "human beings – nature" (to borrow here an expression from *Capital*, the "material metabolism (*Stoff-Wechsel*) between human beings and nature");[93] and the human ecosystem-like organising relations in the nodal circle which is the place of material production—this is none other than the "relations of production".

In *The German Ideology*, at the first stage in the base manuscript, it is consciously asserted that "the major problem regarding the relation of human beings and nature ... the 'unity of human beings and nature', had existed in the situation of industry from long ago, and has existed in different forms in each age according to the degree of development of industry".[94]—The previous Marx viewed things according to the model of the "unity of spirit and nature" = human being,[95] and held to a schema which sought the unity of that dualistic dichotomy in "human being", but in *The German Ideology* and after, he sees the procedural locale for the "unity of human beings and nature" in "industry". Now, the place sublating – unifying through practice the dualistic dichotomous nature of subjectivity and objectivity ... etc. etc. is fixed in "industry".

2.3.3

When Marx-Engels express a mediated unity in industry, it is not the case that they are considering a large subject that is "the human being (human race)" and a large object that is "nature" oppositionally according to the "subject – object" model. (If this were the case, it would mean that they would continue to remain within the bounds of the "subject – object" schema). To understand their conception, it will be convenient I think to take as a conduit the answer

---

93   MEW, Bd. 23, S. 192.
94   D.I. original text edition S.18. Japanese translation edition p. 18.
95   I ask that the citation in the previous section (2) be brought to mind. [Tr. It is not clear what citation Hiromatsu is referring to here].

to the following question: the answer to the likely doubt that, despite such as a "unity of human beings and nature in industry", isn't it the case that the "nature" which enters into a mediated unity in the place of industry, whether it be in the case of agriculture or in the case of manufacturing, is at best no more than the surface of the Earth, and Nature as Nature doesn't in any way unify with human beings?

If people take "nature" referred to in the unity of human beings and nature in the place of industry in the form of simply the nature of physics, in Heideggerian terms in the form of natural objects as "Being present-at-hand" (*Vorhandensein*),[96] then in such a case indeed it would mean that it would only cover one fragmentary area of the surface of the Earth. However, nature primarily appears in the form of what Heidegger calls "Being ready-to-hand" (*Zuhandensein*).[97] In the manner of, for example, the Sun appearing as something which ... brightly illuminates the world, which grows the plants, which warms our bodies, and the moon appearing as something which ... lights our night path, primary nature appears in a form responding to the practical interests of life.

Marx-Engels don't of course use the *expressions* "Being present-at-hand" or "Being ready-to-hand". However, they strongly criticise the fact that Feuerbach puts forward "nature" as the nature of the "scientific view", in accordance with nature in the form "revealed only to the eye of the physicist and the chemist"— precisely in the form of "Being present-at-hand"![98] And they state that "even these 'pure' natural sciences get for the first time not only their material but even their goals through commerce and industry, through the sensuous activity of human beings",[99] and they even go so far as to declare that:

> the incessant sensuous labour and creation, this production, is the very foundation of the entire sensuous world existing in reality today; therefore, if it were to stop for only a year, Feuerbach would not only find

---

96   Heidegger: *Sein und Zeit*, S.69.

97   ibid., vgl. S. 71.

98   D.I. original text edition S. 18. Japanese translation edition p. 18. In addition, in the context of Part 3 〖Tr. of *The German Ideology*〗, in regard to Stirner commenting in the following way—in other words, in regard to his writing: "How little can human beings conquer nature! They have to allow the sun to trace its course, the sea to roll its waves, the mountains to tower to the sky."—in regard to this completely natural thesis when "nature" is seen as "Being present-at-hand", Marx-Engels sternly argue back that "it does not examine the actual relation, determined by industry and natural science, but proclaims a fantastic relation of human beings to nature" (MEW, Bd. 3, S. 169).

99   D.I. original text edition S. 18. Japanese translation edition p. 18.

a major change in the natural world, the whole human world too ... would immediately disappear. Naturally, at such a time, the pre-existence of external nature remains in force, and none of these matters apply to the first human beings who arose through natural generation, yet, however, this distinction only has meaning to the extent that human beings are considered as things separated from nature. Incidentally, this nature which precedes human history is in no way the nature Feuerbach lives in in reality, and, if we exclude the surface of the several recently born Australian coral islands, today it no longer exists anywhere, and as a result it is a nature which doesn't exist for Feuerbach as well.[100]

Having established the standpoint of materialist history, Marx-Engels, in this way, perceive "nature" in the form first and foremost of "Being ready-to-hand", in the form, to put it in a manner more relevant to our point, of fulfilling the role of an internal moment in the human ecosystem (this substantially differs in terms of species difference from fauna and flora ecosystems in general, with the organisational structure being determined by the active factor of production activity, taking industry as the organisational axis) and, as a result, in the form of "historicised nature"[101] "changed" through the activity of human beings.[102]

If we use the *expression* the unity of human beings and nature in the place of industry, it sounds as if firstly something called human beings and something called nature exist, and that after that the two are combined, but the primacy of ecosystem-like relations, indeed, is the ultimate truth. The real state of affairs is that nature exists as manifest nature (ready-to-hand nature) for the first time through being mediated with human beings in the place of industry, and human beings exist for the first time as human beings existing in reality through being mediated historically – in reality – practically with nature in the place of industry.

---

100 D.I. original text edition S. 19. Japanese translation edition p. 19.
101 D.I. original text edition S. 18. Japanese translation edition p. 18.
102 Even though, in this way, we see "nature" primarily in the form of ready-to-hand, it surely doesn't require adding that secondarily the need is brought about to deal with it in the "Being present-at-hand" form. This is the nature which forms the object image of the natural sciences, and is also the nature which the dialectics of nature takes as its subject matter. (Despite being a Being present-at-hand it is from the beginning something mediated in an epistemological sense, and it is not the so-called raw existent itself). However, this is a matter of a provisionally different dimension, and is for the time being outside the bounds of discussion here. [Regarding this matter, I would like reference to be made to Chapter IV of this book "The Historical Reification of the Natural World", and to the "Epilogue" p. 208 f.].

If we turn our gaze here to the side of "human beings", human beings have being-in in an historically determined ecosystem-like world.—In this way of putting things, the regret still remains of human being (the human race) being rendered, as a whole, a grammatical subject = subject. Whereupon, if we express things focused on the individuals, individuals do not exist in (*sein-in*) the present-at-hand natural world or historical world, they have being-in (*in-sein*) the ecosystem-like "to-nature and between human relations", and this ecosystem-like "totality of to-nature and between human relations" is none other than the historical world. The main point being, individuals have being-in in the historical world.—In this, a method of expression still remains in which it is as if individuals are substance-like subjects, but, correctly, it's not that individuals exist independently and enter into a relation state, the "Being there" (*Dasein*) and also the "Being as it is" (*So-sein*) are determined by the histor-ical relations in question, and, to put it most relevantly, the individuals who are "Being there"—who are "Being as it is"—are none other than the "nodes" of the relations in question. (When we say the nodes of relations, people are apt to essentialise and represent the things in relation, and to end up ima-gining that "nodes" are homogenous particles, lacking in individuality. But the nodes of relations are each one unique, and are precisely *individual*. That which people think of as the individuality inhering in an existential, substantial indi-vidual is in no way something inhering in the individual herself or himself but is simply something where precisely the uniqueness of relational "nodes" is taken as a substantial attribute in a misapprehension in terms of "becoming physical").[103]

Theorists of a certain type accept that individuals have being-in in the his-torical world, but having done so they may, perhaps, insisting on the existential individuality of individuals, raise the problem of the individual immanence of "spirit" and "consciousness". This is that spirit or consciousness are things which are immanent in each monadic person, and that they cannot "resolve" into rela-tions. Let us, then, look at Marx-Engels' understanding regarding this matter.

Marx-Engels make a direct break with the modern philosophical view which has seen "consciousness" as a spirit substance or function which inheres self-completingly within each person. Following a concept of consciousness which

---

103   I investigate properly and thoroughly the circumstances of this matter in Chapter 2, Part 3
      of my 『存在と意味 – 事的世界観の定礎 – 』第一巻,「認識的世界の存在構
      造」 [*Being and Meaning – The Foundations of A Koto-Centred World-view*—Volume I—
      "The Being-Structure of the World of Cognition"] due to be published this autumn at the
      latest [published in October 1982].

had already emerged in Hegel,[104] and, moreover, in a form in accordance with the new vantage point of materialist history, they write in the following way.

> My *relation* with my environment is my *consciousness*. Where a relation exists in reality, there, it exists in reality for-me.[105] Consciousness can only be conscious being. And human being means the real process of their lives.[106] Consciousness, in the beginning, of course, is mere consciousness regarding the sensuous environment, ... is consciousness of the relations with other people and things outside of us.[107] – Consciousness, from the beginning, is not such a thing as 'pure' consciousness. 'Mind' from the very beginning carries the spell of being 'charmed' by matter, with matter here appearing in the form of a moving layer of air, sound, in summation, *language*. The time when language was established was, that is to say, the time when consciousness was established, and language is practical, real consciousness which by reason of existing in reality for other people exists in reality for the first time for myself too.[108] Consciousness, in this way, is from the very beginning already a social product, and as long as human beings exist it will continue to be a social product etc. etc.[109]

As can be seen, Marx-Engels do not see "spirit" and "consciousness" as an *internal* substance or function, they understand them as fundamentally *"relations"*. What's more, they understand them as people's relations "towards-nature and mutually" rendered for-themselves, and, moreover, as things which come into existence in reality only in the "intersubjectivity" of the kind which, to put it in the language of today, takes its "real and actual state through linguistic communication".[110]

---

104 See my 『弁証法の論理』 [*The Logic of the Dialectic*] p. 71 f. [I would also like you to see the points made in Takemura Kiichirō's 「哲学的問題構制の転成」 ["A Transformation of the Composition of Philosophical Problems"] (published in 『理想』 [*Ideal*], October 1983)].
105 D.I. original text edition S.28. Japanese translation edition p. 28.
106 D.I. original text edition S.29. Japanese translation edition p. 29.
107 D.I. original text edition S.28. Japanese translation edition p. 28.
108 D.I. original text edition S.26 f. Japanese translation edition p. 26 f.
109 D.I. original text edition S.28. Japanese translation edition p. 28.
110 Regarding this, see my 『もの・こと・ことば』 [*Things – Koto – Language*] (Keisō shobō, 1979) p. 98. For further detail see 『存在と意味』第一巻 [*Being and Meaning*] Vol. I, Part 1, Chapter 3. [Tr. The word translated here as "things", *mono*, refers to physical things only, and the word *koto*, often translates into English as "things" ie. in the sense of events].

In materialist history, human being, including spiritual – consciousness moments, is understood as a state of relation being-in the "historical world".

In this way, now, not only human being as essence but human being as existential as well is re-determined focused along the lines of towards-nature and mutual ecosystem-like – primary relationality. Within the horizon of this new ontology of human being, which is inseparable from a unique ontology of history, "humanism"[111] in general, which takes "human being" as substantial subject (*hupokeimenon*), whether it be "essence"-ist or whether it be "existential"-ist, is directly sublated, and a new world-view came to be opened up.

Although this new world-view based on the overcoming of humanism can, if we render matters abstractly in terms of ontology, be determined *für uns* to be something which put forward a "primacy of relations" understanding of being in place of the primacy of the substance, European, traditional view of being, it is through consideration of the being of "human being" firstly fixed in the place of "history". It, as we have seen through this section, determines an ecosystem-like "towards-nature – between-human beings" relations-state organised with the place of production at the centre, determining human being and locating it as a being-in of this "historical world".

According to our view of things, Heidegger has in no way reached a full understanding of Marx, yet even he acknowledges things in the following way. "Marx ... has reached the *essential dimension of history*, and consequently the Marxist view of history excels the other various writings regarding history. However, Husserl, and as far as I know Sartre, do not recognise in being an essence of the historical. As a result, neither *phenomenology* nor *existentialism* has yet reached a dimension where productive dialogue is possible for the first time with Marxism" etc. etc.[112] (By the way, from the history of philosophy viewpoint unique to Heidegger, this passage of his means that he evaluated[113] Marx to be the most outstanding thinker amongst all the philosophers since Socrates! I would like this fact to be taken note of).—At the time in 1947 when he wrote in this manner in *Overcoming Humanism* ⟦Tr. *Brief über den*

---

111   See footnote 79 above. Incidentally, at the beginning of the essay I referred to in footnote 36 above, Kokubun Kō writes that "it is some time now since notice was given of the death of 'human being' through structuralism, and the overcoming of humanism proclaimed. However, upon reflection, long ago in the middle of the previous century a similar circumstance occurred in the process of development of the Young Hegelians ...", and, I venture to say, this is very much to the point. On reflection, whether it be Feuerbachian, Stirnerian, or, going further back, Straussian or Bauerian, the humanism of the Left Hegelians can be said to have been the culmination of modern humanism.

112   Heidegger: *Über den Humanismus* [Lizensausg], S. 27.

113   Vgl. Heidegger: *Holzwege*, S.193 f., vgl. auch *Vorträge und Aufsätze*, u. *Was heisst Denken?*

"Humanismus"〕, Heidegger had in mind Sartre's *Existentialism Is a Humanism* 〔Tr. *L'existentialisme est un humanisme*〕, and for Heidegger he could not
have dreamt that the later Sartre, completely revising in *Critique of Dialectical
Reason* his evaluation of Marx, would come to "regard Marxism as a philosophy
impossible to go beyond for our current age",[114] but what I wish to pay attention
to here together with this is the fact that Heidegger critiques Sartre's concept
of the "existential" itself. According to Heidegger, Sartre conceives of "the existential" within the bounds of the contrasting schema of "essence (*essentia*)"
vs "existential (*existentia*)" traditional to European ontology,[115] simply moving
from a "human as essence"-ism to a "human as existential"-ism. We too regard
this comment of Heidegger's as having hit the mark. Incidentally, it's the case
that Marx, as we have seen, came, through the occasion of critique of Stirner,
one of the "originators of existentialism", to be the first, at the same time as
overcoming Feuerbachian "human as essence"-ism, to overcome *"existentialism"* ("human as existential"-ism)!—

On reflection, Marx-Engels have a different sense of topic and different problematics to those of Heidegger, with the sense of topic and problematics of
Marx-Engels differing in phase and dimension to Heidegger's "world", "being-
in" and "relations of dealings"[116] and being far more concrete and actual, but I
think that we can go so far as to declare that the world-view and new horizon
of materialist history unfolds located within the stance (*Grundverfassung*) of
what should be called "being-in-history".

3   The Sublation of the Theory of Alienation, and the Theory of
        Reification

In the previous section we provisionally took a cursory view of the fact that
Marx-Engels overcame "humanism" and opened up a new area via the problem
concerning the "essence" and the "existential" of human beings – if we put it
abstractly in the dimension of ontology in general, of the fact that this is understood as a shift from the "substance-ism" view of being traditional to Europe to

114   Sartre: *Critique de la raison dialectique (Précédé de Question de la méthode)*, Tom I. The
      Hirai Hiroyuki translation *Search for a Method* (the Japanese translation 『サルトル全
      集』〔*The Complete Works of Sartre*〕Vol. 25, Jinbun shoin) p. 6.
115   Heidegger: *Über den Humanismus*, S. 15 ff.
116   I would like you to see 「ハイデッガーと物象化的錯視」〔"Heidegger and Reificat-
      ory Misapprehension"〕, the Supplement to Part 1 of my 『事的世界観への前哨』〔*An
      Advance Post Towards a Koto-Centred World-view*〕.

a "relation-ism" view of being—and we now move a step further and arrange
to confirm the course which led to Marx-Engels presenting a new paradigm[117]

---

117   Amongst commentators, there are likely to be those who are derisive of my view that more
than a hundred years ago a new horizon was pioneeringly revealed. People may retort
scornfully, "Why is it that this was not realised for as long as a hundred years!?"—One has
to reply that, essentially, "it was too ahead of its time for ripening", but, for me, with this,
I also cannot but help pointing out the following circumstances as well. It is because for
a long period of time people were unable to decipher a horizon of new thought due to
the fact that the milestone, laborious work, *The German Ideology*, in which Marx-Engels
announced directly the disclosure of a new horizon, had lain hidden for as much as eighty
years, and, to the fact that when the posthumous manuscript was revealed to the public
for the first time in 1926 it was put into print in a form close to being an agglomeration
of discontinuous fragments without the separate layers and internal connections of the
hand-written manuscript being correctly understood, and, next, to the fact that in 1932, in
the Stalin era, a "forging alteration" was inflicted upon the hand-written manuscript, and,
following that, more than thirty years were allowed to go by wherein this "forgery" was
taken as the standard edition. It is only since the second half of the 1960s that people
became able to have contact again with the original state of *The German Ideology*. (It
seems to me that from the first in the Soviet new edition of 1965 and the German new
edition of 1966, and even in the new MEGA pilot edition of 1972, the distinction between
old layers and new layers in the hand-written manuscript and its internal connections
still haven't been correctly grasped, and these editions are hardly without fault) [A partial pointing out of the kinds of inconsistency these editorial deficiencies have brought
about in understanding the world-view revealed in *The German Ideology* is to be found in
the essay by Hayashi Masaji I appended information regarding in footnote 52 above. As a
result, I would like you to see this essay].—This, I believe, is the reason that the Restored
Manuscript – Newly Edited Edition of footnote 3 above came to have to be published,
boldly, in a corner of the Orient [in editing the original text for this, differences with previous editions have been contrasted and noted in detail].

It needs noting, however, that *The German Ideology* is a polemical book, and not one
in which one's position is described systematically. For this reason, one has to know the
thought of their left Hegelian opponents in order to fully understand the thought in the
work. However, because there has been a tendency amongst people, including followers of
Marx, to ignore from the beginning the Left Hegelian philosophers (even though there has
been a little research done, indeed, in regard to Feuerbach), it was doubtful that people
could even reflectingly bring into relief as "background" the thought of Marx-Engels—
Doubtlessly, people can come into contact with the new theory through the works of
Marx's later years, through *Capital* etc. But, it is extremely difficult to represent straight
from *Capital* etc. the horizon itself in the philosophical – ontological dimension which
supports that new theory. We have the circumstance that Marx didn't write a single work
of philosophy after *The German Ideology*, and in regard to the philosophical dimension in
the narrow sense there is absolutely no doubt that we must take *The German Ideology* as
our major source.—

This being the case, the philosophical new horizon which Marx-Engels had gone to
the trouble of revealing remained for a long time unrendered for-itself. And, as is seen in
the bipolar opposition between the "scientism" of "Russian Marxism" and the "humanism"

for a theory of society – history whilst decisively overcoming,[118] inseparably with the turning of sublating self-critiquingly the self-externalisation and self-acquisition which is the composition of the "theory of alienation", the horizon itself on which stands and on which is based the modern philosophical "subject – object" schema; and together with this we will confirm the orientation of the "theory of reification".

3.1
Marx, in *The Holy Family*, written at a time immediately prior to his receiving criticism from Stirner, "exposed" the "secret of the speculative composition" of the Bauer faction, and, going further back, the secret of the speculative composition in Hegel himself, and declared of himself in the following way.

> "If from real apples, pears, strawberries and plums I create the universal representation *'fruit'*, and, taking things further, if I *think* that *'that which is* fruit' is an essence actually existing outside of me, and that it is the *true* essence of pears, apples etc., then at such a time I – to put things speculatively – assert *'that which is* fruit' to be the *'substance'* of pears, apples, plums etc. ... When I do so, this means that I declare apples, pears, plums etc. to be simply the existential forms of *'that which is* fruit' ".[119] "Why then does *'that which is* fruit' appear sometimes as apples, sometimes as pears, and sometimes as plums? ... The speculative philosopher replies: this is because *'that which is* fruit' is certainly not a dead – undifferentiated – static substance, it is a living – self-differentiating – dynamic essence. ... We must no longer say ... a pear is a 'fruit,' an apple is a 'fruit' ..., rather we have to say ... that *'that which is fruit'* proposes itself as a pear, that *'that which is fruit'* proposes itself as an apple .... *'That which is* fruit,' in this way, is no longer a contentless – undifferentiated unity, it is the unity as the *wholeness*, the *'totality,'* of fruits forming an 'organically branched hierarchy.' With each branching of this hierarchy 'fruit' gives to itself a more developed – clearer existence ..."[120] "Behold. Although Christianity knows only the single embodiment [which is the incarnation] of God, speculative philosophy has as many embodiments as things exist. In

---

of "Western Marxism", the situation ended up being such that over a long period of time people came to "understand" Marxism forced within the horizon of modern philosophy.

118   This doesn't mean, of course, that Marx-Engels' thought is systematically complete. This is the reason, I believe, that a continuing development is required.

119   MEW, Bd. 2, S.60.

120   ibid., S.61.

terms of our current example, each individual fruit has the embodiment of the substance, the embodiment of absolute fruit".[121] "The speculative philosopher achieves this sequentially continuous creation through his declaring that his *own* activity of *moving* from the representation of apples to the representation of pears is the self-activity of the absolute subject which is *'that which is* fruit'".[122] "This operation ... is called grasping conceptually *substance* as *subject*, as internal process, as absolute person. And, this 'conceptual grasping (*Begreifen*)' forms the essential characteristic of the Hegelian method".[123]

Marx, in this way, at around the time of the late autumn of 1844, realised the weakness of the composition which makes an essential universal itself the "substance = subject" of self-movement. So then, has he promptly abandoned the proposal in the *Economic and Philosophic Manuscripts* in which he endeavoured to *Begreifen* the whole process with the " 'human being' which is the true state of actuality of the Hegelian 'absolute spirit' " as substance = subject (please recall the earlier point on p. 24 of this book)? Had he already realised at this point that what Feuerbach called "human being as species being" is also a type of "that which is fruit"? Even though there is an aspect wherein he can be said to have been partially beginning to realise it, judging from the praise of Feuerbach in *The Holy Family* and the tone of the work as a whole, it seems that he probably was not completely aware of it.

For Marx at the time, it is likely that he had the intention of developing matters concretely based on "the real human being standing on the base which is Nature" (that which is so called by Feuerbach), based, further, on human beings as the subjects of labour, and that he had set himself the role of having no connection with "speculative composition". From our perspective as third parties, there is something in this which can be acknowledged.

However, nonetheless, if we have Stirner comment, a composition which unfolds the whole process of human history as the forward moving process of the self-alienation and self-recovery of "human being" as "species essence being", is, certainly, a composition which makes that which is "human being", in a separate dimension to mortal individuals, self-unfold as substance-subject, and, regrettably, thus, it does not escape problems. If we consider things carrying its logical composition through to its limit, it is, in the end, essentially

---

121   ibid.
122   ibid., S.62.
123   ibid.

the same as the "speculative composition" of the Hegelian school. (Incidentally, no matter how much they might be speculative philosophers of the Hegelian school it's not the case that they spoke of the *self*-movement or self-*realisation* of "that which is fruit";[124] rather they had the intention of discussing matters concretely – realistically in their own way; what Marx critically pointed out was what would be the outcome if the logical composition of their discussion was carried to its limit). Regrettably, this much we have to admit. It will not do to make "*human being*" as "species essence being" the "substance = subject" of self-alienation – self-recovery in the large path of movement.

Even if one has become aware of this fact, however, this does not *automatically* mean that one should abandon the composition itself of the theory of "self-alienation – self-recovery". This is because it seems that a way is possible of saving – maintaining the logical composition of the theory of self-alienation through making *individual* "fruit" e.g. individual apples or individual pears, "substances – subjects" in place of "that which is fruit". (In Marx-Engels' determining, Stirner, with certain conditions, had the intention of adopting the theory of alienation as conceived along this line of thinking).

So then did Marx-Engels now locate the living, individual being "human being" in the place of "substance = subject" instead of "human being" as species being, and, through this, did they come to adopt a logical composition which makes human history the process of the large path of movement of self-alienation and self-recovery of "human being" as individuals? In summation, no. If we move "substance = subject" from essential human being to existential human being we still can't in the end avoid problems. At the very least, the *simple* existential individual isn't able to be the "substance = subject" of the large forward movement, and we can't speak of an "alienation – recovery" in terms of human history based on such. This is because it is likely that, having

---

124   Hegel himself, in fact, rejects the fallacy of seeing as independent the universal essence as opposed to the particular existential, the fallacy of regarding the universal essence as an independent substance, and, what's more, in doing so he puts forth none other than the example of fruit.—In the Introduction to the *Encyclopaedia* he writes in the following way. "The universal and particular must be differentiated in accordance with their primary determinations. If the universal is taken in terms of form and is placed alongside the particular it itself becomes a particular. If in the case of the objects of everyday life we were to deal with things in that way, it would be clear that it would be inappropriate. For example, a case where a person is looking for fruit but he or she rejects cherries, pears and grapes etc. on the grounds that they are cherries, pears and grapes and *not* fruit is such a case" etc. (*Werke* [Suhrkamp], Bd. 8, S.59).—For Marx, he is probably bringing forth this example of fruit, an example any follower of Hegel would know, to ridicule that the logic of the speculative composition of the Hegelians, no matter what the beliefs of the Hegelians themselves, is in the end ....

made the existential individual a substantial subject, even if we were able to depict the biographies of individuals according to the formula of the theory of alienation, this doesn't mean that the algebraic sum of these "small paths of movement" describes the "history of human being" which is "human history" as the large path of movement of self-alienation – self-recovery.

The Marx-Engels of *The German Ideology* now directly not only reject the way of seeing things itself which grasps human history as a process of self-alienation and self-recovery, they also critically expose the originating elements of the ideological misconception of this composition.

> The philosophers represented, under the name of 'human being' as ideal, individuals in a way of being no longer subordinate to the division of labour, and grasped the whole process [of history] which we have developed up until now as 'human being's process of development'. As a result, 'human being' has been forced on to the individuals of all previous historical stages, and it has been described as the driving force of history. In this way, the whole process has been understood as 'human being's process of self-alienation'. This, essentially, arises from the average individual of later historical stages being one after the other pushed on to earlier stages, and the consciousness of later generations being pushed on to earlier generations. Through this inversion which from the very beginning abstracts the real conditions ... etc. etc.[125]

Amongst commentators there might possibly be those who, having acknowledged the fact that, here, in the theory of human history of the Hegelian school style, even if the existential individual is called the subject of history, in the end, indeed, we end up with the process history of the alienation and recovery of the substantial essence "human being" which "inheres" in individuals, still respond in the following way.—Isn't it an "historical fact" that (A) "an age when people had an authentic way of being, a way of being still not alienated", (B) "an age when people came to have an inauthentic way of being, an alienated way of being", and (C) "an age when people sublate this inauthentic, alienated state and realise an authentic way of being, a way of being which is not alienated", that this (A) → (B) → (C) proceeds directly? Isn't it the case that the composition of the theory of "alienation – recovery" can be actually valid as a descriptive explanation of this "historical fact?"

---

125   D.I. original text edition S.142 f. Japanese translation edition p. 152.

A person, indeed, focusing on this and that historical phenomenon identi-
fying (value judgement) "social ills" and a "bad social state" can, provisionally,
grasp human history according to a schema of the kind, for example, of (a) an
historical stage when the system of private property didn't exist, (b) an historical stage when the "alienation" of the system of private property came to exist,
and (c) an historical stage when this "alienation" is sublated, and the system
of private property comes to no longer exist. And, in such a case, it might be
provisionally permitted that this understanding be pushed into the schema of
thesis-antithesis-synthesis, with (c) not being seen as a *falling* return to (a) but
as a *higher level* recovery of (a). (People have, from long ago, variously imagined
the historical past and the future according to the schema of (a) paradise, (b)
paradise lost, and (c) return to paradise!) However, was humanity ever really
in a paradise state in the past? Even in the state of (b), paradise lost, isn't it in
fact possible to see it as in a certain sense a "better" development stage than
(a)? Isn't it the case that commentators represent in the future, as an ideal
state which ought to be brought about, an "authentic", "non-alienated" state,
and, with this future state which ought to be realised as yardstick don't they
indictingly determine the current state to be an "alienated", "inauthentic" state,
and simply go on, in order to proclaim that this current state is a degenerating
state of being and isn't immutable, to the effect that before this current state
a "non-alienated", "authentic" state existed? Even though (a) and (c) possess a
homogenity insofar as they are oppositional, opposite determining states with
(b), and even though to this extent (c) can be called a higher level recovery of
(a), the point is not in the past with the falling transition from (a) to (b) but in
the fact that the current state (b) *ought to be* sublated and state (c) realized.
Here are expressed dissatisfaction with the current state (b) and aspiration
towards state (c). It's not as if there is no cause for the commentators' conception. In such, historical realities of the type of a current social state where
serious social contradictions have come to be exposed, and, a situation where a
new social way of being which has dissolved existing contradictions has come
to be foreseen, are projected. The composition where the commentators preach
of the fact that the current state is not something absolutely immutable but
is something possible of change, and point out the changeability contained
in the fact that it is not the case that the current state (b) was this way from
the eternal past but is something formed through a transformation from state
(a), and preach of the fact that in view of this (b) too should be possible of
change, can in the first instance be understood. Again, it's not that the circumstances where a consciousness of desire or ought (*Sollen*) where (a) should be
recovered at a higher level with a change from (b) to (c) cannot be understood.
But, just for what reason and how did the change from (a) to (b) occur? And,

how does the necessity or imperativeness of the change from (b) to (c) come into being? One might be able to apply the schema of alienation and recovery to the change from (a) to (b) and the change from (b) to (c), and might be able also to carry out a bestowing of meaning of alienation and recovery to these. However, whether it has been called alienation – recovery or thesis – antithesis – synthesis, with that alone neither why and how the change (a) → (b) → (c) is in fact necessary, nor why and how it is oughtly necessary, is in reality explained.

Certainly, the conception alienation – recovery, because in Christianty, in the case of Hegel, it was positioned in the schema of the religious representation of "God"→ "Human Being (Incarnation)" → "God", carried with it the idea that a process of self-alienation and self-recovery of the substantial subject is apodictic. To the extent that we take this intellectual schema as an assumption, if we just determine that the current state is an alienated state, of itself the implication is that self-sublation of the alienated state, that is to say, recovery of the authentic state, is apodictically assumed. That which Marx exposed as the "secret of speculative composition" of the Hegelians, however, was, precisely, none other than the speculativeness of this speculative schema.—When assuming the Christian schema of "God" → "Human Being" → "God", or, generalising, the schema of the tale of transformation of "authentic appearance" → "altering of appearance through transformation" → "change to natural state through recovery", it is believed, in such, that that recovery of appearance is apodictic by a matter of course, even if transformation is somewhat accidental. To this extent, if a state is pointed out to be an alienated state then return to that which is called the authentic state is a matter of course to the highest degree, and it ends up as if it's unnecessary to explain particularly the necessity or oughtness of such. The opinion of theorists of alienation as if the apodictic nature of "recovery" is explained simply by determining the given state with the concept of "alienated" state, or, the belief that the "theory of alienation" is an explanatory principle, is due to this composition.

This way of putting things, however, is a matter of having from the beginning examined things schematically; despite being theorists of alienation they certainly don't bring things to a close with the few words, "alienation has occurred", rather they attempt to speak with a certain type of concreteness each time of why and how the "alienated state" in question came into existence. And, in the case of the Hegelians at least, they don't do the like of simply seeking the concrete reason for the existence of the "alienated state" in the "intention to become ... myself" of the substantial subject. It is not "explanation" based on such intention, but rather that thereupon "explanation" of why – how the "alienated" state comes into existence through concrete activity under concrete conditions is aimed at as much as possible. (Even in the case of Hegel himself, if we put aside for the present places concerning the foundations of theology, the intention of the substantial subject is not made a direct basis of argument. Although in regard to the *Dasein* state of the human world the "cunning of reason" mediates,[126] he doesn't directly explain this with "cunning", but always strives to set forth his argument based on the concrete activity of people). When this happens, it certainly cannot be denied that a tendency is evident of forcing an "explanation" in a form able to be pushed into the schema of alienation – recovery, but it's not necessarily the case that there is self-satisfaction with a formularistic argument. This is particularly so in the case of the Left Hegelians, and it goes without saying and without unnecessary detail that Marx at the time he was reliant on the theory of alienation endeavoured towards concrete explanation without in any way being self-satisfied with a for-mularistic argument.—This being the case, however, though the case of those placing theological positive significance on the schema of "alienation – recov-ery" itself in the manner of Hegel is separate, for those in the area of using this schema as a conceptual device for at most establishing the argument (a) → (b) → (c), that is to say, a conceptual device for indicting the current state (b) and for explaining the apodicticity of sublation to (c), when they succeed in concrete, "scientific" explanation, the conceptual device of the theory of ali-enation – recovery becomes unnecessary. (In the case of Marx-Engels, in fact, as we saw previously, they realised the irrationality contained in the logical composition of the theory of "self-alienation – self-recovery of the substan-tial subject", and, further, they realised the ideological inversion of such, and further to this we mustn't overlook also the circumstance that they came to suc-ceed in a "scientific", concrete explanation through a new conceptual device. The overcoming of the theory of alienation and the establishment of the the-ory of reification, are, in terms of the process of the facts in the history of their formation, seen not as a linear process but as having been in large measure interlacing).

When commentators come to be able to explain the change from historical state (a) to historical state (b) "in the manner of the social sciences", and come to be able to explain the change from (b) to (c) along the lines of the "law-like nature of the social sciences type",—certainly, in such, whilst labelling (a) → (b) → (c) "in a form easily understood by the philosophers" according, still,

---

126   Regarding Hegel's famous but equally frequently misunderstood "cunning of reason" (*List der Vernunft*), please refer to my 『マルクス主義の地平』 [*The Horizon of Marxism*] (Keisō shobō, 1969) p. 171f., and, the quotations and "exegesis" on p. 164f.

to the formula of alienation – recovery is provisionally possible, the significance of "generative principle of explanation" of such as becoming (b) from (a)
through self-alienation or becoming (c) from (b) *through* self-recovery has now
come to be lost from the conceptual devices of "alienation" and "recovery"—
the conceptual device of alienation – recovery comes to be no longer useful as
the "generative principle of explanation". Here, since historical change from (a)
to (b), and, historical change from (b) to (c), is explained and focused along the
lines of the "composite power" of the concrete, historical activity of individuals, and such as alienation and recovery don't operate as "generative concepts of
explanation", this means that the principle of explanation only lies in the reified
"law-like nature of the social sciences type" focused along the lines of the "composite" of the concrete activity of individuals, and even if the formulaic schema
of alienation – recovery were to be applied to the historical transitions of (a)
→ (b) → (c), it's the case that here the significance and function the theory of
alienation originally had have now come to be lost.

Upon reflection from another angle, even if we have determined the current
state as the alienated state (b), are we able to explain as an inevitability the
transition from this state (b) to (c), the higher level recovered state of (a)? To
the extent that the belief that "since it is an alienated state it ought to return to
the authentic state" is taken as surreptitious assumption, and moreover to the
extent that this is "rendered logic" and the formula "an alienated state necessarily self-recovers to the authentic state" is taken as surreptitious assumption,
there is a tendency to believe as if we have been able to explain necessarily the
transition to (c) simply by pointing out that (b) is an alienated state; but, just
why if it is an alienated state is return to the authentic state inevitable? It's more
than clear, in light of the invalidity, that if we deliberately put things in terms of
a crude example, the type of proposition of: "A broken bowl is an inauthentic
state. For this reason, a broken bowl possesses an inherent inevitability to self-
recover to an unbroken state;" it's more than clear that in general it's not the
case that there is an inevitability of return, because it's an "inauthentic state",
to the "authentic state". Even if one insists on the factuality of the change (a)
→ (b), and even if one determines (b) to be an alienated state, this can't in any
way be persuasive grounds for the inevitability of (c), a higher level recovery of
(a). – The transition (b) → (c), in any case, requires "scientific explanation", and,
when that is achieved, as we saw above, alienation – recovery now loses significance and function as "generative explanatory principle"—The belief that being
an alienated state, a state has an inevitability of self-recovering to an authentic
state is a dogmatic representation implicitly accompanying the idea, not only
limited to its Christian form, of "taking the form of", yet, upon reflection, it cannot from the beginning be valid, and, for this reason, that it was no more than

something which, from its origin, lacks validity as a device explaining the inevitability of an "authentic state" (c) as a higher level recovery of (a) once the current state has been determined to be an "alienated state" (b) is rendered for-itself.[127]

---

127 One might reply here that even if the theory of alienation doesn't have validity as explanatory principle, isn't it, however, an appropriate deployment in terms of self-expressing a particular value judgement, a practical – evaluative attitude regarding the present and the future?—As is acknowledged in the discussion in the body of this essay, in determining the current state as an "alienated state", an "inauthentic state", an implication that an identification (value evaluation) that the current state is something undesirable, that it is something which ought to be repudiated, that it is something which ought to be practically overcome, is made. In addition, the state represented as "recovered state" and "authentic state", is not only a factual future state, it carries the value evaluation of ideal state (or, at the very least, a state far and away better than the current state). But how are the value judgment here and its standard authorised? Isn't it the case that the fact of the matter is that commentators project their own desires and rejections of the current state onto the future and take this projected "desirable" state as their standard, and that, in the end, they make their own, personal desires "objective", "imperative" standards? We can acknowledge that there is sufficient reason for the commentators' desires, and in many cases we have the same desires as they. To that extent, it's not that we don't share the value judgement with the commentators. But when it comes to the stage of reflecting on whether that value judgement has universal validity – objective validity we cannot simply absolutise our own value judgement. The value judgement in question carries class ideological-ness, partisan ideological-ness, and, provisionally, we are aware that, at best, it belongs to a dimension producing an antinomous oppositional postulate between it and the class ideology of the opposing other side. And, in addition, here, a composition of the like of that mentioned on pp. 73–74 of this book is reflected on, and its historical – social – class relativity and the self-sublation through the practical self-realisation of such are thematised for-themselves.—That which the commentators call value judgement does not, at the least, leave the area of antinomous ideological oppositional postulate. For Marx-Engels, they take one step further here and aim at a self-aware – practical sublation of this antinomous level, and this is built in to their theory of judgement – theory of value judgement and in to the method of their system composition.
     I discuss these matters thematically in the main discussion of the next "chapter", 2, so I will leave matters here with, focusing along the lines of *The German Ideology*, the following points.—Marx-Engels re-grasp in a self-aware manner the fact that such as the "essence" or the "authentic way of being" which the commentators take as the criterion of value are certainly neither immutable "essence" nor an "authentic way of being" fixed a priori but are actually simply something where an "anticipated picture of the human being" conceived as an ideal is ideologically imagined as an "essential", "authentic way of being", and they re-grasp the fact that such are goals to be realised for the first time in the future, and that the aim towards such is itself something determined by a particular historical-social existence. From such a standpoint, they ridicule the followers of the theory of alienation: "The philosophers don't say directly, you are not human beings. You were always human beings. But ... you were not true human beings. Your phenomenon did not correspond to your essence. You were human beings and not human beings!" etc.

Marx, in 1845–46, came to render precisely this for-itself, and the circumstance is such that this is interconnected too with the establishment of the "theory of reification".

3.2

In our previous discussion we determined that the theory of alienation cannot be valid as inherent explanatory principle in the large path of movement of the like of human history, but we did not in fact touch on whether or not the theory of alienation has validity as the composition of the process of the "small path of movement" in individual, social activity. In this section, let us aim for the resolution of this task and gradually touch on the composition of the theory of reification.

Materialist history doesn't view that which is human history abstractly and as one bundle, it grasps it focused along the lines of its concretely expressed, segmental arrangement. As a result, such as "social organisation", the "relations of production", and a "unitary economic substance" (*ein ökonomisches Ganze*)

(MEW, Bd. 3, S.232).—In *The German Ideology* not only is a "factual explanation" in accordance with the logic of the theory of alienation not the explanation, the "value evaluation" contained therein is also rendered self-understood as not being able to be ratified as it is, and so, matters are stated in the following way. "Karl Grün, equipped with cloudless faith regarding the fact that (a) the 'human being' is the ultimate purpose of world history, (b) that religion is the externalised essence of human being, and (c) that the essence of human being ... is the yardstick of all things, and, equipped ... with (d) currency and wage labour etc etc. being an externalisation of the human essence, sets out triumphantly to Brussels and Paris with the pretension of the true socialism" (MEW, Bd. 3, S.475.—However, (a) (b) (c) (d) in the text are my organising notations).

The reader will bring to mind, no doubt, that previously Marx himself, in the two essays in the *Franco-German Yearbook*, made statements of the same import as (a) (b) (c) (d) above i.e. that he issued forth with theses of the following type: "the ultimate goal of human emancipation is the human being", "the basis for the human being is the human being himself", "religion is the alienation of the human essence", "emancipation which had stood in the position of the theory which declares human being to be the highest being of the human", and that he asserted, as well, that "currency is a thing where the labour and existence of human beings have become alienated from human beings". And, in addition, the discussion in the *Economic and Philosophic Manuscripts* developed from such a vantage point. However, now Marx sneers at Grün, the theorist of alienation revolution, on the very grounds of these kinds of theses. This is none other than something which equates to a self-critiquing self-sublation of the theory of alienation.

For thematic treatment of the overcoming of the theory of alienation in *The German Ideology* please see my serialised work 「『ドイツ・イデオロギー』と自己疎外論の超克」 [["*The German Ideology* and the Overcoming of the Theory of Self-Alienation"]] I–V (contained in 『情況』 [[*The State of Affairs*]] July, August, September, November 1974, January–February Combined Issue 1975).

are postulated, and the synchronic – diachronic structure and dynamic form of such an arrangement state come to be investigated in the "manner of the social sciences".

Incidentally, scientific knowledge which takes so-called social phenomena as objects of investigation tends to be troubled by a split into two polar opposite positions regarding the *nature of being* of these objects. It is, if we put things in terms of theories of social *being*, an opposition between a social nominalism and a social realism. In the first position, the situation is that that which is existent is only individuals and their behaviour, with it not being the case that society as a particular existent exists, whilst in the second position, the situation is that that which is society has a particular existentiality unable to be reduced to the algebraic sum of individuals and their actions, it being regarded that individuals, rather, are simply branch beings unable to be independent and autonomous. (The first position appears prototypically in the theory of the social contract of the modern period, with the prototype of the second position being the theory of the social organism of and from ancient times. However, changing phase and dimension, the two have come down to us today as an opposition between a so-called methodological *individual*-ism and a so-called methodological *social*-ism). Marx-Engels achieved the formation of their thought right in the middle of the intellectual historical situation wherein social organism theory was reviving, and, for this reason amongst others, they were forced to decide appropriately on an attitude regarding this opposition concerning theories of social being.[128]

It goes without saying that Marx-Engels, as followers of Hegel, started from a social realist viewpoint. But, they freed themselves from the *so-called* Hegelian social organism view comparatively early. Did they, then, move to the position of social nominalism? No. As is known from the Introduction to *A Critique of Economics*, from his later years, amongst other places, Marx has not altered the understanding of his stance that "the human being is in the literal sense a social animal (*zoon politikon*). ... He or she is an animal which can only individualise

---

128 Regarding thematically the items of discussion of the circumstances of the problem of the opposition between "social nominalism" and "social realism" in the modern view of society, the details of the revival of "social organism theory" in the 19th century, and Marx's establishing of a position in regard to this situation, I would like you to peruse 「第III章　唯物史観における社会観の新地平」 [["Chapter III The New Horizon in the View of Society of Materialist History"]] in my 『唯物史観と国家論』 [[*Materialist History and Theories of the State*]] (Ronsō sha, 1982), especially 「第一節　ブルジョア的社会観の視軸との対質点」 [["Section 1 Points of Opposition with the Perspective of the Bourgeois View of Society"]] (pp. 56–78) thereof.

itself in society".[129] So, is a particular *substantial* existence, society, primarily existent? Naturally, no. If we listen to Marx himself, "it's not the case that society is formed from individuals", but that "society is the sum of the *connections – relations* of the individuals".[130]—In the previous section we saw "human being", that is to say, the individuals the social nominalist sees as substance, re-grasped, as "in its essence the totality of social relations", on the basis of a primacy of relations understanding of being, but, as this quotation directly shows, in Marx, the side of that which is society too, which the social realists see as substance, is re-grasped focused along the lines of the primacy of relations, as the "sum of the connections – relations".

In materialist history, in this way, what on the one hand the "individual" social nominalism ("individual"-ism) regards as independent substance and on the other hand the "society" social realism ("society"-ism) regards as independent substance, are not independent *substances*, but are re-grasped as being "the totality of relations" in the two dimensions, and, based on this view of being, the polar oppositionality of social nominalism and social realism is sublated.

In this, however, it is, of course, not possible that that which are the "relations" exist independently. These are, rather, relations which take the branch-like individuals as "terms", and what actually exists are the states of relation which have the individuals as "terms". However, it is usual that these relations do not appear in the consciousness of the individuals involved as mutual relations between themselves, but, rather, in everyday consciousness, they are reflected in the form of an objective object existing independently of the individuals, or, reflected in the form of relations between objective attributes or objective things. Certainly, this is also the reason that that which is the totality of that which is "society" can be seen in an illusory way as if it were a particular substance, and, here, the various social formations (*Gebilde*) come to be seen as existing objectively and independently. Moreover, these social formations, going beyond the region where they are cognized in their externality, even practically regulate, in the form of possessing a restrictiveness towards the activity of individuals, the behaviour of individuals.[131]

---

129   *Grundrisse*, neue MEGA, II. 1. 1, S.22. (Dietz Ausgabe, S.6)
130   ibid., S.188. (Dietz Ausgabe, S. 176)
131   It goes without saying that it is precisely E. Durkheim who, focusing on this fact, put forward in a self-aware manner a methodology which deals with "social facts" (*fait social*) "as things" (*comme de chose*).—As a section where his argument in regard to the distinguishing points I have given is summarised, E. Durkheim: *Les règles de la méthode sociologique*, 1895, 6. éd. 1921, p. 6. et seq.

Grasping the two aspects, the fact on the one hand that from the standpoint of materialist history the relations are reifyingly "rendered independent" for the everydayness of the subjects involved, and the fact on the other hand that these reified formations are, in their true state grasped through scientific reflection, always relation states, is the important and necessary point.—It won't do to settle matters saying that the first of these is, "viewed from the scientific point of view, simply misapprehension". This is because the subjects involved act restricted by the reified misapprehension in question, and because the real execution of social – historical acts and, consequently, the unfolding of history as history, make the "reified misapprehensions" in the everydayness of those involved into, so to speak, positive structural moments. I will, however, put this matter aside for the moment and will return to it in my later discussion.[132] Regarding, then, the second point; it surely doesn't require going into in detail that it is important. Because, in all likelihood, when we overlook this fact we fall into scientific fallacy.

For us, here, the composition wherein the relations reifyingly "become independent" comes into focus. It's not that there are "substantial subjects" of the relations themselves which move of themselves, rather the activity of the individuals gives rise to formations objectively "rendered independent", and thus people may think we can make, can we not, the composition of the self-thing-ification of the subject human being, and, as a result, of its self-alienation, our explanatory principle. However, if we aim at putting our conclusion first, within the horizon of Marx-Engels' materialist history, in the dimension of principles, we can no longer adopt the logic of the so-called "dialectic of subject – object" in which lies thing-ification of the subject and re-subjectification, and, consequently, we can no longer adopt the composition of the self-alienation and acquisition of the subject human being. This is the reason that the composition of the theory of reification is established within the horizon of sublating the "subject – object" schema.

The reason I noted, "in the dimension of principles", just now also lies here, and, having understood the relation state as primary being, in certain kinds of discussion there are occasions when it is convenient to undertake discussion placing the persons or things which are the "terms" of the relation state (appositely, the nodes of the relation) in the position of the grammatical subject. Accordingly, at the level of convenience, it's not the case that Marx-Engels don't also undertake discussion making persons or things the grammatical sub-

---

132   Ch. 2 in this book, "The Composition and Scope of the Theory of Reification", especially Section 2 and Section 3.

ject vehicle. In *Outlines of a Critique of Political Economy*, for example, the expression, "in production the person (*Person*) is objectified, in consumption the material thing (*Sache*) is subjectified",[133] is even used. However, in the same *Outlines*, it is declared that "as theoretical method, [the true] subject [i.e.] society, has to be always represented",[134] and society as the "sum of the connections – the relations" quoted a little while ago, indeed, is made subject = the appropriate vehicle. The declaration that society as the sum of the relations always has to be represented as subject, however, cannot mean that society always has to be discussed as grammatical subject. In cases of discussing individuals as the grammatical subject vehicle, it's not that these individuals are an ultimate substance-subject, rather it seems that it is a cautionary declaration that they exist as the nodes of the relations, that the true subject vehicle is the relation state, that we must always represent this.

In certain kinds of contexts, we discuss the human being as individual substance as generative subject, and use expressions such as she externalises "that which is internal", or, his subjective activity is objectified. To that extent, describing a "small path of movement" by means of the schema of externalisation – acquisition is not necessarily to be prohibited. Be that as it may, however, that which is called the behaviour of the individual substance is not the absolutely autonomous – spontaneous activity of this individual substance, it is something wherein the dynamic state of the "net" of the relations (relations towards nature – between-human beings) in which he is a "term"-like node has been manifested in him (the nodal circle). Even though we can regard his activity as autonomous – spontaneous activity to the extent that we grasp the individual substance in the self-completingly closed form of individual substance, this doesn't mean that, in reality, he is an absolutely spontaneous, generative subject. To quote *The German Ideology*: "People's 'internal true nature' ... is in all ages an historical product, and even if their society is based on 'external compulsions'", we mustn't "forget that their 'internal true nature' corresponded to these 'external compulsions.'"[135]—In this way, when we put the human being as individual substance in the position of a grammatical subject subject and discuss things according to the "subject – object" schema, such as, he objectifies his own activity, or, in the "small path of movement" he self-externalises – self-acquires, and further, when we say that the relations formed between an

---

133   Neue MEGA, II. 1. 1, S.26. (Dietz Ausgabe, S.11) Although in the hand-written manuscript it is not "consumption" but "person" (*Person*), I follow the time-honoured assumption of various schools of thought that this must surely be a writing error for "*Konsumtion*".
134   ibid., S.37. (Dietz Ausgabe, S. 22)
135   MEW, Bd. 3, S.468.

individual and another person or things are reifyingly "rendered independent", in actual fact, that individual substance subject is not a self-completing – independent generative subject, rather, even if there is a limited active subjectivity in that individual substance, it is reflected that the true creative subject is none other than the whole of the state of the social relations.

The composition of the theory of reification is based on reflection on this fact, and it sublates the "subject – object" schema which the theory of alienation depends on, and is not thing-ification of the so-called subjective, but rather it renders for-itself that it is reification of the state of the relations. However, reification of the relations does not mean that that which are the relations transform in a self-moving manner into material things. It means that for the everyday consciousness of the individual being-in the social relations (I wish note to be taken of the fact that these are not simply "something subjective", that, if we express things in compromise with the subject – object schema, they are already "subjective and at the same time objective" existents!), these towards-nature – between-human beings relations which take him as "one term" are not perceived as such an actual relations state but are reflected in the form of material things. (For a definition of "reification" itself see pp. 201–205)

Here, inseparably with the fact that both "individual" and "society", which so-called social nominalism and social realism misperceive as independent entities in a dichotomous form, are, together, re-grasped focusing along the lines of the primacy of relations, the logic is such that neither individual nor society can be accepted as self-moving, generative subject, and, whether it be the "large path of movement" or the "small path of movement", at the level of principles we have reached the stage where the logical composition of the self-alienation – self-acquisition of the substantial subject, and, going further back, the "subject – object" schema itself, upon which the theory of alienation depends, is, focusing along the lines of its true state, sublated in a for-itself manner.[136]

3.3

The sublation of the theory of alienation by the theory of reification mustn't be taken as the theory of reification being something which straightforwardly implies the contention of an historical – stage-like succession of "non-reified state – reified state – state-having-overcome reification". Reification, indeed, in

---

136   Leaving aside the details until Section 2 of the next "chapter", 2, I wish to be forgiven for leaving things here for the moment with my conjecturing remarks above.

regard to a certain type of reification phenomenon, does express its lack – current formation – resolution as an issue of historical fact. However, the theory of reification isn't something which takes on as it is the historical three stage schema of the theory of alienation. If one takes into account what was discussed above in (1) of this section it won't be necessary, I think, to go into detail here again.—Even if the various forms of reification are particular to specific stages of history, the mechanism of reification runs throughout history, and, based on this, a history as history, unable to be simply reduced to the algebraic sum of the activity of the individuals, is able to hold true.

Before we proceed to thematic investigation regarding the mechanism of establishment of the composition of the theory of reification and the historical law-like nature in keeping with such, here, whilst extolling the differences between the common theory of "reification" and the Marxian theory of "reification", and, going further back, inserting a degree of anticipatory footnote discussion, I would like, having done so, to bring this essay to a provisional end, and to aim at the same time at a bridging to the thematic investigation in the next "chapter" (Chapter 2 "The Composition and Scope of the Theory of Reification").

There was a view that, until their extolling by Lukács,[137] the concepts of "thing-ification" (*Verdinglichung*) and "reification" (*Versachlichung*) had been forgotten amongst Marxists—here and now I would like to carry the discussion forward (without at all going into the issue of the conceptual history context of the terminology of Schelling's *Bedingung* and the early Hegel's *das-zum-Dinge-Machen*). These terms had, rather, occasionally attracted attention through examples of their usage in the Neo-Kantian Heinrich Rickert and Max Weber, and also in Georg Simmel and Ernst Cassirer.—Regarding Lukács' "rediscovery" of the words "thing-ification" and "reification" as Marxian terms, it is conjectured that his association with Rickert and the others in Heidelberg might perhaps have been the intermediary opportunity—However, the occasion through which these words came to be used relatively popularly amongst philosophers and social scientists can be said to lie, above all, in their frequent predicative use by Lukács. Yet Lukács went so far, as is well known, as to use on occasion the concept of "thing-ification" with almost the same meaning as the concepts of "alienation" and "externalisation", and, regrettably, he used "alienation" and "thing-ification" in incomplete distinction, without a clear distinguishing conceptually. The origin is unclear, whether it is a problem brought about by Lukácsian usage, or an echo of Neo-Kantian usage, or an act

137   G. Lukács: *Geschichte und Klassenbewußtsein*, 1923.

of simple vulgarisation, but in actuality one frequently comes across still today examples amongst European and American commentators where "alienation" and "thing-ification" are used almost synonymously. In that regard, in our country in recent years, one hardly comes across at all examples of a use of the two terms as complete synonyms, but, one does come across such things as the label of a theory of "alienation = reification" with the implication of emphasising the "continuity" or "complementarity" between "alienation" and "thing-ification", and such things as people saying, "what we call reification is a special form of alienation", and "reification is simply a subordinate concept to alienation".

For myself, I don't have the slightest intention of interfering with the terminologies particular to commentators, but, at the least, I understand the concept of reification of the later Marx to be something which ought to be clearly distinguished from the concept of alienation of the early Marx[138] (which lay within the broad framework of the Hegelian concept)—in the factual process of the history of the formation of the concepts there is, of course, and certainly, a continuity, however—, and that which is the reason for "alienation" and "reification" having little difference in commentators lies, I think, in the concept of "reification" in commentators (it goes without saying that their concept of "alienation" almost unexpectedly puts aside the Hegelian logical composition) being postulated, still within the "subject – object" schema, in the composition of "objective existentialisation of the subjective".

In my view, it seems that when people speak of "thing-ification" or "reification"—this is something I have aimed at presenting[139] in previous works—three layers, of the following type, are primarily represented.

---

138 Entries relating to the concept of "alienation" in such as philosophy dictionaries appear, regrettably, to be extremely unsatisfactory. According to what I myself have seen, J. Ritter: *Historisches Wörterbuch der Philosophie*, 1971 – is detailed regarding examples from the classical world and the Middle Ages but one doesn't avoid the feeling that it is extremely rough regarding usage of the terminology by Hegel and the Left Hegelians. (Incidentally, the situation is such that in the lexicon of the Glockner edition *Complete Works*, the only *completed Complete Works of Hegel* at the present time, the item "alienation" doesn't occur!)

I would be grateful if I might be able to ask that you peruse—not that we can be at all self-satisfied with this—as the most detailed dictionary entry at the present point in time, the entry "the theory of alienation" occurring across pages 1,167–1,171 of the 『現代 マルクス゠レーニン主義事典』上巻 [*The Modern Dictionary of Marxism – Leninism* Vol. 1] (Shakai shisō sha, 1980). This entry, written by myself, might even be called a short essay, and it describes the theory of alienation in the order "1: Etymology and Meaning— Examples From Before Hegel", "2: The Theory of Alienation in Hegel", "3: The Theory of Alienation of the Left Hegelians", "4: Marx's Theory of Alienation", and "5: Contemporary Interpretations".

139 My 『唯物史観の原像』 [*The Original Image of Materialist History*] (San'ichi shobō,

(1)   "Object"-ification of human beings themselves.—For example, situations where human beings are trafficked as slaves (commodities), or where they have ended up becoming a mere accessory to a machine. Here, the way of being of a human being (provisionally another person) is reflected not as a "person" but as something which is of the same type as a thing, and in the sense that he or she is in a situation where he or she is dealt with as something identical to a thing "human beings" are seen as "having ended up being a physical existence".

(2)   "Object"-ification of the action of human beings.—This refers to situations where the movement of people rendered a mass can no longer be affected by the will of the individual members e.g. in the way of being of people in the human stream within a railway station building or within an overcrowded train, and, passing through a distortion, it runs through, as well, to the fixing as custom of forms of behaviour. Here, something which is originally human action has become a state of inertia unable to be controlled by the individual selves, and in the sense of having come to possess an "independent resistance" towards subjective acts of purpose "human action has ended up becoming a physical existence".

(3)   "Object"-ification of the potentialities of human beings.—For example, works of art such as sculptures or paintings, or commodity value conceived in a crude expended labour value manner. Here, with the shade of meaning that we might say that spiritual – physical potentialities which originally inhered in a human subject, flow out of the body, as it were, and solidify having become a physical, external existence, where it is represented such that "human potentialities have become physical existents".

In these "commonly held" conceptions of reification = thing-ification, the schema of dualistic separation between subject (human being) and object (thing) is the major premise, with "thing-ification" being represented with the conception of "something subjective changes into something physical". In other words, this means that the situation is regarded as, in (1), the substantial subject human being existent changing into the physical existent of a commodity or an accessory to a machine, in (2), the subjective action of human beings changing into the physical existent that is inertia, and in (3), the subjective potentiality of human beings being physically objectified and changing into a physical existent, with it being able to be said that, though not being a

---

shinsho edition, 1971) p. 62 et seq, and 『世界の共同主観的存在構造』 [[The Intersubjective Being-Structure of the World]] (Keisō shobō, 1972) p. 124 et seq.—I wish to be forgiven for the fact that the text below partially duplicates with these older works.

literal, real transformation, conceptually it is understood that "something subjective" "changes" into "something physical".

In the case of Marx, cases in his early years where he speaks of thing-
ification – externalisation – objectification in the sense of the above can in
fact be seen. In his later years, too, it's not the case that he rejects from the
beginning including in the extension-range (*Umfang*) of phenomena of reification phenomenal situations of the type illustratively given in (1), (2), and (3)
above. Even so, the concept of "reification" of the later Marx, when we look
at it focused along the lines of the concept content, is something based on an
entirely different thinking and composition to the "thing-ification" spoken of
above.

The "reification" the later Marx speaks of is *not* a concept based on the "subject – object" schema wherein something subjective transforms directly into a
physical, objective existent (*if* it happened to be so, reification would then be,
indeed, a "form of alienation"), it is, in our terms, located in the understanding
of being of the "primacy of relations", and is a determination state dependent
on the composition of *für es* and *für uns*.[140]

In contrast to (1), (2) and (3) above, if we deliberately begin with a crude
point, the reification Marx speaks of refers to the phenomenon where the intersubjective *relations* between human being and human being are mis-cognized
as if they were of the "nature of a thing" (for example, the "nature" of the pur-
chasing power possessed by currency), where the intersubjective social *relations* between human being and human being are seen in inversion as "relations between thing and thing" (for example, the phenomenon of the value
relations of commodities, or, differing somewhat in direction and dimension,
the phenomenon of the fixing of prices through the relation of "demand" and
"supply"). Here, though we say intersubjective relations between human being
and human being, this is, of course, not only the naked relations between
human beings separated off from so-called objective being, to say nothing of
not being static – reflective relations of cognition, it is dynamic mutual involvement within objective activity, functional mutual connection, and a "to-nature
and between-human beings dynamic state".—In the later Marx, it's not that
"reification" is spoken about through the concept of a change from the first
to the second in the modern philosophy style "subject – object" relation. Further, even though we say, "relations between person and person as relations
between thing and thing", this doesn't mean a situation of "the relation of the

---

140 Regarding this thematically see the relevant section of my 『弁証法の論理 – 弁証法
における体系構成法』 [*The Logic of the Dialectic—The Method of System Composition
in the Dialectic*] (Seido sha, 1980).

living pitcher and the living batter as the relation of ball and bat". The total state of connection of people's intersubjective object-involvement activity manifests just as if it is relations between things or the nature of things, and consequently, a physical objectivity; this *für uns* situation, this is what Marx calls "reification".

On reflection, the change to the physical being of the slave-commodity human being referred to in (1) above is also a distorted manifestation of the relation between person and person, not thing-ification of the kind where people who look at the Medusa of Greek mythology turn into stone. Further, it is not just the relation between two people, the slave and the seller. If it were the relation of just these two, the situation of buying and selling slaves as commodities wouldn't be able to exist, even if slavery were possible. The state of affairs called "thing-ification" in the form of the slave-commodity takes as its premise an intersubjective, specific state of connections amongst people—of the manner of this state taking the existence of the slave market as its premise, the existence of the slave market taking a certain mode of production as its premise, and this too taking certain social relations as its premise—and so it is that, as a refracted projection of this, what we are calling a "thing-ification" exists. It hardly needs explaining in detail, I think, that the inertial "thing-ification" spoken of in (2) is, once again, a distortion of an intersubjective relations state. The "thing-ification" into the *Dasein* of the work of art or commodity value referred to in (3), that which is called the "thing-ification" of the subjective potentiality in these forms, doesn't make a "reification of potentiality" in such as simple mud pies, it takes as a premise intersubjective aesthetic consciousness – value evaluation. However, this intersubjectivity is something which arises for the first time with specific historical – social conditions as its premise, and here again, the phenomenon in question exists only as a distorted projection of an intersubjective relations state.

In this way, "the change of something subjective into a physical existence" which was represented in the modern philosophy style schema, that is to say, the crude conception of "thing-ification" itself, similar to the schema of the so-called "theory of alienation", is something requiring exposure for-itself – critically as something in reality bewitched by a refracted manifestation of an intersubjective object-involved state of relations, and, is simply a given requiring at particular times having the secret of its fetishism (*Fetischismus*) investigated. Whilst opening up a new view of being, a revolutionary horizon of the view of the world, Marx constructed, too, a logic able to explicate this "secret".

Without scrupling in terms of being redundant, distinguishing in terms of stages, as things differing in horizon level, the "theory of alienation" of the early Marx and the "theory of reification" of the later Marx, I am one who clearly differentiates between the concept of "alienation" and the concept of "reification", but I am not, however, one who ignores the connection of the two in the process of the history of concept formation. In this context, I have judged very highly the theory of alienation of the early Marx too, ever since my very earliest essay, "Marxism and the Theory of Self-Alienation" (published in 1963 – in my *The Process of Formation of Marxism*).[141] Without the steps of the like of the theory of alienation seen in the *Economic and Philosophic Manuscripts* and the grand systematic thought based on this, the system of the later period would, in all probability, it seems, not, as an issue of fact, have been able to form.— Here, I will refrain from re-asserting this matter in detail; it will be sufficient, I think, if I re-record – make the following point. Marx in the *Economic and Philosophic Manuscripts*, even in cases where he is, when discussing alienation in the place of labour,[142] discussing matters focusing along the lines of the "labourer" titled as the representative singular, and to that extent, provisionally focusing along the lines of the individual, that individual is in-itself "species being", and in terms of logical composition, he made species essence being a "subject = substance". In doing so, basing his approach on, amongst other things, the essentiality of human being as understood in Hegelian terms, and, also, carrying out a unique "reading" (*hineinlesen*) of Feuerbach's view of human being, he places the essence of human being in the collective state – the social (*Sozietät*), and he understood that "the human individual is a social being, and individual life and species life do not differ".[143] Bearing this in mind, it's not impossible that, no matter how undeveloped it was, the situation is such that the human being as the subject of alienation – externalisation can, if we focus along the lines of its species essence, be said to be the totality of intersubjective co-operation, and if we go so far as to re-grasp the subject concept human being as the "whole of social relations",—this is the reason that when we do so the thing-ification of the human essence can be re-grasped as "reification of the total relations of the social relations"—the composition alone making it possible to make the shift to the theory of reification of the later period already existing too in the *Economic and Philosophic Manuscripts*.

---

141 I even think that a "synthetic union" of the so-called "three sources of Marxism" was only possible for the first time through the theory of alienation of the early Marx. In conjunction with the older essay of mine I have cited in the text, "Marxism and the Theory of Self-Alienation", I would like you to refer to the entry, 『経済学・哲学手稿』 [*Economic and Philosophic Manuscripts*], in 『現代マルクス゠レーニン主義事典』 [*The Modern Dictionary of Marxism – Leninism*] (Volume 1 pp. 483–486) of footnote 138 above.

142 As a discussion of mine which analysed this matter thematically and in detail there is Chapter 6 of my 『青年マルクス論』 [*On the Young Marx*] (Heibon sha, 1971).

143 MEW, Ergänzungsband, 1. Teil, S.539. Previously cited Japanese translation p. 135.

This, however, is something we third parties looking back from later are able to say, and it doesn't require going into in detail again that for Marx himself it was something that required a process of thinking fraught with difficulty, and all or nothing leaps. In reality, the re-grasping of the "human being" and the "subject concept" we are speaking of now came to realisation for Marx for the first time, as we saw in the previous section, through the Stirner shock, and through passing through the fiery, difficult struggle of the confrontation between the Feuerbachian view of human being and also again the Stirnerian view of human being. And, with this as the point of entry, Marx was finally able to open up the horizon of a new view of being.

Looked at in terms of the history of the formation of the concept, the leap from the horizon of the theory of alienation to the horizon of the theory of reification, this is precisely inseparable from the establishment of the stand-point of materialist history.—That this materialist history is, what's more, not a so-called view of "history" in the narrow sense, that it can't be covered by say-ing simply that it is "also simultaneously a view of society", that it is in a sense the world-view of Marxism itself; these matters are as was expressed in advance at the beginning of the essay.

People may here once again respond with, what then happens to the view of nature? Let's listen to what Marx-Engels have to say. It will be expedient if the passage already quoted in another context in section 2 be brought to mind; in *The German Ideology*, critiquing Feuerbach's view of nature and con-sequently his world-view, they write in the following way. "Feuerbach doesn't understand that the sensuous world which surrounds him ... is the product of industry and the state of society". He speaks of the "intuition of the natural sciences", and he "thinks of" nature as objective, being "revealed only to the eye of the physicist and the chemist", "of nature as existing from the eternal past, and as an everlastingly constant world of constant things", unrelated to human beings, "but" such a nature is, rather, in actuality nothing more than a fiction.

> The real sensuous natural world is the product of industry and the state of society, ... and, in the sense that it is an historical product, it is the result of the activity of the whole succession of the generations. ... Sensuous labour and creation, this production is the very foundation of the entire sensuous world existing in reality. ... Though, with this, the pre-existence of external nature remains, and it doesn't apply to the primordial peoples who first appear historically. However, such differentiation only has meaning to the extent that human beings are considered as being something distin-guished from nature. Incidentally, this nature preceding human history,

... if we put aside places where coral islands have just emerged recently, no longer exists in reality anywhere today ...[144]

Etc. etc.

In, once again, the passage in *The Holy Family* we looked at briefly a little while ago in section 1, this thought of an "historicised nature", and a reifyingly "naturalised history", critiqued on both sides a "metaphysically re-formed nature separated off from human beings", and a "metaphysically re-formed spirit separated off from nature", and showed there signs of germination in the form of advocating a point of view which dialectically sublates the one-sided position which acts as the principle of each of one side of these two. In *The German Ideology* they now fixed their gaze on locating the yardstick for the ecosystem (*Ökosystem*) arrangement of the "to-nature and between-human beings relations" in the place of practice which is "production" and set to realising such.—To quote Hanazaki Kōhei:

> Through the disassembling of the categories of ⟨the human being as human being⟩, ⟨species essence⟩ and ⟨self-alienation⟩ which had remained in such as the *Economic and Philosophic Manuscripts* and "Notes on James Mill", ... it can be said that removing their Hegelian shackles, indeed, was their major task at the stage of *The German Ideology*. They criticise the fact that Feuerbach grasps the sensual world as non-historical and they contend that it is the ⟨product of industry and the social situation⟩ and that it is the result of the activity of the generations of the human race. And, they reject the dichotomy of nature and history, pointing, as the true world, to the single, total historical world of being of ⟨natural history and historical nature⟩.[145]

—Materialist history is, precisely, the "conception" (*Auffassung*) of this "true world", of this "single, total historical world of being".

Taking such a vantage point—the situation is different if it is as a secondary, subordinate categorisation—there is, in the place of principles, no longer any need to line up hemispherically a view of nature and a view of history, and we can grasp, I think, the reason that materialist history, which brings into scope the totality of an "historicised nature", mutually covers world-view itself.

---

144   D.I. original text edition S.18 f. Japanese translation edition p. 18 et seq.
145   Hanazaki Kōhei 『マルクスにおける科学と哲学』 *Science and Philosophy in Marx* (Shakai shisō sha, 1972 Expanded Edition, p. 69).

On reflection, modern philosophy – the modern sciences, and, to go further back, the modern world-view, lie within the bounds of the horizon[146] of the so-called Cartesian modern paradigm, and have been caught up in the *Wechselspiel* (interplay) of its respective dualistic oppositionalities. The attempt to overcome this modern horizon, in either the form of the "reaction of Romanticism",[147] or the form of the Hegelian enterprise based on the composition of the self-recovering re-unification in the self-alienated bi-polarised split of the active substance, was begun in the early nineteenth century, but its realisation would be far off. Nonetheless, Marx-Engels opened up a new horizon of a view of being proper through a re-grasping of the essence determining of "human being", which forms the *hypokeimenon* of the modern world-view, and locating it in the relations of "production", which are the key to the arrangement of the "to-nature and between-human beings dynamic relations state", which is the reason for the bringing into being of an "historicised nature" and a "naturalised history", they established materialist history, the *Grundverfassung* of a new world-view, of a "single system of knowledge (*Wissenschaft*) which unifies natural history and social history", and, dependent on this, they strengthened a position for overcoming the horizon of the dualistic oppositionalities of matter and spirit, objective and subjective, species and individual, essence and the existential, ... nature and human beings, ... etc. etc.

The horizon of materialist history opened up by Marx-Engels is, exactly, the new horizon of a contemporary world-view which sublates the horizon of the modern world-view, and the situation is such that, for us, we extol "materialist history" as an epoch-making *Auffassung* which discloses a new paradigm, and this materialist history is none other than the very "composition of the theory of reification", the composition where we can grasp in a unifying way the mechanism of establishment of "nature for us" (*Natur für uns*), of "historicised

---

146   Regarding the characteristics of this I would like you to see Section 1, Chapter 2 「近代的世界観の地平－その特質」 [["The Horizon of the Modern World View—Its Characteristics"]] in my 『マルクス主義の地平』 [*The Horizon of Marxism*], Section 1, Chapter 1, 「近代合理主義を支える世界了解の構図」 [["The Schema of the World Understanding Supporting Modern Rationalism"]] in my 『マルクス主義の理路』 [[*The Logic of Marxism*]] (Keisō shobō, 1974), and Sub-section 1, Section 2, Chapter 1, Part 1, 「近代哲学の諸前提」 [["The Assumptions of Modern Philosophy"]] in my 『事的世界観への前哨』 [[*An Advance Post Towards a Koto-Centred World View*]] (Keisō shobō, 1975) etc.

147   That this is not simply a "reaction", and regarding its positive motifs, I would like you to see the discussion in op. cit. 『唯物史観の原像』 [[*The Original Image of Materialist History*]] p. 17 et seq.

nature", and, in addition, the mechanism of establishment of social – historical – cultural formations, that is to say, "naturalised history".

For us, in order, here, to guarantee the concreteness of "extolling materialist
history" we have thematised the "composition of the theory of reification"[148]
verified through internal sublation of the Hegelian "theory of alienation", and I
take the next step to be a surveying of its "scope".

---

148   I describe the "schema" of this matter not only in the next "chapter" but in the "Epilogue—
      Expansion of the Theory of Reification", and so I would like to ask that you see these.

CHAPTER 2

The Composition and Scope of the Theory of Reification

For some years I have been expressing my view that it is "the composition of the theory of reification"—which Marx-Engels in their early years established in overcoming internally the "logic of the theory of alienation" of the Hegelians—which marks the new paradigm in Marxist social theory – the theory of history – cultural theory.[1]

On reflection, however, I still haven't completed the task of tracing in detail the "shift from the logic of the theory of alienation to the logic of the theory of reification" during the period when Marx-Engels were forming their thought, and nor have I fulfilled[2] the task of expounding systematically from the per-

---

1 In, for example, the essays contained in my 『マルクス主義の地平』 [[*The Horizon of Marxism*]] (Keisō shobō, 1969) and my 『資本論の哲学』 [[*The Philosophy of* Capital]] (Gendai hyōron sha, 1974).

2 My 『青年マルクス論』 [[*On the Young Marx*]] (Heibonsha, 1971), which traced the process of Marx's thought formation, was brought to a close having analysed – considered in detail the *Economic and Philosophic Manuscripts*, and 『マルクスの思想圏 ― 本邦未紹介資料を中心に』 [[*Marx's World of Thought—Centring on Material Not Previously Introduced in Our Country*]] (Asahi shuppan sha, 1980, co-authored with Inoue Gorō), which traced the biographical facts of Marx, the social *environmental* situation in which Marx was placed, and the thought and trends of the Left Hegelian group etc, and which analysed Marx's notes from the time, and which can be said to be a major revision of the older work, only reaches to the period of the *Rhenish Newspaper*. My old work 『エンゲルス論』 [[*On Engels*]] (Morita shoten, 1968) does provisionally trace things up until *The German Ideology*, but since then notes from the young Engels and other new material has been unearthed – made public, and I am currently entrusting an expansion – revision – correction of our work to Inoue Gorō.

   However, as the first shot in an historical critique against the view that takes it that the theory of alienation is maintained in the later Marx, there is my academic essay 「『ドイツ・イデオロギー』と自己疎外論の超克」 [["*The German Ideology* and the Overcoming of the Theory of Self-Alienation"]] (serialised in the journal 『情況』 [[*The State of Affairs*]] from the July 1974 edition to the January–February 1975 joint edition), and, also, regarding the relationship with the circumstances of the "internally violent" debate within the Left Hegelians which gave Marx the incentive to overcome the theory of alienation, my essay 「『ドイツ・イデオロギー』とその背景―文献学的研究から内容的討究への架橋のために」 [["*The German Ideology* and Its Background—For a Bridge from Philological Research to Content-Based Investigation"]] (serialised in the journal 『知の考古学』 [[*The Archaeology of Knowledge*]], published by Shakai shisō sha, from the inaugural edition of April 1975 to the third edition) has been published.

spective of the theory of reification the social theory – the theory of history – the cultural theory – the theory of revolution of Marx and Engels.[3] My existing published works partially deal with these matters, and for me I am left in the situation of these matters still being unresolved.

This essay is not something which from the beginning attempts to respond to these unresolved matters square on, but for the time being aims, as a precondition for such, at an extolling of the composition and scope of the theory of reification.

Further, this essay also has the feature of being a continuation of "An Extolling of Materialist History [a previous essay which was the model for the previous chapter of this book]", although I do not here go into the task of tracing in terms of the history of its formation the *process of sublation* of the theory of alienation. In addition, in this essay I omit going into in detail the fields[4] of

---

3   However, as a provisional sketch, there is my 『唯物史観の原像—その発想と射程』 [*The Original of Materialist History—Its Conception and Scope*] (San'ichi shinsho, 1971), and as a thematic discussion of the relationship of the theory of organisation of the revolutionary movement and the theory of reification there is my essay 「大衆運動の物象化と前衛の問題」 [*"The Reification of the Mass Movement and the Problem of the Advance Guard"*] (first published in the 1970 『京都大学新聞』 [*Kyoto University Gazette*], and contained in my 『新左翼運動の射程』 [*The Scope of the New Left Movement*] Nagoya yunite, 1981).

4   In recent years, detailed research in these directions from a theory of reification vantage point has, it seems, already reached a considerable level of accumulation in our country. Jotting down here only those whom I ought to have quoted within the discussion of this essay, but whom I will have you allow me to deliberately omit, there is such as Takahashi Yōji's 『物神性の解読』 [*Deciphering the Fetish Character*] (Keisō shobō, 1981), Ishizuka Ryōji's 「商品世界における物象化について」 [*"On Reification in the World of the Commodity"*] (Senshū daigaku daigakuin kiyō *Keizai to hō* [the Graduate School Bulletin of Senshū University, *Economics and Law*]) No. 12, 1980) and the series of essays published in the same bulletin thereafter, the series of essays by Masaki Hachirō culminating in 「マルクスの価値形態論と労働の抽象化」 [*"Marx's Theory of Value Form, and the Abstraction of Labour"*] (*Keizai kenkyū* [*Studies in Economics*] Vol. 33 No. 1, January 1982), Abe Isao's 「市民社会＝国家論の再審」 [*"A Re-Examination of Bourgeois Society = the Theory of the State"*] (carried in Shakai shisōshi gakkai nenpō *Shakai shisō shi kenkyū* (the Yearbook of the Association for the Study of the History of Social Thought, *Studies in the History of Social Thought*) No. 6, 1982), and the series of essays published in the *Bulletin of the Osaka University of Pharmaceutical Sciences*, and Yamamoto Kōichi's 「協働・役割・国家」 [*"Co-operation – Role – State"*] (contained in 『唯物史観と国家論』 (*Materialist History and Theories of the State*) co-authored with myself, Ronsō sha, 1982).

I won't touch on overseas material which should be referred to in the context here, but it seems that an essay by Faccarello introduced by Yoshida Norio is worthy of attention: 「マルクス商品論の一解釈—G. Faccarello 論文の紹介を兼ねて」 [*"An Interpretation of Marx's Theory of the Commodity—Together with the Introduction of an Essay by G. Faccarello"*] (contained in Daitōbunka daigaku *Keizai ron shū* [Daito Bunka University *Collected Essays in Economics*] No. 33, March 1982).

the various theories such as economic theory and the theory of the state, and I wish to focus on what might be called the "philosophical dimension" of the view of society – the view of history and the "schema of systems theory".

1   The Reification of Social Relations and the Nature of Being of Cultural Forms

In this section, for convenience of discussion, whilst exposing for the time being the synchronic – structural projection of the reificatory existence of social = historical phenomena, I will confirm the reason why the theory of reification opens up a new horizon in *social* ontology, and, at the same time, I will verify that the theory of reification opens up in a trailblazing way a new era in the theory of social forms (*Gebilde*) and in the theory of cultural value proper.

1.1

To render the composition and scope of the theory of reification for-themselves, the making clear beforehand of the comprehensive implications of the concept of reification performs a necessary condition. For that reason, in this item of discussion I would like to begin from this provisional process.

Marx and Engels do not describe in the manner of a definition the concept of "reification", and it is not necessarily the case that they use the concept frequently. Even so, when considering a series of usages to be seen in their texts from their "later period", it will be easily acknowledged that the state of affairs where the social relations between persons (in these relations causes in terms of things mediate and are mediated) appears in the form of "relations between things" or with "the characteristics possessed by things" or, yet again, in the form of "an autonomous thing-like being"; it will be easily acknowledged that this state of affairs is referred to by the word reification. With this as evidence, as a provisional representation prior to the determining of the concept we can for the present call the state of affairs where the *relations* between persons appear

---

Further, as works of mine in this regard, I would like you to see, apart from 『資本論の哲学』 [*The Philosophy of* Capital], 「貨幣論のためのプレリュード」 ["Prelude to a Theory of Money"] (the journal 『現代思想』 [*Modern Thought*] October 1977), 「市民社会 ─ 国家体制」への視角」 [["A Perspective on 'Bourgeois Society – the State'"] contained in my 『マルクス主義の理路』 [*The Logic of Marxism*] (Keisō shobō, 1974), and the Addendum to my previously cited 『唯物史観と国家論』 [*Materialist History and Theories of the State*].

in the form of the relations – the characteristics – the forms (*Gebilde*) of *things* the phenomenon of reification.

That when we spoke of "relations between persons" just now these are certainly not naked human relations but that naturally causes in terms of things mediate in such, and also that person is not a reference to the body as thing, but is a knowing-active "subject" "possessing consciousness" and what's more "acting", and as a result that it is not simply cognizing relations – relations in terms of consciousness but relations of praxis which are at issue; these matters need to be borne in mind.

The phenomenon of reification which we are considering here is *not* a state of affairs appearing only for an observing third person, but is a state of affairs which appears for the persons involved themselves in the everyday. This state of affairs where the relations between persons are understood in the form of relations – characteristics – forms of things, in a form entirely different to the relations between persons, is certainly illusion – delusion viewed from the standpoint of scientific reflection, but it is certainly not, however, such a thing as coincidental – random, deluded hallucination. It is no exaggeration to say that it is an illusion which emerges appropriately under the given conditions, and it is a delusion which the everyday consciousness of people "necessarily" falls into. This point also needs to be borne in mind (together with the previous one).—Incidentally, isn't it the case that the states of affairs where relations are cognized in the form of thing-ness or where on occasion relations are cognized in the form of an entity, aren't limited to relations between persons? Isn't it the case that a certain type of "natural relation – relation between things" also is cognized in delusion as made-into-things, made-into-entities? And, what's more, isn't it the case that this is a delusion which emerges virtually of "necessity" for everyday consciousness? Absolutely so. Isn't it the case that such a matter was also discussed by Hegel early on in his work in his discussion of determination of reflection (*Reflexionsbestimmung*) and elsewhere, and that it is something which Marx and Engels too were quite well aware of? Indeed. So why not not fix the concept of reification to the reification of the relations between persons but enlarge it to the making-into-things and the making-into-entities involved in the relations of the determination of reflection between objects? I myself am one who deliberately plans this enlargement, and I don't consider that such is incompatible with the method of thought or the understanding of being of Marx and Engels.[5] Nevertheless, however, considered from the perspective of the use of the word "reification" it is a textual fact that Marx

---

5 I myself have occasionally given expression to this "understanding", and have published 『存在と意味』 [*Being and Meaning*] (Iwanami shoten, 1982) with it as a premise, and I have

and Engels do not expand the extension of the term that far. To this extent, in this essay, which is focused on a discussion of Marx and Engels, I wish to use the concept of reification limited to the reification of intersubjective, social relations between persons, and moreover, primarily in the form of such which appears to the direct consciousness of the subjects involved. (Between limiting things in this way and my manner of expanding things some difference arises in dealing with the form of the "real – ideal" and the determination of the features of the thing [see pp. 96 and after in this book], but we need not, I think, go into this matter here).

We aim, therefore, in this way, in accordance with the use of the term by Marx and Engels, to discuss the composition and scope of the "reification *of relations*" under the limitation "relations between persons" (intersubjective, practical social relations). At this point, however, a certain kind of thinker might interrupt our discussion and enquire in the following way. Isn't it the case that in the texts of his "later period" there are occasions where Marx uses the expressions "reification of the person (*Person*) and personification of the thing (*Sache*)", and he doesn't necessarily always say reification "of relations"? Viewed in light of this, isn't it the case that the accent is not on the *relations* between persons, but rather the point, even in instances where the word relations is inserted, is the reification = objectification of the person = *the subjective*, and the conception of the self-alienation – self-externalisation of the human subject of the early period is more or less maintained as it is? Etc. etc. To reply with the conclusion first, the answer is no. As we investigated in some detail in the previous essay, "For an Extolling of Materialist History", the Marx of the "later period", if we take that famous phrase from the "Theses on Feuerbach" as a symbolic catchphrase, expresses his argument having re-conceived the "human essence" as "the totality of social *relations*", and the "person" when the "reification of the person" is spoken of is not the "person as entity" spoken of in the view of the human being of modern philosophy but is itself already a determined state of reflective relations. For that reason, the situation when he speaks in the texts of the later period of the "reification of the person", if we follow things back to the fundamental determination, is rather simply a mat-

recently seen the appearance of bibliographic positivistic research in a form which indirectly supports my "understanding". Such is Hayashi Masaji's essay 「『自然弁証法』の意義と編集問題―マルクス主義唯物論の復権のために―」 [["The Meaning and Editorial Issues of *The Dialectics of Nature*—For a Reinstatement of Marxist Materialism—"]] (carried in the journal 『インパクション』 [[*Inpakushon*]] No. 21 Izara shobō, January 1983), which, based on a textual criticism investigation of Engels' vast work, which was re-edited during the Stalin period, includes a chapter which discussed Engels' view of "matter".

ter of the "reification of the state of the determination of relations". Indeed, on such occasions, a continuation can be seen in terms of a schema of form with the schema from the early period of the self-externalisation of the human essence (*Wesen*). It is not that the theory of alienation and the theory of reification are completely unrelated; with the latter having been formed precisely in the dialectical sublation of the former, it is only natural that there is a relation of continuation there. Schematically this continuation is naturally to be acknowledged. Nevertheless, even though they speak of the same human essence, between understanding such in the subjective entity form of the Hegelians and understanding such in the nodal relations form there is a difference of ontological horizon. The situation is that in the latter, in the recasting of the subject in terms of person in terms of relation-ism the former is sublated. Incidentally, the "thing-like being" when the "personification of physical phenomena [anthropomorphising autonomising]" is spoken of is also not the "thing-like being in general" but is a special thing-like *Dasein* of the commodity – money – capital – profit – land rent type, and the determinate-ness which is the reason that these special physical phenomena are things *more than* a mere physical product, a mere piece of metal, a mere type of machine ... etc., more than a mere natural physical existent, is once again posited in a state of reflective relations.[6] Here, too, if we go back to the essential determination it is none other than the "personification" of the *relations determination* state.

1.2

So then, what kind of state of affairs is the reifying of relations referring to? Leaving the concrete aspect until later in the discussion and examining the matter gradually, let us here for the time being determine things conceptually.

Although we say reification of relations, that that doesn't mean the *thing* that is relations literally transforms into a thing-like being entity; this point, I'm sure, doesn't require being made here again. Re-"ification": this "change" is not a process directly known in the everyday consciousness of the people involved but is, for the moment, a matter identified upon reflection from the standpoint of scientific reflection. In the everyday consciousness of the people involved the things which appear before them in the form of relations between things – physicality – formations, are, viewed from the vantage point of scientific reflection, projections of refracted relations between persons, are provisional phenomena; what exists as an existent is for the moment this synchronic – struc-

---

6 I'd like the fact to be brought to mind that Marx repeatedly stated clearly, in regard to "money" and "capital", that they are "not *things* but particular social relations", and the thrust such that these were not legal relations but "relations of production".

tural state of affairs. Here, to the extent that we view things from the vantage point of scientific reflection, the mechanism where the relations determination state which is the true reality appears to the direct consciousness of the persons involved *transformed – changed* into a thing-like being form is identified. With this mechanism of a change into the appearance of a thing-like being form as proof, this is the reason that from the vantage point of scientific reflection re*ification* is spoken of. – People can also perhaps understand the composition of "true reality – provisional phenomenal" here as a composition of "essence – phenomenon".[7] But the relation we are speaking of here between "essence (*Wesen*) = true existent" and "phenomenon", in the manner reasoned in the usual theory of "essence – phenomenon", differs in ontological implication from the relation of "entity – outward appearance". "Essence" is not a "substantial entity", nor is it an autonomous entity which is an "original form corresponding in the *same form* to a copy form", rather it is a "relations determination state" which is completely unlike the phenomenon. This needs to be borne in mind.—In the state of affairs of "reification" in this sense, to the extent that we are viewing things from the viewpoint of scientific reflection, the thing-like being which absolutely exists in an objective – object-like form is no more than an illusion, and is not something which exists as it is. Even so, even viewed from the vantage point of scientific reflection, the illusion in question is certainly not simply arbitrary delusion but has its being-structure foundation in the state of existent relations. And, for the people involved themselves, the "thing-like being" in question is not simply perceived as actually existing, but precisely as an "actually existing thing-like being" existence it in actuality regulates their practical behaviour. No matter in what way it is identified from the vantage point of a scientific observer, for those who are the subjects involved the "thing-like being" is completely a thing-like being actually existing objectively, and this "thing-like being" directly regulates their practice in everyday life.

No matter to what degree it appears in an objective form for everyday consciousness, we notice, if we reflect to a certain degree, that nonetheless the state of existence which is the reification of relations between persons carries a special being-structure characteristic. It is rare that the state of existence which is

---

7   In *Capital* Marx says "if phenomenal form and essence were directly in agreement, there would be no need for science at all" (MEW [Tr. *Marx-Engels Werke*—MEW hereafter], Bd.25, S. 825), and assigns, indeed, investigation of essence to science, but it should be brought to mind that "essence" here is in Hegelian philosophy precisely a "reflective relations determination state". Regarding this matter, it would be convenient to have you refer to the place where I investigated Hegel's theory of essence in my 『弁証法の論理』 [*The Logic of the Dialectic*] (Seido sha, 1980).

reified is perceived in the everyday in an isolated form, and usually, in a form secondary to the natural thing, it is perceived in the form of "some thing" due to the given objective existence being something *more than* a "mere natural thing". In determining the characteristic of being of this "some thing" it would be useful to listen to what Marx points out regarding "value", which is typical of reified being.—"In the value objectivity of the commodity there is not a single atom of natural substance".[8] That value is not a material, physical entity is a matter of course, and it cannot possibly even have physical properties. The natural properties of the commodity exclusively involve use value, and value itself "cannot have natural properties, such as the commodity's geometrical, physical and chemical properties".[9] Marx makes this point, and says that value is a "*supra*-natural property (*übernatürliche Eigenschaft*)".[10] Not concerned that quick-to-judge commentators, that "crude materialists",[11] would show lament and surprise that a materialist of all people would do such a thing, he deliberately even goes so far as to call value "a ghostlike objectivity (*gespenstige Gegenständlichkeit*)".[12] When elucidating the characteristics of being of the value of a commodity, having rendered *that which is value* autonomous, it has to be said that it is a "supra-natural" something, a "*supra*-sensual" something. It is in this form in itself reified. Whereupon, for Marx he even expresses the commodity "formed" from the "two elements" of use value and value as "a sensual – supra-sensual thing (*ein sinnlich übersinnliches Ding*)".[13]—Marx hasn't left any texts discussing thematically the characteristics of being regarding states of existence of reification apart from "value". However, that when the characteristics of being of such are investigated *in a form where they have been rendered autonomous*, so-called cultural value in general, in other words so-called "philosophical value" in general (apart from economic value), the values which value philosophy calls truth – the good – beauty – the sacred, that they are a something which "doesn't contain a single atom of natural substance" and

---

8   MEW, Bd.23, S. 62. In this essay, quotations from Marx-Engels are according to the MEW volume numbers and page numbers. However, in the case of the *Grundrisse*, which is not included in the MEW, I provide the page numbers of the neue MEGA and the Dietz edition together.

9   ibid., S.51.

10   ibid., S.71.

11   A "fetish worship" "coarse materialism", the like of which is also "simultaneously a coarse idealism", where "the social relations are regarded as a determinateness inherent in things and are made to belong to things, and through this things end up being mystified" etc. *Grundrisse*, neue MEGA, II. 1. 2, S. 567. (Dietz Ausgabe, S.579)

12   MEW, Bd. 23, S.51.

13   ibid., S. 85.

are entirely different to "the geometrical, physical, chemical, physiological ... natural properties", and which for the time being can only be called "*supra-natural – supra*-sensual"; this fact should be easily accepted. Although, it is not the case that that which are cultural values exist in themselves independently and separately from real existents, rather the true situation is that on each occasion they are "carried" by real existent states and *Dasein* in the form of "properties" (*Güter*). But this "property" i.e. "cultural property", can be said, precisely, to be "a sensual – supra-sensual thing". In this way, Marx's point focusing on the commodity – the commodity value, for the time being is valid for cultural properties – cultural values proper. The validity of Marx's point does not, however, stop at the domain of "philosophical value" in general. Systems – norms – power ... etc. etc., so-called social formations (*Gebilde*) in general, although they are "carried" on each occasion by a real (*real*) given and exist in the form of a "sensual – supra-sensual thing", when their characteristics of being are investigated having intentionally separated off the "formation itself" and rendering it autonomous, these too present the appearance of a "*supra-sensual – supra*-natural something". This surely no longer requires going into in detail nor discussing and determining.

In this way, the practical, intersubjective relations between people in a reified state of existence, in other words, so-called cultural – social formations (*Gebilde*), whilst, in the main, *Dasein*-ing "carried" by sensual – natural *realität*, when the characteristic of being of these "things themselves" are determined, they present, for the moment, an appearance which should be called a "supra-sensual – supra-natural something".—Since Marx's time philosophers have done none other than attempt to refer to this peculiar characteristic of being with concepts such as "appropriate (*gelten*)" or "ideal existence (*Bestand*)". Although, they have not had in mind the mechanism of reification, and, for that reason amongst others, it can't be agreed that they achieved a separation from a "metaphysical existence".—In the case of Marx, he does not maintain the metaphysical assertion that the "supra-sensual – supra-natural something" actually exists, rather he points out that the peculiar "thing-like being" which appears "objectively" with this kind of an appearance to the everyday consciousness of the persons involved is in fact a refracted projection of certain intersubjective relations, and he reveals the "secret (*Gehemnis*)" of this "mysterious characteristic (*der rätselhafte Charakter*[14])" through focusing on the mechanism of reification,[15] and by means of this he overcomes the traditional oppositional horizon of "realism vs nominalism". Regarding this matter,

---

14   ibid., S. 86.
15   His provisionally thematically carrying out this task within the discussion of the "world of

however, let us come back to it later and discuss it then.—To change direction, following on from de Brosses[16] what Marx calls *Fetisch* (I am willing to use the idiom 「物神」 [[*busshin*]], but this translation is quite misleading and so when necessary I also use the translation 「呪物」 [[*jubutsu*]]) is a "supra-sensual" existence, and if we consider it, what's more, to have the implication of existence which regulates in a "supra-natural" manner the consciousness and action of persons then this means that the reified state of existence determined in the manner of Marx immediately has a fetishistic characteristic, and it means that the theory of reification and the theory of fetishism in a broad sense are tightly bound together. (On this point, in the theory of reification expanded in the manner I have done, going so far as to locate the "mechanism of reification" in the area of *so-called* "sensual – natural *Dasein*", the theory of fetishism becomes a subordinate division of the theory of reification).

In the above, it is the case that we have attempted to provisionally render for-itself that which ought to be rendered so in the implications of the concept of "reification" in the sense in which Marx uses it, and we have ended up in an outcome wherein many matters have already been brought forward during the discussion. In this essay, whilst pointing out point by point the fact that cultural – social formations are in general reified states of existence, it will be difficult to expect us to go so far as to undertake the task of concretely investigating the mechanism of reification in each particular case, yet even so we are now at the stage where we have to express our points of discussion as concretely as possible and we should provide a foundation for matters brought forward and conjectures.

1.3

Here let us turn our gaze directly to that which is so-called "society" as a unified whole. It requires no reflection that in the history of theories of society a "theory of social realism" which says that a particular existent called society actually exists and a "theory of social nominalism" which doesn't recognise the actual existence of a particular existent called society but which regards that

---

the commodity (*Warenwelt*)" is none other than "Section 4 The Fetishism of Commodities and the Secret Thereof" established thereafter in the first chapter of the second edition of *Capital*.

16   Sakisaka Itsurō gave attention to this matter first, but as a major work dealing with it there is Imamura Hitoshi's 「フェティシズム論」 ["On Fetishism"] (the journal 『情況』 [[*The State of Affairs*]], published in the May 1974 edition). Further, regarding Marx's notes from his period in Bonn, including notes extracted from de Brosses, as a beginning please see the long footnote on pp. 427–431 of 『マルクスの思想圏』 [[*Marx's World of Thought*]] cited in note 2 above.

which actually exists as simply a composite of individuals, have come to stand in opposition. How does Marx's theory of reification respond to the horizon of the dichotomous opposition between so-called "society"-ism and "individual"-ism in theories of the being of society?

Marx declares decisively that "society is not formed from individuals".[17] When reading this sentence alone or bringing to mind the fact of his writing that "human beings are, in the literal sense with which Aristotle says it, social animals (*zoon politikon*). Not stopping at saying that they are simply social animals, they are animals who are able to be individuated [become an individual entity] only in society [this actually exists in a pre-existing way!]",[18] and together with this when recalling the inheriting relationship to "Hegel's view of society", crudely prevalent, thoughtless people may think that it is as if Marx is siding with the point of view of a "society as organism" style of "social realism". However, since his early period Marx states clearly that "at the very least we must avoid placing that which is "society" in opposition to the individual and thus fixing it. The individual is a social being. ... The individual life and the species life of human beings are not separate things",[19] and he strictly rejects the conception which sees "society" as if it were an individual "entity"-like existence.—Marx rejects both "social nominalism", of the type of which the theory of the social contract is typical, and "social realism", of the type of which the theory of a social organism is typical. From a different perspective, he can be said to be rejecting both the theory of "the individual = an entity" and the theory of "society = an entity". He establishes a third point of view. In doing so, however, he *doesn't* put forward a third way of seeing things from *within the same plane* as the "nominalism" and the "realism". He goes beyond the horizon itself of this dualistic opposition.

"Society is the totality of the connections (*Beziehungen*), the relations (*Verhältnisse*), of individuals mutually involved with one another",[20] determines Marx. This essentialist determination, if viewed superficially, may appear to be a type of social nominalism. Indeed, Marx rejects the "society = entity" view. However, this determination is established following on from the proposition quoted above that "society is not formed from individuals", and Marx rejects in advance the "individual = entity"-istic social nominalism which views "society as a composite of individuals-as-entities".—The element of "reification" becomes involved here. The "connections – relations" mentioned don't

17   *Grundrisse*, neue MEGA, II. 1.1, S.188. (Dietz Ausgabe, S.176).
18   ibid., S.22. (Dietz Ausgabe, S. 6). [Tr. Parenthetical material by Hiromatsu].
19   MEW, Ergänzungsband, 1. Teil. S.538.
20   *Grundrisse*, neue MEGA, II. 1.1, S.188. (Dietz Ausgabe, S.176).

appear as phenomena in their true form as it is, they appear as phenomena in a reified form, presenting to individuals an appearance as if they are external – autonomous individual existent entities. From this reified appearance, and from, what's more, confirming the fetish form, the theory of "society = real existent" is formed. This "society = entity" theory in principle – essentially is of course a reificatory misconception, but it is not a mere delusion, and it won't do to conclude matters by ignoring it. (The "individual = entity" theory is, once again, none other than another reificatory misconception, but regarding this aspect let us move the discussion forward leaving it aside for the time being). When it comes to the dimension of the reification of the totality which is "society", even though it is the case that it at least is a problem in the situations of scientific reflection and historical observation, the reified projections of social formations are an everyday fact, and in reality whilst being-in this reified "environment world" people carry out their everyday activities and through this they constantly reproduce reified reality, and so even in cases where thinkers attempt to investigate the actions of individuals in an "understanding sociology" way, taking provisionally the point of view of such a thing as "methodological individualism", it is first of all necessary to cast one's gaze on the reified system of the human "environment world" which regulates the consciousness and behaviour of the subjects involved.—Persons who are unaware of the mediated existentiality which is that for human beings the "real" environmental world is a reified product, just persons who follow what we might call "methodological naturalism",[21] ignore the reified product-nature of the "stage" of social acts and the what should be called deep hypnosis motive-assigning or restrictiveness of this intersubjective "place" and are able to rush around under a *mis*understanding of motive".—This means that, using a method which *seems as if* it "confirms" the very thing itself of the "society = real existent" view, what is required is an attempt at an analytical positioning of the social relations – social structure which appear before us reified.

In this way, in the dimension of principles – an essentialist dimension of the view of "human beings – society", determining so-called human society focusing on the ontological primary dimension of "the connections – the relations" and locating "individual = entity"-ism and "society = entity"-ism as misconceptions corresponding to a dichotomous *reification* of the relations, Marx goes beyond the horizon of the dualistic opposition of "individual"-ism and

---

21   Wanting to use "naturalism" here, I choose the words in order that there not be confusion
      with the terminology of Tanaka Yoshihisa. His terminology refers to a position which takes
      the position of "the subject, facing the simple object, acting from a completely internal –
      internally generated motive" as its methodological scene of departure.

"society"-ism, but he doesn't remain with this essentialist determination, rather he moves for the present towards an analytical positioning of the reified structural form of social relations.

Although expressed in the one phrase of the social connections – relations of people, such are multifarious and within them layer – dimension distinctions can be identified. And, though we say reification of relations such is multilayered and these layers intersect three-dimensionally. For this reason, in research of the social science type, whilst analysing the social structure as a reified totality, one has to begin with an ascertaining of universal structure and special structure, and foundational stratification and secondary stratification. Incidentally, and also, even though in the actual state of relations the category of dialectical "interaction" (*Wechselwirkung*) exclusively holds true, in the reified existent the reified category of "causality" (*Kausalität*) in the understanding "holds true", and the relations determining and functioning in the understanding of "cause – effect" are to be "discovered" between event moments. Marx and Engels, as in the details of which we saw in the previous essay, "For an Extolling of Materialist History", see the fundamental relations of human existence as the place of "human ecological relations" in the place of the production of material life.

> In production, people not only act on nature, they act on each other as well. Human beings only produce through co-operating in a fixed form and through exchanging mutually their activities. In order to produce, human beings enter into fixed mutual connections – mutual relations, and it is only in these social connections – social relations that acting on nature, in other words production, is carried out;[22]

with this as evidence, Marx and Engels grasp relations in this situation, that is to say in "relations of production", as the foundation of people's social relations. These relations of production which are the foundational relations act as the "base" (the so-called "base structure") for reified things in the complete structure of reified society, and on this "base" people's political, religious ... etc. various reified formations of intersubjective – co-subjective relations, in other words, the political superstructure and the formations of social consciousness appear spanning it from above. And, in this reified total structural form the economic base structure manifests in the form of the launching part.—As is evident from the "formula of materialist history" and elsewhere, Marx for the

---

22   MEW, Bd. 6, S. 407.

time being and generally shows a structuralist grasping of the social form in a structuralised form in this way.

This synchronic – structural positioning (in this the *thing* which is the "economic structure" is in the lower part whilst the *thing* which is the "superstructure" is in the upper part and the two are reified as if there is a *cause and effect determining relation* between them [in other words, with the mediated-ness through the conscious – significant acts of *human beings* set aside from consideration, the situation is represented as if there is a *direct relation of action* between the two] and it is the case that this structure is represented as if it is *self*-operating but it) is, however, only a temporary formula and Marx aims at concretely investigating the true actual form. But, and in order to do that, it is necessary to grasp this synchronic – structural form in terms of its diachronic – dynamic form.—When this task is attempted in a thorough way, researching concretely dividing up the reification of the various formations into their respective fields, economic, of customs, political, of spiritual culture ... becomes an issue as a matter of course.

In this essay, however, focusing on the dimension of "society" as a structural totality, and focusing on the reification form which is the historical transition of this "society", we will have to make do with the area of rendering for-itself the general schema of this configuration. To this extent, let us now shift our axis of view to the characteristic of being of "history".

2   The Law-Like Nature of the Historical Dynamic and the Significant Action of the Subjects Involved

In this section we are at the stage of outlining the being configuration of people's intersubjective – co-operative activity, focused on the diachronic – dynamic transition which is the reason for its being reified in the form which the particular nature of being of "history" has. Here, the issues are on the one hand the "law-like nature of history" and on the other hand the "acts of will of the subjects",[23] and the relationship of the two is the point of investigation.

---

23   I would be grateful if I could have you peruse together with this essay my old essay 「歴史法則と諸個人の自由」 [["The Law of History and the Freedom of Individuals"]] (contained in my 『マルクス主義の地平』 [[*The Horizon of Marxism*]]).

2.1

Within the horizon of modern knowledge, the fact of "whether or not history has from the start a law-like nature" is to begin with a major problem. Which is to say that, modern knowledge, on the one hand, understands all things in nature as being things which change in a law-like way in accordance with a cause and effect necessity, imagining to this extent a "determinism" (*Determinismus*) based picture of the world, whilst, however, on the other hand, understanding, inseparably with the "autonomy of the modern self", that human individuals are things which are free acting subjects possessing free will, and to the extent that human activity violates cause and effect necessity, it sees that there is no deterministic necessity in history and sees the world of history as based on "indeterminism" (*Indeterminismus*), and so here an ambivalence arises between a determinism and an indeterminism.—"Common sense" on occasion establishes vaguely a "coexistence" between a "law-like nature of history" on the one hand and the "freedom of individuals" on the other hand, but from the point of view of scientific reflection such vagueness is not permitted. So, *modern* scientific knowledge fell into the dilemma of a dichotomous opposition between a standpoint on the one hand which, viewing the free will of human beings as a mere illusion, accepts the law-like nature of history through a thoroughgoing application of a deterministic view of the world, and a standpoint on the other hand which denies the law-like nature of history through a positive acceptance of the free will which destroys cause and effect necessity. What kind of attitude then does Marxism take regarding this dichotomous opposition?

In society, the crude view that Marxism is an "economic determinism" holds sway. Also, amongst thinkers of the Russian Marxist stream, although certainly not an economic determinism, a tendency certainly exists for such to take upon themselves a type of determinism. However, I'd like to verify matters here as a precondition for later discussion, and say that it is not the case that Marx and Engels in any way take a position of determinism.

Engels resolutely rejects "the *determinism* (*Determinismus*) which has transferred from French materialism into natural science, and which tries to bring matters to a close by simply rejecting contingency [and consequently also 'freedom']",[24] and ridiculing this "scientific determinism", he writes in the following way.

> According to this view, in the natural world, a simple, direct necessity rules completely. That the pod of these green peas contains five peas,

---

24   MEW, Bd. 20, S. 487. [Tr. Parenthetical material by Hiromatsu].

and that there are neither four nor six; that this dog's tail is 5 inches long and is neither more nor less, ... that it was 4 a.m. last night that I was bitten by a flea and not 3 nor 5, and, what's more, that it was my right shoulder which was bitten and not my left thigh, all of these events are facts brought about through a *firm, immovable chain* of *cause* and *result*, through *immovable necessity* ... etc. With this necessity and the like we still haven't left a theological view of nature. ... whether it be called fate or whether it be called necessity ... What is called necessity here is simply an empty catchphrase, and as a result that which is called contingency remains here unchanged.[25]

In opposition to these two views [indeterminism and determinism], Hegel appeared with the following thesis, a thesis which was completely unheard of previously. Namely, that the contingent is necessary, and that the necessary determines itself as contingency. And that, in another aspect, this contingency is absolute necessity, etc.[26]

Natural science ignored this thesis without difficulty, as a nonsensical joke, as self-contradictory nonsense. And, in terms of theory ... it adheres either to a metaphysical lack of thought of the style of Wolff, or it adheres to an equally thoughtless type of mechanistic determinism etc.[27]

Engels, in this way, resolutely rejects determinism, and also at the same time rejects non-determinism as well. He became aware that "with existing concepts being unable to serve" in regard to the "contingency" and "necessity" which serve as preconditions for the opposition of "non-determinism" and "determinism", and critically continuing the work already done by Hegel, he re-determined "how it is possible that the contingent is necessary, and the necessary is contingent",[28] and through this, he attempts to go beyond the horizon itself of the opposition of determinism vs non-determinism.—I have already discussed thematically in a separate essay the matter of how the concepts of "necessity", "contingency" and "freedom" are to be re-determined in Marxism and, dependent on this, under what kind of deployment the opposition of determinism and non-determinism is sublated,[29] and it won't do, I think, in the current context of discussion to follow this different line of thought.—Viewed

---

25   ibid., S. 487 f. [Tr. Italics by Hiromatsu].
26   ibid., S.489. [Tr. Parenthetical material by Hiromatsu].
27   ibid.
28   ibid., S.486.
29   My essay of note 23 above and Chapter 2, Part 3, of my 『事的世界観への前哨』 [*An Outpost Towards a Koto-Centred View of the World*] (Keisō shobō, 1975).

from our current aim it will be sufficient if we verify as a precondition that the world-view – the view of history of Marx and Engels is not "determinism" and (having said that that it is also not "non-determinism").

Well then, that the world-view – the view of history of Marxism is not determinism is not, however, grounds for such a view denying the law-like nature of the world and history. Of course, in the intellectual, conceptual devices of modern knowledge, denial of determinism leads directly to denial of law-like nature. However, Marx and Engels inseparably with the dialectical re-determining of the categories of "necessity", "contingency" and "freedom" re-propose the notion of "law-like nature", and accordingly establish a law-like nature of history under a new understanding of law-like. The key here once again is none other than the mechanism of "reification".

2.2

How then is the law-conforming progression of history formed? This is a fundamental problem for the philosophy of history which ought to be solved separately from the abstract problem dimension of determinism – non-determinism. Regarding this fundamental problem, Marx and Engels respond precisely through the use of the theory of reification.

Here, placing the so-called "history of nature" outside the sphere of discussion, I wish to limit discussion to the "history of the human world" exclusively, but for the present, including the "history of nature", if one was to posit a "transcendent commander" (God or world reason or fate) it would be relatively easy to state a law-conforming nature of history. However, this is very much prior to modern science and is for us outside the bounds of consideration. Incidentally, within the horizon of modern knowledge, even if we took the position of a mechanistic determinism, it is not possible to draw out from there directly a law-like progression appearance *of history*. From the position of non-determinism matters are even more troublesome. Cases where thinkers assert a non-determinism to an extreme degree and obstinately insist that not even tendency exists in history are a separate matter, but to the extent that thinkers accept that at least a "probable law-like nature", what might be called certain tendencies, in history exist, the matter of just how the *free* acts of individuals manifest this "probable law-like nature" can't but help become an issue. Here, the relationship between on the one hand "spontaneous acts based on the free will of individuals" and on the other hand the *"probable* law-like nature of history appearing as the result of the activity of individuals" is therefore the issue. Conversely, even under determinism the relationship between on the one hand "the *apparent* free acts of individuals" and on the other hand the "law-like nature of history appearing through the acts of individuals" has to in the end become an issue. This being the case, even though there is a mutual diverging depending on whether one takes the two concepts of "spontaneous acts of will" and "historical law-like nature" rigidly or takes them roughly, in either case, the problematic of how the acts of individuals manifest the law-like progression of history remains in theories of history regardless.

Let us listen to what Engels has to say.

> In the history of society, the actors are all equipped with consciousness, and are all human beings who act with deliberation or passion aiming at a specific goal. Without conscious intention or an aimed at goal nothing whatsoever would take place. ... Through each pursuing his or her own consciously aimed at goals, human beings make history.[30] – These wills working in many and various directions, and also, the *resultant force* of the multifarious acting of these wills in regard to the external world is precisely none other than history. For that reason, what the multitude of individuals is aiming at becomes the issue at hand. The will is decided by passion or careful deliberation. There are various levers which directly decide this passion or deliberation. It is possible that it might be an object in the external world, or a motivation from ideas, or fame, or a "genuine feeling for truth and justice", or personal hatred, or a purely individual delusion. ... However, if we question one step further, what kind of activating force lies behind these motivations? What kind of *historical* cause transforms into such activating forces in the minds inside the heads of actors? There was no precedent of the *previous* materialism proposing this question. ... The inconsistency of the previous materialism lies not in accepting activating forces in the mind, it lies in not searching behind these activating forces in the mind, in not tracing things back as far as the cause which activates these forces".[31]—In this way, if searching for the motive power which acts as the true, ultimate activating force of history lying behind the motivating force of human beings acting in history is indeed the issue, ... it is not the motivation of individuals, but the motivation which moves the masses, all the members of a nation, all the classes in a national people which is the issue. Furthermore, this motivation has to be something which realises continuous, grand historical change. ... Investigating this *activating cause*, this is the very thing which alone can guide us when researching the laws of history as a totality, naturally, and

---

30   MEW, Bd. 21, S. 296 f.
31   ibid., S.297 f.

also when researching the laws which control the history of individual ages and individual countries.[32]

What is called an "activating cause" here is none other than a reified "social force" mediating as an "external restriction" in regard to individuals.—To quote Marx,

> Just to the extent that the totality of the movement appears as a social process, the whole of the process appears as an objective relation which emerges at last as naturally born. What's more, despite being something which emerges from the interaction of conscious individuals, it is not in their consciousness, and nor as a whole is it subordinate to those individuals, rather it *appears* as an objective relation. The mutually *combined force* of the individuals themselves gives birth to an alien social force in regard to them and which stands above them.[33]

What Marx calls here an "alien social force (*fremde gessellschaftliche Macht)*" and what Engels calls an "activating cause", can be called in the final analysis the "productive forces", even though they can take a variety of mediating – mediated existent forms. However, in doing this, we mustn't represent in a crude way the concept of the "productive forces". The "productive forces" referred to by Marx-Engels, as a fundamental category of materialist history, differs in dimension ontologically to the like of "technological productive forces" referred to in the bourgeois economy—indeed, there are cases where they also adopt the usage of it in classical economics or by List, using it in this sense as a "generally accepted idea". The re-grasping in the form of the potency of the dynamic relations of intersubjective co-operation in the place of production, (the grasping of this in a synchronic arrangement form – relations form is the "relations of production"), is the "productive forces".[34]

So, if we quote here the famous section from *The German Ideology*, the "social forces (*die soziale Macht*), that is to say, the forces of production (*d. h. die vervielfachte Produktionskraft*) which have been refracted through several layers" are none other than something "which comes into being (*entstehen*) through the co-operation (*Zusammenwirken*) of individuals". Even so, the situation is

---

32   ibid., S.298.

33   *Grundrisse*, neue MEGA, II. 1.1, S.126. (Dietz Ausgabe, S.111). [Tr. Italics by Hiromatsu].

34   Regarding this point, please see the discussion considering the circumstances of the formation of this concept in Marx-Engels on p. 97 and following of my 『唯物史観の現像』 [*The Original of Materialist History*].

limited to such that in these "social forces, that is to say, forces of production
which have been refracted through several layers ... the co-operation itself, is
not of the free will but is natural (*naturwüchsig*)", and this means that

> in regard to the individuals involved, they no longer appear as a phe-
> nomenon of a combination of the power of they themselves, they appear
> as a phenomenon as an alien force (*Gewalt*) existing outside of them. ...
> Rather than they being no longer able to rule these forces, on the contrary,
> it is these forces which are particular, are independent of people's inten-
> tions and movements, and on the contrary they rule people's intentions
> and movements, displaying a series of unfolding forms and development
> stages.[35]
>
> This self-adhesion of social activity, this very coagulation which is a
> power as thing where a product of our own selves controls us, ... is an
> important factor in previous historical progression.[36]

It is precisely through the mechanism of this reification that the law-like progression of history appears.

To review, we "explain" the law-like nature of history through the "combined
force" of the activities of the multitude of individuals and the mechanism of its
reification, and in the composition we have looked at above, the mechanism of
the law-like nature existent is what might be called "thermodynamic". To put
it more crudely, it can be said to be analogous to the composition where in a
"river" whilst the individual molecules of water move in all directions free and
disconnected, as the "combined movement" of the total they form a defined
stream.—This analogous mechanism[37] is, however, limited to being simply a
schema, and it is not the case that an explanation in reality of why and how the
law-like nature of history is established is fulfilled in any way in the above. The
"law-like nature of a river" is decided by "gravity" and the "shape of the riverbed", real existent elements which for the molecules of river water are external.
(Indeed, the "shape of the riverbed" may change through the movement of
the water molecules, but at the very least "gravity" "exists externally", and this
"external force" which is gravity acts as the "driving force" *affecting uniformly* all
the molecules). However, in "history", it is not the case that an "external force"
driving uniformly all the members of a society exists *in reality*.—In that case,

---

35   S.36 of the original text, and also p. 36 of the Japanese translation, of my 『手稿復元・新
      編輯版*Die deutsche Ideologie* 』［Restoration of the Handwritten Manuscript – New Edi-
      tion *Die deutsche Ideologie*］(Kawade shobō shinsha, 1974, New Corrected Printing, 1983).
36   ibid.

through what and how are the "direction" and "size" of the "combined force" in history determined? We now must proceed to examine the mechanism of

---

37   I'll provide here again schematic discussion of an analogous composition in my old paper "The Law of History and the Freedom of Individuals". "As an analogy, rather than as an example, of the law of history, let us, with the so-called law of supply and demand as our key, have a glance at how such is realised.

In the form of ⟨price being decided by the relationship of demand and supply⟩, the law of supply and demand is always, in other words, a formularisation of a cause-and-effect relationship of determination between two objective facts. However, it goes without saying that it's not the case that that which is price is self-moving, separated off from the act of human beings of buying and selling. In order for price to be decided, that is to say, in order for 'cause-and-effect' relationships of determination in an historical, objective scene to be able to be established, there has to be a mediation of a *conscious act* of human beings. Precisely, 'without an act of human will nothing arises' (Engels), and in this sense, human beings decide price.

People can sell things below a 'reasonable price', and can buy things above a 'reasonable price'. To this extent, it's *not* the case that the act of buying or selling of people is *uniformly and without exception* controlled by the relation of supply and demand and the law of supply and demand. In this regard, it differs decisively from such as the law of parabolic movement of a physical object. Saying that the *law* of supply and demand *controls* price is not saying that extending a mysterious, physical effect on the subjects of buying and selling such *unequivocably* decides the act, it is only saying that buying and selling price as a collective phenomenon, on the whole accords in a cause-and-effect-statistical manner with the 'law of supply and demand'.

What's more, in this, it's not necessarily the case that the subjects of buying and selling transact having grasped in fine detail the actuality of the relationship of supply and demand. Consequently, it's not the case that *knowledge* of reasonable price determines the act of buying and selling. Further, persons *will*ing the realisation of the law of supply and demand do not exist. It is not something aimed at by anyone. A person may make it their principle to sell cheaply thinking to have their customers be delighted, and a person may always pay extra in terms of change to show that they are generous. Etc. Buying and selling is precisely a 'free contractual act' supported by a great variety of consciousnesses, and the content of consciousness and the goal aimed at do not have a direct relationship to the relationship of supply and demand. The *realisation of the law* of supply and demand, viewed from, too, the characteristic of consciousness, is a result brought about, as it were, by chance.

In the above two senses, a *direct* relationship of determination between the 'law of supply and demand' and acts of buying and selling isn't formed. In this sense, again, in the sense of the realisation of the law not being the realisation of an aimed at goal, the act of the buying and selling subjects has no necessary relationship, but rather is *accidental*, in regard to the law of supply and demand. Of course, it's not an accident in an absolute sense. Nevertheless, provisionally, through 'accidental' acts in these senses, in a resultant manner – statistically, the law of supply and demand proceeds to be realised. (Strictly speaking, for the law of supply and demand to be able to be established, buying and selling doesn't stop at being simply 'accidental', it has to be 'free'. If buying and selling is coerced extra-economically, the law of supply and demand cannot be established. In this sense, the control of buying and selling by the law of supply and demand takes, rather, the 'freedom' of buying and selling as a presupposition).

establishment of this "combined force", to examine the mechanism of establishment of the reifying composition itself.

2.3

As constituting elements deciding the "direction" and "size" of the historical "combined" vector, people may put forward the "movement" and "capacity" of the various classes. Certainly, at a certain level of historical explanation or prediction fixing attention on these "elements" is in accord with reality, and in scientific thought as well research focused along the lines of these "elements" is necessary. However, if we analyse going back to first principles, the "movement and capacity" itself of "each class" is already a "combined vector", and is a "reified product". For that reason, in the dimension of a "philosophy of

---

The situation seen in the law of supply and demand above can, I think, be extrapolated to the manner of realisation in general of the 'law of history'. And, when extrapolating this, isn't there something between the 'necessity' of the law of history and the 'free acts' of individuals which vividly reminds us of Hegel's ⟨cunning of reason⟩?—Hegel's world reason 'doesn't of itself enter into the process and ... leaves people to act as they please'. Although the scheme of the face of the die being one in six is fixed, this doesn't interfere with the trifling, every move of what the face of each respective die may be. People act with various interests and passions, according to their character, and through behaving 'as they please', they proceed to realise the goal of rationality, in a total – resulting way. It's not the case that an absolute freedom is recognised here, but human beings are granted provisionally free acts, and for the goal of rationality of these parenthesised 'free acts' they proceed to actualise world reason through accidental acts.—When we remove a metaphysical world reason (God) from the thought of Hegel's ⟨cunning of reason⟩, and render a law-like nature inherent to the world, the relationship between the law-like nature and particular events which appears there is, I think, analogous to the relationship between the flow of a river and the movement of the molecules of water.

It's not the case that the individual molecules which make up the stream of a river are unequivocally determined directly by gravity and the state of the bed of the river, by, in other words, the law of the stream. It's not the case that the molecules flow uniformly, rather it's the case that they move in all directions at great speed. However, if we look at the movement of such water molecules as a whole and as a resultant, the current flows by at a speed of several kilometres an hour, determined by the state of the riverbed and gravity.

Incidentally, for the river to flow at a speed of several kilometres an hour requires the 'free movement' of the water molecules as a precondition. In this regard, it is the same as the realisation of the law of supply and demand requiring the 'freedom of buying and selling' as a precondition. Further, the movement of the individual molecules is 'accidental' in regard to the law of the stream. It is precisely as only the 'combined power' of this 'accidental', 'free movement' that the stream is formed.

From a different perspective, the form of realisation of the law of supply and demand, nay, the relationship of the law of history and the acts of individuals to the extent that such can be extrapolated to it, is precisely this kind of thing." Etc.

society" – "philosophy of history" view of history, it isn't acceptable to rest at this level, we must consider matters moving back to a more fundamental situation.—Whereupon, the level of the "productive forces" and the "relations of production" comes into focus as the issue at hand. Research at this level is not simply the cornerstone of the "class struggle view of history", it has an actuality in the dynamic grasping and observation of history, and it is certainly the case that it is a necessary level of research. However, if one represents the situation as if there are the two *things* of the "*thing* of the forces of production" and the "*thing* of the relations of production", with the movement and laws of history being decided through the direct relation between the two, in principle these too belong to a level which has as its precondition a "combined force" and "reification".—For us, that concrete research is necessary at these various levels – the level of interrelated dynamic relations between "societies as units", (whether such is a "state defined by land", a "people", a "communitas based on a relationship to territory", or whether such itself is a multiclass "communitas based on kinship"), the level of the oppositional relations between the classes, the level of the forces of production – the relations of production, etc—and, that such research possesses actuality in historical research, and having affirmatively acknowledged and stated clearly these facts, the point here, however, is to methodologically go back to a more fundamental – basic principle situation.

We are at the stage, here, of going back to the situation of the practical activity of individuals, and considering the mechanism of the reificatory establishment of the historical law-like nature.—But we must undertake this bearing in mind ourselves that when this is undertaken lacking a methodological self-awareness it is an extremely dangerous process. The individuals are not a *homogenous entity*, and even though they are an "active subject of practice" they are not an "absolute subject" of "causeless spontaneity". The individuals, who are an "active subject of activity", exist in their true state as a "nodular whole of relations towards nature and between human beings"; and in reality, through an already reified set of relations, not only so-called "individuality" and "character", and "conditions of behaviour" and "forms of behaviour", but even the "motives" and "goals" of acts are controlled. Also, whilst in the current context they can be treated as "spontaneous activating subjects" equipped with "free will", from the dimension of analysis of cerebral physiology, they don't possess true spontaneous activating-ness but rather the *possibility* that their action is no more than of a "conditioned reflex kind" wherein action is decided unequivocally through physical stimuli and first and foremost the state of the brain, is possible. We are not ones to forget this fact, and we bear in mind that consideration in this dimension is separately necessary, but, to the extent that it doesn't directly resonate with the tenor of our current discussion, here, I wish to develop our discussion for the time being on the basis of a "common sense" "methodological" arrangement wherein individuals are knowing, acting subjects equipped with free will who behave appropriately in response to given conditions.

Further, though it isn't necessary to reconfirm this again, in materialist history, the laws of history are not of the type of thing where they transcendently pre-exist and directly control the activity of individuals.—In a certain type of understanding of laws, for example in regard to the parabolic movement of an object, the situation is represented in a manner where that which is "the law of parabolic movement" pre-exists eternally unchanging, and the movement of an object on a particular occasion is said to be "ruled" by or to "obey" this law. Here, rather than existing rails, the "law" has an effect on the moving object just like a beam guiding the flight of a missile and it can be said to be conceived in the form of a fixed something which "makes" the moving object forcibly "obey" a specific flight path. Materialist history, even though it "predicts" a specific image of a future society, "predicts" the form of history developing into the future, but this certainly doesn't mean that it conceives of a fatalistic rule by an established law in this way.—The law-like nature of history in materialist history is what might be called something which can be illustrated by the traces of the reified "combined force" of the activity of individuals, a "wake"-like formation (*Gebilde*) which proceeds to result in all probability under specific given conditions. For us, for this reason, we didn't develop our discussion in the reified perspective of how the *laws* of history make the activity of individuals follow them, rather we began our task of investigating how the probable "direction" of the vector-like combination of the activity of individuals results.

Now, to the extent that human individuals are animals, the continuation of direct – indirect reproduction of *Leben* is given a probable tendency, and this practice of life is regulated by given conditions. Engels says:

> The first condition of the whole of human history is, it goes without saying, the existence of living human individuals. For that reason, the constituent requirement which first ought to be determined is the system of the bodies of these individuals and alongside this the relation between these individuals and the rest of nature given through this system.[38]

However, "here, of course, we can neither enter into matters regarding the physical features of human beings themselves, nor regarding the natural con-

---

38   ibid., S.23. p. 23 of the Japanese translation as well.

ditions human beings discover before them, regarding the geological, land-scape, climatic etc. relations".—However, as a confirmation from basic prin-ciples "records of history must all begin from this foundation of natural history along with changes in such undergone through the activity of human beings in the progression of history".[39]

When we consider matters from this standpoint,

> no matter what stage we are at in history, a physical result, the totality of the forces of production, a relation created historically towards nature and mutually between individuals are discovered. This is something which is transmitted to each generation from prior generations, but these forces of production and the sum total of the environment, even though in one aspect indeed they are changed by the new generation, in another aspect they designate in regard to this generation life conditions peculiar to it, and they also endow this generation with a specific development, and certain special characteristics. In this way, human beings create their environment, and in the same way, their environment creates human beings.[40]

Here, if we might venture to make for the present an abstract-formulaic com-ment, truly a human ecological succession forms here in reality, and a law-like nature of history as ecological succession results.

Even though the human ecosystem is determined by the way of being of the relation towards environment and intra-species relations, by, in other words, the way of being of what Marx calls "relations towards nature and relations mutually between individuals", in the human ecosystem, the subject individu-als are conscious beings acting with *a sense of purpose*, and the action of these subjects is carried out as conscious, significant activity. As Engels also states clearly in the passage quoted above, "in history, without conscious intention, without a desired goal, nothing would occur".[41] And, what's more, this inten-tional practice is not a direct drive of simply desire. It is not only restricted "as an existent" and "in fact" through objectified *environmental* conditions, but is also bound "in terms of ideas" and "normatively" through reified inter-subjective relations – co-subjective forms. However, even though up until the point of restriction through *existent* environmental conditions this is a rule in common with ecology, the moment of *normative* restriction (although it

---

39   ibid.
40   ibid., S.50. p. 50 of the Japanese translation as well.
41   The same as note 30 above.

can't be said to be exclusively characteristic of human beings, in essence) is a species differentiating major feature in human ecology. And, this normative restrictiveness is not *sein müssen* but belongs to the realm of so-called *sollen*.

In discussing, here, the tendency toward a "combined force" formed from *human* ecological co-operative activity, we face the necessity of giving consideration to normative imperative-ness, to this conscious restrictiveness.—To the extent that we refer to a narrow view, Marx and Engels unfortunately have not developed a thematic theory in regard to the theory of normative restriction *in the narrow sense*. Despite simply saying norm, such takes truly multifarious concrete existent forms, in regard to society, in regard to an age, in regard to a class, in regard to a group ..., and it is not something which can be discussed easily and put aside. However, at the level of consideration we are facing in the current item of discussion, it will be, I think, sufficient to cast our gaze at the general composition.—We use the concept of "normative restriction" in an extremely broad sense. Despite calling it a conscious restriction, I would like to include also "pre-conscious self-restriction" not accompanied by a clear self-awareness. Amongst the restrictions on human behaviour, apart from restriction which is existent—as a fact *sein müssen*, despite the fact that transgression is possible as an existent—in fact, I include in "normative restriction" all "restriction by custom (*nomos*)" (*für uns*, self-restriction based on internalised sanction-involving restrictions) which due to so-called "social pressure" makes us usually obey. (Without fear that it may be too crude, if we deliberately aim at being "illustrative", aiming at the convenience of contrast, of a different type to that where at the location which is the "stage condition" of agricultural fields the activity of fishing cannot be carried out, and under the "equipment condition" of a fishing rod the activity of farming cannot be carried out; of a different type to such existent – in fact restriction is, for example, "not being able at all to appear in front of people stark naked", or "not being able at all to eat human flesh", situations which although in terms of existents they are in reality possible, and it is the situation that I call here restrictions in terms of custom – in terms of folk usage – morally – in terms of rules – in terms of the law ..., all binding through imperative controls, "normative binding").

Now, no matter how "free will based" and "spontaneous" the behaviour of people may be said to be, in addition to behaviour being restricted and oriented "in terms of existents – in fact" by "stage-like environment" and "equipment conditions", even though being restricted in this way, within the zone of behaviour possessing rather the possibility of enlargement in fact – in terms of existents, the type and form of behaviour is "normatively" restricted. As a

result, the behaviour of people under given "stage – equipment conditions",
is considerably multifarious viewed microscopically, and is something which
viewed macroscopically ends up being largely contained within an extremely
limited large-scale boundary, and this is the reason that the "direction" of the
"combined force" is demarcated.—In the above sentences, we have written in
a manner which is as if "conditions of factual restriction" and "conditions of
normative restriction" differentiate dualistically, but the fact is the two are not
things which should be differentiated dualistically. Though we say "stage environment", within such even so-called "natural" moments are of a "nature transformed" by the activity of preceding generations, and other people also appear
on the stage, and although it appears in an established objective existent form,
the "stage environment" is, in fact, none other than a reification of the "functional relations towards nature and between human beings". And, as a problem
in reality, this stage environment itself already *also* carries "normative restrictive force". That the same is the case for "equipment conditions" hardly, I'm
sure, needs detailed comment. "Normative conditions" too are formed through
the activity of preceding generations, and are none other than intersubjective
forms "reproduced" at the place of sanctioning intersubjective relations, and
for individuals these again are perceived reified in the form of a certain thing
existing externally and independently and exerting a restrictive force. And, to
the extent that normatively restricted behaviour becomes a factor in the trans-
formative reproduction of stage conditions, and, again, to the extent that stage
conditions restrict the way of being of norms, the two are mutually mediating. However, to the extent that we speak focusing along the lines of reified
forms, "stage – equipment" existent – in fact conditions are the foundation,
and "normative" in-the-mind – value conditions are positioned as secondary
forms.

Now readers will, I think, recall – confirm that the composition in the above
series of quoted sentences where Marx and Engels discuss and describe the
mechanism establishing the law-like nature of history has become a composition of explanation formed by "stage – equipment conditions of restriction"
and "normative conditions of restriction" brought into the discussion above as
explanatory devices.

If we venture to check again, Marx and Engels say:

> In history no matter what stage we are at, a specific material result, the
> totality of the forces of production, a relation towards nature and mutu-
> ally between individuals created historically, are discovered. Even though
> these forces of production and the totality of the environment are indeed
> in one aspect transformed by a new generation, in another aspect they

designate for this generation its own conditions of life, and they also endow this generation with a specific development and a special characteristic.[42]

This, if we put it in terms of our explanatory devices, is none other than something which speaks of a succession of reified existent conditions of restriction which are "stage-environment – equipment-conditions" *created historically* and which are pre-existing for the generation on each occasion. However, with this alone, the schema of the existent – in fact restrictiveness of the ecological succession of a generation has been shown as a necessary condition only, and the way of being of the activity of the individuals of each generation still hasn't been positively determined.

Thereupon, Marx and Engels, whilst taking these existent conditions as a precondition, introduce the point of argument that "social forces, that is to say, the forces of production refracted through several layers"—even though these forces "come into existence through the co-operation of individuals"—"appear as phenomena as an alien, powerful force to individuals, existing independently and outside of them", and that "it is this force which directs (*dirigieren*) the intentions and movement of individuals". This expression of view is of a form where the gaze is directed towards reified "social forces", and in terms of our explanatory devices it is none other than something which speaks of "normative binding".

In this way, the meaningful action of individuals in history is given direction by "stage-environment – equipment-conditions", and, moreover, it is the case that as a result of this direction being limited by "normative restrictions", the "direction" and "unfolding" of the "combined force" are demarcated.— Although, as I qualified above, the "stage-environment – equipment-conditions" themselves already in fact carry as well "normative restrictiveness", and the two-stage presentation of the argument here is simply a methodological division.—What we are calling "normative restrictions" are "observed" in that form where in a reified form "social forces" existing independently outside of individuals "control (*dirigieren*)" each person, and, to this extent it seems to have an analogous composition to the effect of gravity on the molecules of a river, but, in truth this is in no way the case. Whereas gravity actually exists externally and acts physically and directly on each molecule, it is not the case that "social forces" exist independently and externally to individuals, nor is it the case that they exert a direct physical force. What exists in reality is a

---

42   The same as note 39 [sic –40] above.

situation where individuals, who are conscious existents, restrict themselves, despite this being based on a reificatory delusion. When we bear this fact in mind, not only does history present a reified progression in regard to the standpoint of an observer, (because real history progresses in the subjects involved acting in a self-restricting way while they themselves perceive "stage – equipment – normative" conditions in a reified form) the situation of reification for the subjects involved forms a constituent moment in historical progression.

We can now confirm the following fact. Marx and Engels, in a certain regard, say that, regarding the viewpoint of non-determinism which denies that there is lawfulness in history (in other words, regarding the viewpoint which regards *for reason of* human beings being subjects of free will that laws etc in history *cannot* exist), that *despite* the fact that human beings are provisionally "subjects possessing free will", through the mechanism of reification the law-like nature of history is established. However, this is one aspect of the matter, and in another aspect they, more positively, say that *for reason of* human individuals carrying out somehow "meaningful" action in a self-restricting manner, under given reified conditions (even though *für uns* in a deluded manner or a preconscious manner), the real progression of history appears in a law-conforming manner.[43]—Indeed, in the texts left to us by Marx and Engels, in comparison to the laying bare of and the formula of the law-like nature of history and the pointing out that this law-like nature is a product of reification, there are not many instances of a carrying out of concrete analysis of the process of people's activity "producing – reproducing" the reified law-like nature of history. The carrying out of this concrete analysis can be said to be a task left to we who have come after them. However, Marx himself declares that pointing out that a given certain situation is a product of reification and is a delusion is relatively easy, and that the elucidation indeed of why and in what way the reification arises is difficult but important [vgl. MEW. Bd. 23, S. 392 f. (Anm. 89)]. Even though he himself left the concrete task unfinished, it seems certain that he had put

---

43   Takahashi Yōji discerningly brings this problematic to light in the aforementioned 『物 神性の解読』 [*Deciphering the Fetish Character*], and he has started the task himself of unfolding a concrete examination into this matter. It is likely that my stance of a lack of what ought to be a separation between "what ought to have been" and "what was" will be reproached by Takahashi, and I wish to beg forgiveness.—Presenting clearly and ascertainingly this problematic, which is the key for the methodological unfolding for a social science type of research which stood on the standpoint of the theory of the fetish character – the theory of reification, and, moreover, implementing the concrete task in response to that, needs to be taken note of as a ground-breaking achievement of Takahashi's. Further, my plan to introduce a "role theory composition" is based on a consciousness of problematic of the same type as Takahashi's.

forward a composition of explanation that ... it is *for reason of* such and such intentional acts of people under reified such and such conditions.

Above, our discussion in this section takes as a precondition the fact that the co-operation of persons is "natural" and "in-itself". What about situations where co-operation is carried out "for-itself"? In order to respond to this problem, amongst other reasons, we need to relaunch our discussion with an investigation of value evaluation in regard to the situation of reification and, going further back, with an investigation of the methodological significance the situation of reification had for Marx.

3   The Systematic Method of the Critique of Reification and the
      Standpoint of Value Judgement

The theory of reification, for Marx, is not only something of an area which delineates his view of society and view of history—to say nothing of the fact that it doesn't stop at being of an area of explanatory principles of economic phenomena and political phenomena—it is something which extends its scope to his theory of knowledge of the humanities and the sciences and his methodology, and, from a different perspective, it is of a type which provides the foundation for his theory of revolution as well.

3.1
The special characteristic of Marx's system of knowledge of the humanities and the sciences, for the time being, can be seen I think in the composition of the type where it is "simultaneously a description of the system and a critique of the system through description",[44] which he describes in a letter addressed to Lassalle. A composition of the type where a systematic description of the given – objective situation at the object level is simultaneously and inseparably a critique of that system at a meta-level; it is to be understood that Marx aimed at a system of scientific knowledge possessing this kind of composition. We see in reality in *Capital* examples where systematic description of a reified situation is simultaneously and inseparably a critique of the reified systematic situation.

Upon reflection, in the Hegelian system, it is of a schema where historicity and logicality are matched, and based on this, there was a deployment where a confirming systematic description of historical progression and a sequential

---

44   MEW, Bd. 29, S. 550.

overcoming – critique in regard to previous stages are carried out simultaneously and inseparably. This in its own way is of a composition of "systematic
description = systematic critique".—To the extent that ascending unfolding in
Marx succeeded in a critiquing manner the Hegelian dialectic there is no doubt
that there is an aspect where this deployment is sublatingly taken over, but
Marx, as is evident from his statement in the Introduction to *A Critique of Classical Economics*, strictly rejects the Hegelian understanding, which overlays historicity and logicality.[45] Marx in his later period can no longer take the Hegelian
static stance (*zusehen*) in regard to the spiral like self-progression of alienation – recovery. He has now reached a position where a new law of composition
of a dialectical system which sublates Hegel's is the matter of concern.[46]

The objective situation which Marx systematically describes – critiques, is
on a particular occasion different for both on the one hand the system internal
= non-critiquing consciousness of those involved (and, system internal "scientific knowledge" to the extent that such is unable to go beyond this system
internal standpoint), and on the other hand system external = critiquing scientific knowledge. That which appears – manifests as a phenomenon in the
form of a relation between things – characteristics – a form (*Gebilde*) for those
involved internal to the system (and system internal "scientific knowledge"),
is sensed as a relation between people (relations between people which also
depend on the mediation of physical factors) for Marxian scientific knowledge
which takes a system external standpoint. The objective thing-like being which
appears to system internal consciousness is cognized in reality in Marxian scientific knowledge as a *reified state of relations*.—Here, *description* by Marxian
scientific knowledge regarding the reified *objective situation*, inseparably
accompanies a *critiquing* identification that it is a *reified* hypothetical phenomenal. Of course, it's not that each line of text is carried out as "description – critique". Having first carried out analytical description of the *für es*
situation which projects as a thing-like being, it's possible that a method of
argumentation is taken wherein a *für uns* critiquing identification is carried out

45   Although if one focuses superficially on Hegel's wording this criticism appears unreason-
      able, elucidation of the fact that it is actually valid will be made with reference to 「弁
      証法の唯物論的顛倒はいかにして可能であったか」 〖"How Was the Materialist
      Inversion of the Dialectic Possible?"〗 contained in my 『マルクス主義の成立過程』
      〖*The Process of Formation of Marxism*〗 (Shiseidō, 1968).
46   See my 『弁証法の論理—弁証法における体系構成法』 〖*The Logic of the
      Dialectic—The Method of System Composition in the Dialectic*〗 (Seido sha, 1980). In addi-
      tion, I would be grateful if I could have you also peruse my "What Was 'Philosophy' for
      Marx?" [included as Chapter 5 in this book] 〖Tr. The chapter title is actually "Philosophy
      in Marx"〗.

step-by-step in the manner of a "solving of a riddle". In actuality this method is adopted in *Capital*.

Upon reflection, the composition of *für es* (for the consciousness involved) and *für uns* (for scientific knowledge) was something Hegel introduced in *The Phenomenology of Spirit*. However, in his case, we have the appearance of scientific knowledge statically observing the process of the consciousness involved accumulating experiences on its own initiative one after the other, and things are constructed such that the reader along with the author, Hegel, observes. Scientific knowledge does acknowledge with the concept of a third-party the level attained by the consciousness involved, but it was determined to be something which for the time being is not related to the self-awareness of the consciousness involved. *Für uns*, in Hegel, to the extent that scientific knowledge has the appearance of a static observer, performs no kind of positive role for the *progression* of systematic description – critique. To put things the other way around, because the scientific knowledge which the author Hegel embodies was of an appearance where a positive change of stage is not carried out, the consciousness involved has in-itself to move *upwards*, and a composition has to be adopted where logic advances in conjunction with this chronological (historical) upwards movement.

In the case of Marx, in contrast to this, the scientific knowledge which the author Marx embodies positively performs a change of stage. Scientific knowledge is not a static observer it is a systematic describer and a systematic critic. He no longer needs to depend on an autonomous upward movement of the consciousnesses involved. Consequently, there is no need to affirm as-it-is historical progression. In response to the demands of logic in systematic description, he can select the order of description. (Even though whether or not historicity and logicality partially are in accord "depends on the conditions", and in Marx's upwards unfolding as well, as a broad framing schema, indeed the situation is similar to a form where the consciousness involved moves upwards sequentially. Yet, this "pseudo generative theory" schema is only something which responds to the system – logical unfolding brought about through the hegemony of the author, and is not confirmation of the self-movement of the consciousnesses involved.—In Marx's case, even though the historicity of tracing the "self-movement" of the reified situation is at issue, the Hegelian "appearance" of an historical tracing of the self-movement of the consciousnesses involved is avoided). In Marx's systematic unfolding of description = critique, the reader too is not simply a sharing observer, but, in response to Marx's stage changing, and at the level of each occasion, is formed into a "*wir* (we)" with Marx the author.—In Marx's dialectic, the composition of *es wir* which Hegel introduced but was unable to make positive use of, in this there is a deployment in which the moment of "author and reader" is made good use of methodologically.[47] Although we can't go so far as to say that this is something which makes the theory of reification as a first step possible, we need to take note of the fact that it is a method of system composition which was established inseparably with the composition of systematic description = systematic critique of reification.

Incidentally, in this new method of system composition of Marx, inseparable to the theory of reification, a new "problem" arises. With the appearance of only statically observing in the manner of Hegel it is possible to insist that it is "value-free (*wertfrei*)". However, in the Marxian system in which description – critique is carried out from a standpoint external to the system, whilst the "author" "pretends" to "embody" scientific knowledge, isn't it the case that the author's ideological value position and evaluating attitude are baldly brought into the situation? Moreover, isn't it the case that similarly the "author", purporting to respond to the demands of a logical systemicity which is not of the continual arising of history, can to quite a degree "freely" select the objective situation which needs to be described? To take things further, isn't it the case that the arrangement is such that in Marx's method of system composition, the "author", whilst directing the "puppets" marked as the subjects involved, "bewitchingly" controls the "reader" as well?

How would Marx respond to these possible doubts? Would he respond stiffly with the comment that in the end systems do not escape when all is said and done being of such an ideological make-up? The matter is not so simple. Including this problem within our purview, let us now turn our gaze to the problem of values in the theory of reification and to the problem of ideology critique.

3.2

When the theory of reification points out that a thing-like being considered to be a true form not only for the everyday consciousness involved but for "scientific knowledge" internal to the system is *not* as it is a *true form*, and, moreover, when this point is made from a critiquing standpoint external to the system, is it then that such a pointing out is based on different values to a system-internal pointing out? Or is a pointing out of reifying misconception or explanation of the reifying mechanism a "value free" "judgement of fact", with "value judgement (*Wertung* = value evaluation)" not being particularly included within such?

---

47   Regarding the differences between Hegel and Marx concerning the composition of *für es* and *für uns*, the composition of "author and reader", which I have pointed out in an abbreviated way above, I would like to have you supplement such through the full discussion of such in my work cited in the previous note.

A certain kind of thinker regards the theory of reification as if it is "value free", in contrast to the theory of alienation forming a unity with value evaluation, and they intimate dissatisfaction with the theory of reification saying that in the case of the theory of alienation indictment of the status quo and the *sollen* (imperative) of revolutionary rising up can easily be drawn out, but that with the theory of reification motivation for revolution is not established. Indeed, for the theorists of alienation when a given is determined as an alienated state the fact that, immediately, it is "something *bad*", that it is something where "its authentic nature *must* be recovered", may well be implied in an "analytical judgement manner". In contrast, the understanding of reification certainly doesn't contain as it is in an "analytical judgement manner" a value evaluation of *good and bad* or the imperative of being "something which *must* be self-sublated". However, this certainly doesn't mean that the theory of reification system as systematic description = systematic critique is completely value free. Rather the fact that it *can* be extremely ideological is as was shown in the questions at the end of the last item.

When the theory of reification regrasps as reificatory *delusions* the "situations" or "propositions" which appear "objectively" for the consciousnesses involved within the system or for "scientific" consciousness from the vantage point within the system and which for them are "universally valid", the theorist of reification asserts that consciousnesses internal to the system have fallen into a type of *error* and the theorist is convinced that it is he or she indeed who understands the true form of the matter. From the point of view of the theorist of reification, a consciousness internal to the system who thinks that reified forms are, just as they are, true forms is a consciousness which has fallen into "falsity (*Falschheit*)", in other words, it is a "false consciousness (*ein falsches Bewußtsein*)". Immediately, here, we have to say that a "value" evaluation of "truth – falsity" mediates.—So does, then, the theorist of reification attempt to solve things by saying that the reified situation is simply a falsehood? Does he or she solve things by saying realise the error and focus on the true form? Matters are not so straightforward.

In the systematic description = systematic critique of reification, "truth – falsity" and the issue of the "criterion" of such are both built into the system in a self-aware manner. Even though we speak of critique *external* to the system this is certainly not transcendent critique. Without requiring a bringing to mind of the wisdom of Hegel, the dialectic is something which renders the Kantian "critique" into steps and aims at this critique being built into the system,[48] and it is

---

48   I would like you to bring to mind the famous passage (Section 41 Appendix 1) "defining" the dialectic in the *Enzyklopädie*.

something which *for the moment* internalises as well the criterion for truth and falsity within the system. Indeed, Hegel's dialectic and Marx's dialectic are not the same just as they are. In Marx's case, things do not unify at the heights of "absolute knowledge", rather, *in the final analysis*, "a human being must verify truth, that is to say, the reality and power, the worldliness, of his thought in *practice*. The debate regarding the reality – *ir*reality of thought divided from practice is purely a problem of the Scholastics",[49] says Marx, with the verification of truth and falsity shifting to the place of "practice". Despite this, this is a matter of *in the final analysis*, and it certainly cannot mean that the problem of truth and falsity within a theoretical system is completely shelved. In a form corresponding to the composition of verification in the place of practice, a practice which has gone beyond the boundaries of the theoretical system, Marx has built in the problem of truth and falsity within the theoretical system. Apart from the values of truth and falsity, the same applies to the values (problems) of "good and evil" and "right and wrong".

Let us look at matters from the problem of truth and falsity. A reificatory error for Marxian scientific knowledge is *für uns* purely an error. However, whilst it is naturally the case for those directly involved, for those who cannot go beyond a perspective internal to the system, that is to say, for the overwhelming majority under a given system, it is reflected as the very reality – truth. Even if scientific knowledge suddenly pointed out that the matter in question is simply an error, the result is likely to be simply a pointless argument. A reificatory error which for consciousnesses within the system is virtually inevitable, is not so simple and contingent a thing that with only a small amount of pointing out by another they notice the mistake. From a paradigm within the system, it can even be said to be the truth. The reificatory error in the dimension we are focusing on at the moment differs completely in terms of dimension to an individual error within a homogenous paradigm; it is of a kind involving the paradigm as a totality itself.

Although it is crude, the point may perhaps be more easily seen if we introduce by way of illustration, here, the case of the opposition of the theory of the heavens moving and the theory of the Earth moving. For those involved who stand in a position internal to the surface of the Earth system, the ground doesn't move, and it is the Sun which revolves. If it is pointed out that this is an error they are not easily convinced. It is through taking a position (even if it is as a performance within the mind) *external* to the surface of the Earth

---

49   MEW, Bd. 3, S. 6.

that a person for the first time can know that the Earth revolves and that the theory of the heavens moving is an error. However, even if for example a person has understood the correctness of the theory of the Earth moving, to the extent that he exists in actuality within the surface of the Earth system, to his eyes the situation will remain that the Earth does not move and the Sun revolves. For him, the theory of the Earth moving is at most no more than "knowledge", and he conducts himself in accordance with the "objective" "reality" that the Earth does not move and the Sun revolves. No matter how much he is told it is an error, for a person internal to the surface of the Earth system it is the "phenomenals of the theory of the heavens moving" which indeed are truly "reality", and different to "simply knowledge" they are "stage givens" controlling in actuality his daily life = practice. To the extent that one exists within the surface of the Earth system one simply brings ruin upon oneself if one tries to act ignoring this reality. This "illusory reality", which is analogous to a reified situation, limits – restricts in reality the consciousness – life – practice of those involved. For a standpoint within the system, it is truly "objective reality" and it is "valid universally".—By the way, let us imagine that there is in the same way an understanding within the paradigm of the heavens moving that "the Earth is a vast flat surface, that pillars stand in its four corners, and that these support the heavens". From the perspective of the theory of the Earth moving, a perspective which is external to the surface of the Earth system, the "stationary Earth view" and the "flat surface of the Earth view" are both together identified as fallacies. However, are the two really fallacies at the same level? No, they are not. Whereas the "flat surface of the Earth argument" is already a fallacy within the paradigm of the theory of the heavens moving, within this paradigm the "argument that the Earth doesn't move" is a correct argument. The two differ in level. Analogously to this, within paradigms as well which correspond to reified standpoints internal to a system, exist many contingent misconceptions of the type where they are already fallacies within the bounds of such paradigms, and so it is necessary to differentiate "apodictic" reificatory mis-cognition from such contingent misconceptions.

How does Marx deal with this problem? In the section on the theory of the fetish character in *Capital*, he takes up a group of reified forms, and having shown by investigation that these existent forms are reificatory inversions (quid pro quo) he relates in the following way.

> These kind of forms indeed form precisely the categories of bourgeois economics. These forms indeed are the socially valid, and for this reason, objective (*gessellschaftlich gültige, also, objektive*) forms of thought of

these historically determined social forms of production, of commodity
production, in relation to the relations of production.[50]

—People may be surprised here and may respond with retorts: Isn't "socially
valid, and for this reason, objective forms of thought" a reference to "truth"
put another way? If that is the case doesn't it mean that Marx is recognising
the reified forms which make up the "categories of bourgeois economics" as
the "truth"? If we end up recognising this as the "truth" what on earth was
the description in the preceding section pursuing the view of reificatory inversion for? Isn't the investigating of the secret of the fetish character wasted?
Marx does, in fact, although with certain conditions, recognise the "truth" of
the reified forms. With the condition of it being from a standpoint internal
to "these historically determined forms of production", he provisionally recognises the "truth" of these forms. This, if we look at things in terms of the analogy
above, would be equivalent to the confirmation of "truth" internal to a system
of knowledge of the type of the "theory of the stationary Earth" which we differentiated from such as the "theory of the Earth as a flat surface". However,
this "truth" is certainly not "truth" from a vantage point external to the system.
The investigation is necessary of what and in what way such is inverted, and in
actuality Marx carries out this investigation. However, this investigating knowledge *still* hasn't obtained a "socially valid, objectivity". Here, if "social validity –
objectivity" is taken as the criterion for "truth", to that extent, on the contrary,
it is the reified forms which have to be taken as "truth". And, the investigating
knowledge comes to be no more than the "thought" of at best a minority, or of
Marx alone. To put things in accord with Marx's method of system composition, under the present situation, things are still in actuality treated this way.
He certainly doesn't insist, in this situation, that his own system external criteria and knowledge are uniformly true. Marx's descriptive critique = critiquing
description is, within the theoretical system, for the moment and in this way
self-relativised. This is the reason, I think, the criterion itself of critique follows
stages dialectically and ought to be self-scrutinised and rendered to a higher
level.

   If, provisionally, we give an interim response here to the problem which
arose at the end of the last item of discussion regarding "value free-ness" etc,
it is certainly not the case that Marx advocates value free-ness; but, as we saw
above, he self-relativises the critiquing criterion itself, and, moreover, he carefully moves forward with his investigation in a way that ensures he doesn't

50   MEW, Bd. 23, S. 90.

depart transcendently from system internal "truth", and it is certainly not the case that he decides on *arbitrary* ideological conclusions.—This applies not only for the values of true and false, it is the same in regard to the values of good and bad and just and unjust. In *Critique of the Gotha Programme*, Marx retorts,

> Do not the bourgeois claim that the present-day distribution is "fair?" In fact, based on the foundations of the present-day form of production [I would like the reader to take note of this condition – Hiromatsu], isn't it then the only "fair" distribution? Isn't it the case that economic relations are controlled by the concepts of the Law (*Recht* = justice), or in the opposite direction, that the relations of the Law (justice) arise from the economy?,[51]

placing the value criteria for "fairness" and "justice" *for the moment* on system internal validity. Marx doesn't do such as suddenly arbitrarily introducing system external value criteria.

Marx's systematic description = systematic critique is not, of course, completed with the above composition. Let us now look at the next logical step.

In the discussion above, there was a tacit assumption that from a system internal standpoint and within paradigms in accord with system judgements of true and false, judgements of good or bad or right or evil, ought to be settled in a uniform way. However, this assumption is not correct. Based on the "insight" that all concepts, that all judgements, fall into antinomy, Hegel relativised contradictory causality and took up the dialectic. In the realm of social – historical phenomena which Marx took as the object of his description – critique of reification, through the fact that class oppositionality exists, antinomy appears in the knowledge of the people involved themselves within the system. Antinomy, it goes without saying, refers to a logical situation where whilst being based on assumptions of a common paradigm, truth or falsehood (good or bad, right or evil) cannot be unequivocally decided, with the affirmative proposition S is P and the negative proposition S is not P both claiming truth and refusing to yield to the other.

In situations where antinomic opposition emerges among the people involved themselves internal to the system, it is no longer possible to confirm as it is system internal "truth" criteria (the criteria of good or bad or right or evil) and make judgements. It is, I think, because of the very fact that while the two

---

51   MEW, Bd. 19, S. 18, vgl. auch S. 359.

sides stand in opposition to each other sharing the "criterion" of "socially valid, and for that reason, objective", a decision (logically) cannot be made through a referring to that criterion; this is the reason it is an antinomy.

How does Marx respond in this situation? Let us bring to mind an all too famous passage in the discussion of the "labour day" in Chapter 8, Volume I of *Capital*. He describes the propositions of both the capitalist and the labourer, in opposition concerning the labour day, with both understanding in common "labour power" as a commodity, and with both understanding "commodity value" in the manner of the theory of labour value; ... showing that, based on these assumptions in common, both are able to argue for the "truth" and "validity" of his or her own assertion, he says the following: "So an antinomy arises here. In other words, it is an opposition of right (*Recht* = justice) versus right with both equally guaranteed by the law of commodity exchange. Between equivalent rights force (*Gewalt*) decides the matter".[52]

A certain kind of thinker would say in surprise: If the assertion on the labourer's side is theoretically mistaken be that as it may, but in this situation where an assertion of complete "truth" can be made why on earth doesn't Marx align himself with the labourer's side? This indeed would be, wouldn't it, faithful to Marx's class – ideological position?—Another thinker would say the following: It is the case that to the extent that Marx "recognises" provisionally a system internal criterion it can only but be said to be an antinomy, but from the criterion of his essential system external – critiquing position there ought to be a recognition that the labourer's side is correct, etc.

These are both rash views. Indeed, to the extent that the labourer's side also here recognises as preconditions the determinant of "labour power = commodity"[53] and the "theory of labour value" they fall into antinomy. Because of the very fact that internal to the system another "correct criterion" does not exist a

---

52   MEW, Bd. 23, S. 249.

53   With this, if I take the opportunity to add here a few words, the "commodification of labour power", i.e. when speaking of the *change* of it into a commodity, is represented as an historical *transformation* which occurred in a specific, historical period. However, nevertheless, it's not that the *thing* which is labour power literally changes form into the *thing* that is the commodity. The *establishment* of commod*ification* is an instance of the *establishment* of the phenomenon of re*ification*. Such corresponds to social relations (intersubjective relations) where quid pro quo regarding labour is carried out according to such and such a general principle (in summary, the same general principle as that which governs commodity exchange) being historically established. And, "the labour power commodity" and "labour power as a commodity" are forms of reification of such and such social relations determination, and, the "commodification of labour power" in the sense of the state of "labour power being commodified", is also simply a reificatory expression.

decision cannot be expected in a logical struggle of theories and this means that the non-theoretical – practical method of "solution" which is *Gewalt* (force) is all that remains.—To put it another way, it is not possible for Marx to present another correct criterion and to rule on – arbitrate the opposition between the two theoretically. Marx indeed does have another criterion. But, it cannot possibly be held in common by the two parties involved in opposition. If the labourer, one side of the parties involved, had taken on Marx's criterion, this means that he sublates the existing criterion itself, and sublates as well the existing assertion, and so he is no longer caught up in an antinomy indeed, but now it is an opposition of criterion versus criterion, and because a common greater criterion doesn't for the moment exist there there is in the end no choice but to settle things by *Gewalt*. Moreover, on this occasion, because the labourer has sublated a system internal criterion and has made a system external criterion his own he now stands at a standpoint beyond the class-ness of "labourer" which is of a dimension of opposition of system internal equal points, the opposition of "capitalist versus labourer", and although as a living person he remains a "labourer", his "class-ness" and "partisan-ness" ought to have become a higher level partisan-ness which has gone beyond the level of ideology of the opposition of equal points, the opposition of "capitalist versus labourer".

Marx, precisely, brings in a self-aware manner the composition of this kind of antinomy and its sublation into his system. That he planned to bring the final chapter of *Capital* to a close with the class *struggle* has been historically investigated,[54] but his theory of reification reaches the resting point of being a theoretical system as "theoretical system" not through confirmation, needless to say, of the system internal criterion as it is, but through an argumentation that within the bounds of this criterion antinomy is necessitated.

To dissolve this antinomy, the crucial point, theoretically, is to sublate the paradigm itself possessed as a precondition in common by the two sides, and to establish a new paradigm. This new paradigm indeed, still hasn't system internally had its "social validity – objectivity" ("truth") confirmed, and it is that which is for the time being simply treated as "thought". In order for this "thought" to show its truth as "truth", "social validity" has to be practically obtained. For reason of its being for the present still system *external*, it becomes "internal" truth only in the realisation of a different social system from the current one. For this reason, in the Marxian method of system composition, it is the case

---

54   See Yamasaki Kaworu 「マルクス経済学の確立―経済学主義批判」〖"The Establishment of Marxian Economics—A Critique of Economics-ism"〗 (carried in 『批評精神』〖*Critical Spirit*〗 No. 4, 1983).

that theory internally too, sublation in practice of the current system, and the realisation of a new system, are tasks.

In this regard, sublation of the antinomic situation depends on a theory external practical solution, on precisely *"Gewalt"*. Who is this then carried out by? It's obvious to say that it isn't done by a transcendent third party. It is for the present moment borne by one side of those involved in the antinomy. If they reach a zone of sublation in theory – in thought of the preconditions of the antinomy they become beings who have now gone beyond the level of system internal class-ness. Even so, within the current system, as an actual problem it is difficult to complete the practical solution at a stroke and simultaneously at the level of the masses. In the zone, for the time being, of one side of those involved in the antinomy, the masses, based on system internal criteria regarding the values of truth and falsehood – good and bad – right and evil etc., condemn the current situation and aim at the "realisation" of the "true" value of right.[55] Marxian scientific knowledge, to the extent that it is one pole of an antinomy, doesn't confirm this theoretically as it is.[56] However, this antinomic class struggle, and the ideological struggle in that dimension as well, are deployed appropriately in the situation of "practice".[57] Since "truth, that is to say, the reality and power of thought, its this worldliness, must be proven in practice",[58] that is to say, since the this worldliness of truth is not proven simply within the bounds of the theoretical system, Marx's *total* system just completes reliant on practice. The system of *theory* of the theory of reification as systematic description = systematic critique confirms logically an antinomy, and historic-

---

55   It is said: "true freedom", "true equality", "true fraternal-ism", "true fairness", "true human-ism", "true welfare" etc.—The pathos of the mass movement, in the beginning, is insep-arably generated with critique of the current situation based on value criteria idealised within the system. As a problem of historical fact, that idealised ideas within the system are taken as the value criteria for critique of the current situation is always the case for the first struggle in the in-itself class. And it is the case too that the accompanying intelligent-sia may in general remain permanently at this level.

56   I'd like the "freedom – equality – Bentham!" Marx announces repeatedly in a derogatory manner be brought to mind.—Engels, going beyond such which correspond to the bour-geois social order, re-grasps ideas such as "freedom" and "equality" under a new paradigm. For example, see *Anti-Duhring* Part 1, Chapter 10, Chapter 11 etc.

57   Although they critique reform*ist* movements, they tactically take part in the so-called struggle for reform, and tactically, positively organise such. It's not the case that the revolu-tion comes into completion as a simple extension of the struggle for reform, but rather that such is *able* to become an aid in polarising the antinomous nature of the situation, and in exploding the social contradictions. Through this, in addition, such is *able* to stimulate paradigm change in the masses.

58   The same as note 48 above, the *Theses on Feuerbach*.

ally an explosion of a system contradiction which has "self-motion" in a reified form, and making this consequential situation a conscious – in fact generative – stage condition, and having confirmed the "reificatory" and "binding" necessity of the "wriggling"[59] of a proceeding towards a movement where the subjects involved sublate the system itself, it opens out to a theory of practice – a theory of revolution. It is not closed in a self-completing way in a "theory of absolute knowledge", but truly forms a theoretical system opened out to "practice".

3.3

Now we are at the stage where we should survey the scope of the theory of practice of the theory of reification. Through such, we will be able, I think, to investigate the issue of the law-like nature of history in a future society as well.

Even though reification is *für uns* a misapprehension, it is something which has its basis of being in the "real relations towards nature and between human beings" under the current system, and, analogous to the misapprehension of the "stationary Earth – revolving Sun", it is "necessary – real" to the extent that it is internal to the said system, and it is not something which can be overcome through the simple activity of the consciousnesses involved in a change in recognition (in a theoretical correction of the fallacy).[60] To overcome reification, a real transformation in the real relations which form the basis of being of the reification is the essential, crucial point. As long as the existing real relations are not disassembled the phenomenon of reification will continue to be produced – reproduced.—For example the reified "social power" which is the

---

59   Z.B. MEW, Bd. 23, S. 789.
60   The following is stated in the "Preface" of *The German Ideology* as a symbolic declaration of this situation. "That which has been given birth to in the heads of people has grown and come to go beyond their heads. They, the masters of creation, have come to bow down before their own creations. We seek, do we not, to free them from these delusions, ideas, dogma, imaginary beings, from, in other words, the yoke under which they are suffering, we rebel, do we not, against such rule of thought? Teach them to replace these imaginary things with thought corresponding to the essence of human being, says one, teach them to take a critical attitude towards those imaginary things, says another, teach them to knock them out of their heads, says a third. They say that if this happens, the existing reality will collapse. These foolish, naive delusions, this is what forms the core of recent Young Hegelian philosophy.
        ... once a commendable man believed that human beings drown in water because they are possessed with the idea of gravity. Declaring that gravity is a superstitious representation, a religious representation, he maintains that if only the representation of gravity is knocked out of people's heads then human beings ought to avoid all drownings; so he fought with the illusion of gravity his whole life, and all statistics presented him with numerous and new proof regarding the dangerous consequences of the illusion of gravity" etc.

"power of money", inevitably continues in a different form with only abolition of the physical thing of money; it cannot be dissolved without sublation of the social arrangement itself of commodity economics. Again, the reified power which is "state power" cannot be abolished, as the anarchists plan to do, as if it itself were a thing; it cannot be abolished without radical rearrangement at the fundamental place of production of the social relations which bring about the reification in question.—Reification which has its basis for existence in the capitalist relations of production, the antinomic contradictions which emerge in reified form, and the various conflicts which arise further from here; these can be overcome for the first time through sublation of the capitalist relations of production themselves. Marx and Engels simply don't point this out they also present the new social arrangement which ought to replace the capitalist relations of production. This too they don't simply proclaim as a utopia, but based on scientific investigation of the fact that the reified tendencies of capitalism, and further back of human history, have prepared in reality its conditions of realisation, and rather than as an alternative plan, it is presented as an historical vision of the future. Needless to say, this presented society is communist society.

On the point of the fact that the communist future society, which is a new form of relations by reason of overcoming – dissolving existing reifications and their contradictions, is not an arbitrary conception but is precisely something which the reified progression of human history is tending towards in a law-like way, it is to be strictly distinguished from a mere utopian rough sketch. However, the "law-like self-motion of human history and its results" is a reified representation, and in truth it is not the case that that which is history has self-motion. In truth, the practice of persons forms history, and a communist future society will be created through the practice of persons—This practical creation of a communist future society, in other words, this communist revolution, is not, indeed, aimed at purposefully by all members of society. However, a section of the members of society do aim purposefully at it. In reality, Marx too is one such revolutionary. The revolution, however, is not something which can be realised by only a small number of revolutionaries. The revolutionaries have to rely on the co-operation of the masses. In this, the strategy – tactics of revolution and the activity of the organisation come into focus as issues.

To the extent that the revolutionary movement is a conscious – intentional practical activity, the subjects involved must be able to stand at a system external – critiquing vantage point, and relativising the reality and real thought of the current system, they must be able to represent in an intentional manner a vision of the future society. Here, precisely, is where the difficulty arises. Is it really possible for persons to stand at a vantage point *external to – critiquing* the system whilst in reality living within the social system concerned? Is it really possible in this situation to establish anti-establishment thought? If it's a matter of the extent of being one pole of the antinomy discussed above, that is to say, a matter of proposing, based on a system internal paradigm and "criterion", an anti-thesis to the narrow, particular ideology of the ruling class, a matter of rebelling against the naked pursuit of the particular interests of the ruling class, if it's a matter of being to this extent then under certain conditions it is probably possible at the level of the masses. However, in order to truly establish anti-establishment thought a paradigm change is required and that is an extremely difficult thing to do. In actuality, those who truly are able to arm themselves theoretically with anti-establishment thought are *for the time being* limited to only an extremely small number of "enlightened persons". Their gaining the masses as comrades in terms of thought – in terms of the movement is in reality extraordinarily difficult.

Marx and Engels declare:

> The thought of the ruling class is in every age the ruling thought. That is to say, the class that is the ruling material force in society is, at the same time, the ruling spiritual force of that society. The class which has in its hands the means for material production, controls through this, at the same time, the means for spiritual production, and so the thought of the [ruled] classes who lack the means for spiritual production is, as a rule, subjugated by the ruling class. The ruling thought is the ideological expression of the ruling material relations or, to put it another way, it is none other than the ruling material relations which have taken the form of thought, and it is the ideal expression of those relations which make a certain class truly the ruling class. ... in this way, that the thought of the ruling class is the ruling thought of the present age, is naturally evident.[61]

If that is the case, isn't it so difficult as to call it almost impossible for the vast masses to awaken to anti-establishment revolutionary thought? That is so. Is then a revolutionary movement of the masses impossible? It's not.

Marx and Engels first and foremost render for-itself the fact that the movement of the masses itself progresses for the time being in a reified form.

---

61   The text of note 35 above. Original text S. 64. Japanese translation p. 66.

What this or that proletarian, or even the whole proletariat, imagines as his or her or its goal is not the issue. The issue is, what, determined by its existence, is the proletariat forced to do historically.[62]

The communist knows that revolution, no matter when or where, is the necessary result of causes which do not depend on the will and leadership of individual parties nor even, further, on the will and leadership of the classes as a whole.[63]

With this kind of in-itself movement of the masses isn't it the case that true revolutionary thought can't be expected? Are you saying that even so a "cunning of reason-" like communist revolution will be realised? Even if we put that aside, how does the advance guard leadership intervene in the movement? Marx and Engels soon come to actively conceive of the *engagement* of the advance guard organisation regarding the movement of the masses which progresses in a reified form. Whereupon that which is formularised for the present is the strategic tactic of "permanent revolution", which is a formula for the gradual advancement of a minimum programme acting as a preconditioning step for the maximum programme.[64]

Marx and Engels, having discerned that the thought of the vast movement of the masses is certainly not something which can suddenly reach a true anti-establishment state, and that in the early stages of the movement of the masses it is difficult for it to go beyond the pole of the aforementioned antinomy, they nevertheless plan a successive advancement in the manner of permanent revolution of the level being aimed at even though it is within the bounds of the antinomy. And they anticipated – aimed at the involvement (here theoretical, enlightening activity naturally occurs) of the advance guard organisation with the movement of the masses which unfolds in a reified form and an eventual grasping by the advance guard organisation itself of hegemony. With the process of this permanent revolution as a precondition, in the furnace of the proletarian dictatorship, the existing theoretical – thought paradigms which had grasped the masses up until then, and the existing values, undergo on the scale of the masses a gestalt switch to the paradigms and values suitable for the new society.[65] This can, I think, be said to have been Marx and Engels' understanding.

---

62   MEW, Bd. 2, S. 38.
63   MEW, Bd. 4, S. 372.
64   Regarding this tactical strategy and method please see my 『新左翼運動の射程』 [*The Scope of the New Left Movement*], Chapter 2, especially the material in Section 4 thereof.
65   The final "criteria of truth" and "criteria of value" of Marx's systematic description = sys-

Many matters remain to be discussed concerning the theory of revolution, but I have used up the space available to me, so, lastly, I will bring things to an end with an aiming at a simple description of the problem of the law-like nature of history in a future society.

The law-like nature of history was established in a reified manner through the "co-operation" of individuals being "natural" and "in-itself". If this is the case, will a law-like nature disappear from history if a social order is established in which in the future co-operation amongst people is carried out for-itself? Even in a future society it is difficult to expect that co-operation amongst people will be completely carried out for-itself, and for everyday consciousness a certain kind of reification will probably remain. Reification of linguistic meaning, reification of the regulatory force of social customs, reification of moral norms, etc; these kinds of reificatory phenomena will, albeit in a loose form, be likely, in the end, to arise. In addition, human beings will not escape ecological limitations, and submitting to fixed normative restrictiveness (although the content of the norm will indeed be completely changed) will, as to be expected, continue. Human action will in the future as now certainly not possibly be completely free and easy, but will be limited – restricted by certain natural – social conditions. However, the direction of the "combined force" discussed above will no longer *be established as a result*, as the combination of multifarious vectors oriented by class – strata special interests, but will be the realisation of an *aimed at direction* from the beginning in the goal-consciousness co-operation of people. To this extent, though under ecological and other limiting conditions, through goal-conscious co-operation which takes this into consideration, people will come to "create history" in a

---

tematic critique only self-sublate the "intellectual" (*Vermeinung*) assertions of the author, and only receive so-called "authorisation" (*Rechtfertigen*) epistemologically, dependent on the realisation of such. The proposition of "proving the this-worldliness of thought [judgement and value judgement] through practice"—although it applies as well to "objective activity" in general in the relation to the natural object, from the broad perspective—is to be understood through being placed within this kind of composition. I'd like to give thought once again to the significance that this composition, which opened out to practice, practically closes, being deployed to block "the vicious endless progression to a meta – meta – meta ... level of the authorisation of criteria" has for the Marxian method (theory) of system composition.

Further, if we re-grasp this system composition, which opens out to practice, from a subject point of view, we can say that the "we (*wir*)", dependent on the dialogic composition of "author and reader" and formed in an attaining way in the place of theoretical description = critique, takes the form of the leap of decision which commits towards a theoretically confirmed tendency of outlook forming the ring of mediation of the discontinuous continuity between theory and practice.

goal-conscious manner. If you want to call the traces of this the law-like progression of history you can, but this is no longer a so-called "necessary law". To
put it in the style of Engels, human beings escape the "realm (*Reich*) of necessity" and realise the "realm of freedom".

If we listen to what Engels has to say, through society grasping the means of
production and the consequent abolition of the production of commodities,
the "rule of products over the producers is abolished".

> In place of the anarchic state internal to social production, a planned –
> conscious organisation appears", and "the complete range of the condi-
> tions of life which up until now had ruled human beings now submit to
> the rule and control of human beings. ... Until now, the laws of the social
> acts of human beings themselves [appeared reified and] stood in opposi-
> tion to human beings as external natural laws which ruled over them, but
> from now on human beings will come to apply these laws, and will rule
> over them. Until now, the social union of human beings themselves ... has
> stood in opposition to human beings, but now that will become a free act
> of human beings themselves. The objective, external forces which until
> now had ruled history will yield to the control of human beings them-
> selves. The struggle for existence will come to an end", and "human beings
> will move from animal conditions of existence to truly human conditions
> of existence.[66]
>
> From this time for the first time, human beings will be fully conscious
> and will come to create their own histories themselves. From this time
> for the first time, the social causes enacted by human beings will come to
> bring about results for the most part desired by human beings, and, this
> will come to be so more and more with time. This in other words is a leap
> of humankind from the realm of necessity into the realm of freedom.[67]

Here—even though the mechanism itself of reification will continue, and certain kinds of reification will newly emerge—it is predicted that the reification
which held people in bonds and which was almost universal in the "previous
history of humankind" will now be sublated.

---

66   MEW, Bd. 20, S. 264.
67   ibid.

CHAPTER 3

The Theory of Reification of the Historical World

I have affixed the title of the being-structure of the historical world[1] and so it is in accordance with this that I will put forward my views, but in order that I might not invite unnecessary misunderstanding because of this title, in advance I would like as preparation to spend some time putting forth a partial frame of consciousness of the issues concerned, and, at the same time, to delineate my main theme.

Saying the "historical world" here isn't reference to a certain, particular part or aspect of the world—such as the "world of history" in a differentiation with the natural world, or the "world situation" of today. The matter is such that there is no problem at all in directly calling it "the world" instead, with the limitation of "historical" being exclusively involved in what kind of thing this world is to be understood as, in the method of this understanding.

What kind of thing this world is to be understood as—to put it more appropriately, how the old understanding of the world is to be re-made, how it is to be re-grasped—this indeed, is, in addition, none other than the frame of consciousness of the issues concerned supporting the discussion below.

Speaking in this way, it is likely I think that many of you will think of Heidegger. However, I have no intention at all of following Heidegger's lead. In addition, I have no intention of making it my business to engage in *Auseinandersetzung* [debate] with Heidegger.

Yet, as a key to having you represent then what kind of problem from what kind of perspective it is that I am planning to consider things—to that extent—, if I make Heidegger a "vehicle for discussion", it is I think appropriate that the matter of how we go beyond the so-called horizon of the understanding of the world of the early modern (of the modern) world itself—rather than the *Subjekt—Objekt—Schema* ["subject—object" schema], the kind of "horizon of the modern understanding of the world" which produces as a matter of necessity the *Wechselspiel* [see-saw game] between *Subjektivismus* and *Objektivismus*—can be agreed to as forming the fundamental issue of present-day philosophy. Whether Heidegger, however, is in fact able to establish an orientation in which he is in truth able to solve the particular problems he

---

1 〚Tr. Although no explanation is given, it would seem that this may have been the title of the original lecture of which this is the text, with the above chapter title having been affixed when the material was prepared for publication〛.

proposed is something I cannot help but doubt. In the *Grundverfassung* [basic stance] of "being-in-the world" taken in *Being and Time* and after, in the facts themselves of this *Grundverfassung* [basic composition], facts which are able to coincide with his frame of consciousness of the issues, arises it seems to me his limitation.

Heidegger's *Verfassung* [composition], which grasps the world in the way of being of primordially *Zuhandensein* [Being ready-to-hand], which grasps human being as "essentially Being-with [*Mitsein*]", is certainly of a different nature as compared to the horizon of the modern world-picture, and is of a stance aimed at overcoming it. Nevertheless, if I might put my view forward, rather than their being one-sided, a problem lies in his method of grasping of *Zuhandensein*, his method of grasping of *Mitdasein* [Being-with], in the fact that they are not understood in the aspect of actuality.

As I stated before, I do not have an intention of undertaking a thematic critique of Heidegger's philosophy, nor do I have an intention of attempting a critiquing continuation of him, but in regard to the determining content of "being-in-the world", concerning its above-mentioned two moments which ought to be called the "two foci of an ellipse", it is necessary I think, in exactly the same way that he took aim at the Cartesian ⟨world⟩ ontology, to show the orientation of these as "transformations" of the true way of being, of the true way of understanding. For that reason, amongst others, however, the situation gives rise to the need to affirmatively present then in what way for us we understand the world, and the attempt to come is in particular concerned with this.

When considering matters through this kind of frame of consciousness of the issue, for me it isn't possible to overlook the new world-view opened up by the "later" Marx-Engels. In the so-called orthodox school interpretation the horizon opened up by Marx-Engels is once again concealed and is taken as something which doesn't have all that much of a difference to eighteenth century style materialism—and even Sartre, who had reached the point of "I regard Marxism as a philosophy which can't be surpassed in the present-day age", doesn't it seems to me necessarily clearly understand Marxism—, but in my view, Marx-Engels were blessed with a certain historical good fortune, and they established a perspective which had to be able to overcome the horizon of the "modern" world-view, something they have left to us in note form.

As regards this, I discussed it as a main theme in two (miscellaneous) essays last year, 「マルクス主義的唯物論とは何か」 [["What is Marxist Materialism?"]] (*Shisō* [[*Thought*]] June edition) and 「人間主義対科学主義の地平を超えるもの−世界·内·存在と歴史·内·存在」 [["A Going beyond the Horizon of Humanism vs Scientism − Being-in-the World and Being-in-History"]] (*Gendai no Riron* [[*Contemporary Theory*]] July edition), so I won't, however, repeat it here [the above two essays were later included in my 『マルクス主義の地平』

[[*The Horizon of Marxism*]], the discussion to come being, in complementarity with 『世界の共同主観的存在構造』[[*The Intersubjective Being-Structure of the World*]] being published in *Shisō* in instalments at present [later contained in a volume with this same title], a modest attempted discussion aimed at rendering for-itself the fundamental being-structure of the world with Marx-Engels' "notes" as the *Leitfaden* [guiding thread].

I said "notes", but I count *Capital* as primary amongst these. As has been pointed out since long ago, *Capital* is not simply a "book of economics" in the usual sense, it is in itself a "work of philosophy" announcing a particular world-view. According to what Marx himself relates, *Capital* was written with a new world-view – view of history, which he had arrived at, as the *Leitfaden*, and we are able to plan a reconstruction, working backwards from it, of the world-view he had arrived at. Whilst in many places making statements in a fragmentary fashion involving the core of his world-view, Marx hasn't left a unified exposition concerning his world-view itself. But, through a working backwards from *Capital*, we can in an integrating way understand what seem at first glance "eccentric" passages he has written here and there.

The discussion below, however, does not take the form of a hermeneutics of Marx's texts. I will take the method of discussion of first undertaking a self-understanding outline of the being-structure of the "world of the commodity" (*Warenwelt*) analysed in *Capital*, and keeping this in mind, I will then re-view the reality of the "world occurring historically".

1   The Being-Structure of the World of the Commodity

The *Warenwelt* [world of the commodity] which *Capital* takes as its object is, certainly, simply one *Phase* [phase] of the "historical world". However, here the being-structure of the historical world in general can be seen to be directly appearing. For that reason, first, regarding the being-structure of the "world of the commodity", we will, whilst confirming Marx's position, take a quick glance at this structure and—whilst stating indirectly as well the reason why I said before that Heidegger's *Zuhandensein* grasps only one aspect of things—I'd like to establish a standpoint for use in later discussion.

1.1   *The Twofold Nature of the World of the Commodity*
The world of the commodity, that is to say the world opening up existing in people's ken in the way of the occurring of interests which ought even be called *homo oeconomicus*, appears before us *provisionally* as a totality of "Being ready-to-hand" *Zuhandensein*.

"The commodity, provisionally, is an external object which through its attributes satisfies some kind of desire of human beings". This usefulness "makes the thing a use-value (*Gebrauchswert*)". However, this useful, that is to say, the commodity entity (*Warenkörper*) which does not become a simple physical entity, "must in no way be understood as if the 'aspect' of usefulness has been imprinted into a 'presence-at-hand' (*Vorhandensein*) and as if it is a thing where material of the world present-at-hand in-itself is ⟨subjectively coloured⟩". According to Marx, the "commodity entity itself is use-value".

In the commodity as use-value its usefulness is exclusively at issue and the matter of what kind of thing it is as a "present-at-hand", of what kind of thing it is in terms of physics-chemistry, is not in itself at issue. For example, whether a pen is something made by cutting a feather, or is made of simply iron, or has iridium attached, or is made of glass; these kinds of materials themselves are not at issue. Mass and shape themselves too are not directly foci of concern. The way of being of these "present-at-hands" is at issue only when matters are limited to when such involves the ease of "use" of the pen, when such involves the usefulness of the pen as an implement. To be precise, material, mass, shape etc. etc. do not come into focus here as "present-at-hand" characteristics but rather come into focus in themselves as moments of usefulness, and only to that extent.

In so far as it is concerning the commodity as use-value, it has "appropriateness" (*Bewandtnis*) as *etwas um zu* ... (something for ...) and it exists within the "totality of the implement" (*Zeugganzheit*), etc. etc., so we can cover the situation with Heidegger's so-called *Zuhandenheit*.

However, what we can cover with Heidegger's *Zuhandenheit* stops at being limited to the commodity as use-value. However, the commodity is not simply use-value, for the commodity as commodity, use-value is in the end simply the "material bearer of exchange value".

In the world of the commodity, all commodities appear not as simply use-value entities, they always appear as things which had a certain exchange value (the money expression of this is "price"). Not only the commodities lined up in the shops, even those currently in use, for example the car I am using, the house I am living in, are understood as things which can be sold at such and such a price at any time, as things which have in-themselves an exchange value. In the commodified world, even things which would originally not be commodities come to have a price—through the establishment of the so-called "false value" in economics—from virgin land to works of art, all things have come to have a certain price.

Having value, if we anticipate things, refers to a *way of being* completely separate to the commodity being use-value. We can, for the moment, verify three things.

Firstly, the fact that all commodities are reduced to a certain common quality, measured through the unit of price. We do not do such things as measure length using grams nor do we measure mass using feet. The carrying out of a common measure has as an assumption that an amount having a certain common quality exists.

Secondly, that price (exchange value) is held only by things which have use-value. If there isn't use-value = usefulness no one will exchange (purchase) the *thing* in question. Only things having use-value can have exchange value, and in this sense it can be said that "use-value is the bearer in terms of the material of exchange value".

Thirdly, that exchange value and use-value are decisively of a different nature, however. Even if we put aside the earlier point that in terms of use-value commodities of a different quality reduce to a common quality, if as use-value two things are exactly the same people would not be expected to exchange them. Two commodities to be exchanged, that is to say, two commodities equal in terms of exchange value, implies that they are different in terms of use-value.

We will, henceforth, call that "common quality"—something which though borne by use-value is nonetheless a straightforwardly different quality— assumed in-itself in the commodity price, in, to go further back, commodity exchange, that quality of a commodity in which it gains its quantitative expression in price (exchange value), the "commodity value" or "value".

What we are calling "value" = "commodity value", is not, from the beginning, a thing which is able to cover "value" in general as it is designated in the so-called philosophy of value. That, however, it might have the same "being-structure sphere" and being-structure features as the "value" referred to in philosophy, and, what's more, that in the understanding of things which is Heidegger's *Zuhandensein*, this thing called value has its unique objectivity overlooked— through being indiscriminately subsumed—, and that because of and through this it may be a factor in causing a *verkennen* (ignoring— misrecognising) of the true form of the "objective world"; I think that I can hope that these points at least are from the beginning borne in mind.

That the world of the commodity, in any case, *erscheinen*s [appears] under the two appearances of object-nature as use-value and object-nature as value; for the moment what I want to confirm is this twofold nature.

1.2   *The Problematics of the Theory of Value*

Just what then is the value of a commodity? As far as we posited things in the previous item of discussion, the matter of what kind of being-structure characteristics such is has not yet been settled. To begin with, concerning the existence of the commodity value—rather, *even* concerning it—as is well known, an opposition exists between subjective value theory = value nominalism and value realism, but in this opposition whether that which is value actually, in the end, "objectively" exists is an undecided issue.

According to subjective value theory = value nominalism "that which is value" does not exist objectively but rather it is simply something believed individually. As a result, the *Was Frage* [the question of "just what is?"] essentially has no meaning, and the situation is regarded as such that it is sufficient if we ascertain experientially the price on each occasion and if we investigate the factors and laws determining price fluctuation.

Here—leaving aside for the moment criticism of this theory—I'd like to verify the following fact. Namely that in the subjective theory of value value judgement carried out in accord intersubjectively, the object-nature of value "believed individually" in this, is at most simply ⟨subjective colouring⟩ "projected" on to the commodity entity as a "present-at-hand", and in the subjective theory of value value is thought of as a thing of a kind similar precisely to the "secondary qualities" occurring in modern thinking.

On the other hand, value realism, in its simplest form, can be said to have regarded value as an attribute possessed by a certain type of natural object, to have regarded it as so to speak a "primary quality" which the physical entity itself possesses. However, such a primitive theory of value, faced with the empirical fact of price fluctuation caused by the relation of demand and supply, is eventually forced to look for the essence of value elsewhere.

As long as value realism, in any case, asserts a certain "quality" held in common by commodities of completely different qualities as use-value entities, as long as it asserts the objective reality of *etwas* ⟦Tr. something⟧ separate to the natural qualities of the commodity, and, moreover, if it asserts this within the traditional horizon, it will inevitably encounter the connected problems existing since Greek philosophy and vociferously argued in the "debate of universals".

The opposition between value nominalism and value realism is not simply an opposition existing in economic theory, it is precisely a dispute in terms of philosophical world-view. It is likely then that this is the reason too that the true solution to the problem of "what is value?" is inseparable from the indicating of a new philosophical horizon.

To grasp this "solution"—and the essence of Marx's theory of value—it would be a shortcut when all is said and done to return to the scene of what might be called the origin of the labour theory of value and to then reconfirm an historical certain circumstance.

The labour theory of value, it goes without calling to mind, was not, originally, something which appeared in order to sublate the opposition between value nominalism and value realism. It is a fact that, viewed historically, the labour theory of value was established—through a critique of *simple* value realism—before this opposition emerged.

The classical labour theory of value put forward the major thesis that it is labour which is the only source of wealth. However, it is not the case that the thesis of labour = value entity was simplistically derived from this. The explanation of the proper ratio in two kinds of commodity being exchanged can be said to have been the direct moment of the labour theory of value.

Based on *"Robinson Crusoe*, based along the lines of the eighteenth century world of the commodity", the classical economists undertook a "pure" investigation of the fact of exchange, putting forward the following argument.

Under the condition that people can produce any product themselves, they will not exchange a product A which required two labour hours to produce with product B which required one labour hour. This is because instead of the two hours expended to make A, he or she produces B himself or herself through one hour of labour. Exchange is carried out between products requiring the same hours; the in-itself ultimate thesis of the expended labour theory of value can be said to be fully represented by this.

In reality, of course, there are differences in people's labour productivity, and in addition, labour is not carried out with one's bare hands but rather it is generally the case that it is carried out using implements, and it is generally the case that from the beginning that which is being called the object of labour is already a product of labour. As a result, when calculating the necessary labour hours, we have to calculate the labour hours needed for the production of raw materials and equipment and to take into account how many hours of labour the wear and tear of equipment is equivalent to etc etc. In this way—without waiting for the higher level problem of the establishment of the "market price"—, in terms of logic a complicated calculation is required, but, be that as it may, it is understood that under imagined pure conditions, using the yardstick of how many labour hours in the final analysis are required people "ought to" carry out the exchange of products.

In this final situation, the entity of value is not necessarily at issue, and the required labour hours only have the functional meaning of determining the ratio of exchange. Actually, even though, referring to required hours, we refer to an objectification of labour, despite the fact that it was a product which previously doubtlessly objectified ten hours of labour, if productivity has increased and it has come to be such that it can be now reproduced in five hours, that ten hour product is now exchanged as a five labour hour product, and so it is not the case that the *expended* quantity itself of labour is rendered an entity.

However, the value of the raw materials or of the wear and tear component is "contained" in the value of a product, with the value of the raw materials "transferring" into the product. When this calculation is made the substantial "value" which "transfers" is logically presupposed. Also, the "fact" of the social distribution of wealth, that is to say, of the social distribution of the value acquisition of the use-value object which isn't distributed, takes as a precondition the existence of a substantial certain something which ought to be distributed. All things aside, the "fact" of social wealth increasing through the accumulation of labour products—because "it isn't the case that even a single molecule of the natural world increases" through labour—encourages the idea that a *certain something* separate to the natural thing accumulates and increases.

Because of such circumstances a tilting towards a *hypostasieren* (hypostasizing) of "value" arises of its own accord. From an intellectual history point of view, it's the case that in the process of putting forward an antithesis in regard to the fetishism of money–currency of bullionism–mercantilism that the true content of wealth is labour, is objectified labour, an hypostasization of labour, an hypostasization of labour value, came to be carried out.

Here I won't go into the relationship between the expended labour theory of value and the ruling labour theory of value etc., into points of issue from the scholarly history point of view, but rather what I want to take note of is the two points of the fact that the labour theory of value is, essentially, a functional proposition for explaining the ratio of exchange, and the fact, however, that pressured by the like of the above-mentioned "experiential fact" labour value came to be hypostasized.

1.3　　*The Objectivity of Commodity Value*

It is the case that Marx, as is well known, carries forward critically the labour theory of value of classical economics, and he provisionally—and only provisionally—determines the content of "value" by carrying one step further the way of thinking that hypostasizes labour.

Although I say that human labour becomes objectified, becomes hypostasized in the product, it's not as if people carry out an abstract, general "thing which is labour"; the labour actually carried out by people is concrete, useful labour, is construction labour, spinning and weaving labour, iron manufacture labour, etc. etc. Nonetheless, these concrete, useful labours are labour where, through such, the usefulness, the "use-value", of a product is created, and in this sense, concrete, useful labour can be said to be objectified and become use-value. However, labour limited to this has "no connection" to the value of the commodity, and so we cannot continue on with as it is the concept of labour value of classical economics nor in addition with its concept of labour.

Hereupon Marx distinguishes a twofold nature of labour, making such correspond to the two primary factors of the commodity, that is to say, to the
twofold nature of use-value and value. That is to say, he distinguishes "concrete,
useful labour" and "abstract, human labour". And he asserts that the objectification of concrete, useful labour is use-value, and that the objectification of
abstract, human labour is value.

A series of questions can immediately arise in regard to the "fundamental
thesis" of Marx's theory of value which is that that which is commodity value
"is a coagulation of abstract, human labour". Does an "abstract, human labour"
separated off from concrete, useful labour really exist? Is such a thing as such a
thing coagulating and forming the entity of value really in reality possible? Isn't
Marx's argument the same nonsense as the argument which says "this concrete,
useful fountain pen draws a line, and an abstract fountain pen writes the alpha-
betical letters?"

If we regard the determination "abstract labour" as simply logical abstraction, in other words, if we regard it as the residue left after the concrete determinations have been abstracted from real human labour, even if we had accepted
such an abstract, human labour, it is the case that that which is its objectification would at most only be likely to be able to be sufficient as "abstract, general
use-value"—it cannot possibly be value.

The abstract, human labour Marx speaks of, however, is not such a logical
abstraction. We need to pass on positive determination to the next item of discussion, but if for the time being I state the general gist that it is "an abstraction
carried out daily in reality",—in the same way that the das Man that Heidegger
speaks of is not the abstracted person der Mensch drawn out through logical
abstraction from real human beings—that, in societies where commodity production is universal, it is something which corresponds to the real situation
where labourers have transformed into as it were das Man or das Arbeiter, I
think I should be able to obtain a provisional understanding from listeners.

"Value" presents a unique being-structure characteristic,—Marx himself
uses the description "a mysterious character" (der rätselhafte Charakter)—with
no relation for the moment to the determinant of the coagulation of abstract
labour.

Value, certainly, approaches us with a kind of "objective reality". When it
comes to the stage of actually exchanging – buying and selling, even an economist who takes the subjective theory of value position—although he or she
may be able whilst engaged in speculative thought to continue thinking that
one fountain pen and one car are of equal value—ought to be made to realise
that just as the volume and weight of a fountain pen and a car are "objectively" different, the value of the two differs "objectively". The size of a value

appears before us as an immovable "objective" determinateness unable to be influenced by the value evaluation of the individual. Touching on one part of the "law of value", even if the maxim of always selling above value and always buying below value has been proposed, or, even if the opposite philanthropic maxim has been proposed, it's surely no exaggeration to say that in order that one doesn't go to wrack and ruin one has no choice but to obey the "law of value"—in the same way that one has to obey "natural laws". Value, in this way, not only controls people's consciousness but appears before us as an "objective object-ness" controlling action as well.

Value is, however, certainly not a so-called real thing (*realitas*).

> "Completely opposite to the objectivity responsive sensibly to the com-
> modity entity", – Marx says – "in the value objectivity of the commodity,
> there is not even a single atom of the natural object. As a result, no mat-
> ter how one pulls individual commodities this way and that their value
> remains as always un-graspable". "The physical attributes of commodities
> come in to issue only in so far as they make the commodities useful things,
> as they make them use-values", and value "is not any kind of natural, indi-
> vidual attribute of a commodity, not geometrical, physical, chemical etc".

In short, the determinatenesses as the *realitas* possessed by the commodity are in each and every case things tied up with use-value, and, according to Marx, in the commodity as the value thing there is not "even an atom of the natural thing". This is the reason Marx put forward the concept of "abstract, human labour" and it is also, in addition, the reason he speaks of a "ghost-like objectivity" (*gespenstige Gegenständlichkeit*), and so value is not a natural-thing-like – real-existent-thing-like objectivity it is an *irreal etwas* [[Tr. unreal something]].

In this way, whilst "value" is an immovable "objective" object-ness, it doesn't require going into detail that it is nevertheless not a real, existent thing as a *realitas*, nor also, having said that, is it a metaphysical existent. In the end, "value" is a thing referred to by philosophers with such expressions as a "third empire of meaning" and a "value zone", and it is the case that it has in common the same being-structure characteristic as such as Hermann Lotze's *Geltung* [validity].

As for Marx, he firstly positively understands such an aspect of the world of the commodity which is "value"—the *irreal* object-ness of the world of the commodity, an object-ness which isn't able to be fully covered by the under-standing that is *Zuhandensein*—, this *Geltung*, through the determinant which is the *Objektion – Objektivation* [objectification – objective object-ification] of "abstract, human labour".

1.4   The Fetish Nature of Commodity Being

A commodity "seems at first glance to be a very ordinary thing", yet it exists in one aspect as the sensuous object-ness that is use-value, whilst in another aspect, and moreover simultaneously, it exists as the supra-sensuous object-ness that is value, it exists as, in other words, a real and irreal *ein sinnlich über-sinnliches Ding* [sensuous and supra-sensuous thing], and as Marx writes, "if one analyses it one realises that the commodity is an extremely troublesome thing, packed with metaphysical tricks and full of theological nastiness [[sic]]".

In order to grasp the being-structure of the world of the commodity we have to unravel this "fetish character of the commodity and its secret" (*Der Fetischcharakter der Ware und sein Geheimnis*)—this also connecting at the same time to "abstract, human labour", and to the riddle of Marx's thesis of "value" as the "coagulation" of such.

Marx, in the following way, poses a question and then answers it.

"Where does this riddle-like characteristic ... which arises immediately that a labour-product takes the form of a commodity arise from? ... In the commodity form the equivalence of human *labour* takes the *reified* form of the equivalent value objectivity of the labour-product, the quantity arising through the chronological continuum of the expenditure of human labour power takes the form of the size of the value of the labour-product, ... and the relations of the producers take the form of the social relations of the labour-products". "The mysterious way of being of the form which is the commodity simply lies in the following point. Namely, the commodity form lies in the point that, to people's eyes, with the *social characteristic* of their own labour as an *objective characteristic* of the labour-products themselves, these things are caused to be reflected as social attributes held by them as natural things, and subsequently in addition, the social relations *of the producers* towards total labour is made to reflect as the social relations of *object things* lying outside of them". "Through a quid pro quo of this illusion the labour-product—becomes a sensuous but also supra-sensuous, or a social, thing—becomes a commodity. ... Here what appears to people's eyes taking the illusory form of the relation between a thing and a thing is none other than a *specific social relation between people themselves*. ... In the world of the commodity, products of the human hand are endowed with a particular life, and *appear provisionally* as if mutually between themselves, and also between them and human beings, they are independent forms forming relations mutually".

Earlier, focusing on the, as it were, labour of an individual, we came to regard it as if it were in one respect, as concrete, useful labour, use-value forming, whilst at the same time, regarding it as if it were in another respect, as abstract, human labour, value forming. That is to say, we discussed things as if the labour process itself was use-value forming and simultaneously value forming. To that extent, I think that the doubt was able to naturally arise that isn't it the case that Marx's view which grasps the world of the commodity as the objectification – object-entity-ification of the labour that is the subjective activity of human beings, isn't this indeed a confirmation of the "technological civilisation" which completes the modern *Subjektivismus*, isn't it none other than a "completed metaphysics?" In addition, having brought in the *problematisch* [problematic] concept of "abstract labour" doesn't lead to an explanation of "value". Because of this, I think I will have provoked the surreptitious criticism that this does not amount to a rejection of value nominalism, to say nothing of also not amounting to an authorising of value realism. However, the labour process itself which has abstracted its social determinants is in no way value forming. According to Marx, "labour-products *within their exchange for the first time* take on *value* objectivity—separated from use objectivity, and socially equivalent". The expression "coagulation of abstract, human labour" itself was none other than in fact an expression focused on the universal fetish character in the world of the commodity where "specific social relations of human beings themselves appear taking the form of a provisional physicality".

If this is the case, is that which is the objectification – reification of abstract, human labour, and as a result also "value objectivity", no more than simply an illusion? The Marx of *Capital*—rather Marx after the *Grundrisse: Outlines of the Critique of Political Economy*—when discussing the objectification of labour, no longer uses the logic of in the Hegelian sense objectification, externalisation and alienation. The series of expressions of the substantialization, the hypostasization, the coagulation of human labour, to this extent only have now an, as it were, metaphorical meaning. Even in regard to the expression the "objectification" of concrete, useful labour, Marx in fact deliberately clarifies things in the sense of it being "simply no more than a bringing about of change of the form of the physical material", to say nothing of in regard to the expression the coagulation of abstract labour. Value objectivity doesn't even allow analogy with the "projection" of so-called secondary characteristics such as colour. In reality Marx emphasises that

> the impression of brilliance a thing gives to the optic nerve indeed doesn't appear as a subjective stimulus of the optic nerve itself, it appears as an objective form of a thing outside the eye. However, in the case of sight it

> is a relation of the thing and the thing ... of the external object and the
> eye. ... But the commodity form ... bears absolutely no connection to a
> physical relation. It is none other than a specific social relation between
> people themselves,

and he stresses that

> value is none other than the relation of labour mutually between indi-
> viduals, is none other than the objective expression of a special social
> labour form.

Value is not a physical formation created through the direct relation of subject –
object, nor is it, in addition, a secondary characteristic-like thing "projected"
from the subject to the object, it is in fact "a social relation", "a social formation
[*Gebilde*]". This is the reason that the "logic of subjective – objective" of the
theory of alienation and the logic of the "theory of reification" differ decisively;
with, in addition, that which is value being simply a thing where in this way an
in-itself *social co-operation* amongst people has been *reified* and has appeared
phenomenally provisionally as an *etwas Objektives* [objective something].

   If that is the case, shouldn't we call that which is value objectivity simply a
fiction? Shouldn't we say that Marx, in the final analysis, stands in the position
of value nominalism? Marx, however, criticises "mercantilism which resurrects
a position of seeing only exclusively social forms in value, of seeing only illusion
without an entity for the social forms". If Marx had been a positivist empiricist
of the kind who doesn't recognise real existence apart from *realitas* as *realitas*
he may have been tripped up by Bailey's nominalism. However, his philosophical position makes possible a positive assertion of an "objective" object-ness
of value. As we verified earlier, in the world of the commodity "value" appears
as an external – restricting objectivity as regards individuals, and the "size of
value is independent from the will – foreknowledge – acts of those exchanging", and, "for example, that one tonne of iron and two ounces of gold are of
equivalent value is as if it, despite one pound of gold and one pound of iron
differing in physical – chemical attributes, appears as if it is the same thing
as their being of equivalent weight". It has to indeed be a *realitas*, and to the
individuals involved it exists as an immovable "objective" object-ness. It is certainly not the case that this objectivity exists supra-historically – supra-an age,
rather, that "it is socially valid in regard to the relations of production of this
historically determined social form which is commodity production, and for
that reason that it is an objective form of thought (*gesellschaftlich gültige, also
objective Gedankenform*)"; to the extent that Marx takes a position within the

world of the commodity he positively acknowledges the *Bestand* [existence] of "value" as a socially *gültig* ⟦Tr. valid⟧ and for that reason *objektiv Gedankenform* ⟦Tr. objective form of thought⟧.

"Value" is certainly not a "third empire of meaning" existing directly independently of human beings, nor is it an autonomous objectivity grasped in an "essential intuition". Marx rejects a "fetishism" (*Fetischismus*) which mistakenly sees "value" as if it is such an autonomous object. But, at the same time, he also rejects with a double blade the view that causes it to fall to being a mere illusion. (*In-der-Warenweltlich*) In the world of the commodity "in the exchange relation of the products of private labour, the labour hours socially necessary for the production of these ... just like such as the law of gravity ... penetrate these themselves as a regulating natural law", and in the hypostasized appearing of the functional relation of the necessary labour spoken of in the foundational thesis of the labour theory of value,[2] Marx places the real foundation here, and to that extent this is the reason he postulates[3] the thesis of the "coagulation of abstract, human labour".

Under particular historical – social conditions, when people's intersubjective (*zusammensubjektiv*) relations of co-operation are reified (*versachlichen*) being-structure-restrictively and appear as phenomena *intersubjektiv*-ly (intersubjectively), co-subjectively (*Gemeinsubjektiv*)—the being of value being the archetype of this—Marx stands, whilst understanding for-itself the secret of that "reification", in a position of understanding which recognises phenomenally its existentiality—a standpoint differing in dimension from the traditional oppositional plane of nominalism and realism—and it is in taking such a position that he grasps the being-structure of the world of the commodity.

1.5   *The Fourfold Nature of the World of the Commodity*

The world of the commodity, provisionally, appears as a world of thing-like being, but that things in the thing-like being form, or, things appearing as a relation between a thing-like being and a thing-like being, are in fact the co-operative activity of people and their relations; this we have already implicitly seen via the discussion through to the preceding item of discussion. Here,—to

---

2   We can say that it is the same logical structure as when, regardless of the fact that the entity of weight (correctly mass) does not exist, with it being simply a determining of inertial acceleration, we are able to say this and that in regard to the same masses, hypostasizing the functional relation.

3   That Marx himself carries out value determination in *A Contribution to the Critique of Political Economy* primarily as a "coagulation of necessary labour *hours*" would seem to be related to these earlier matters.

the extent necessary for a foreshadowing of what might be called a key to later discussion—I would like to elucidate the fundamental structure of the holistic relations of the world of the commodity.

First, we have the moment of "use-value"; earlier, we discussed it as if it is a natural objectivity. However, correctly, we can't overlook the fact that from the beginning even this use-value is a social, historical form. For example, things such as stone implements or bows and arrows are no longer a use-value for us today, and things such as televisions and aeroplanes were not until very recently use-values. Use-value can be said to be "usefulness satisfying some kind of human desire", with desire itself being historically – socially determined, and being a type of cultural form—as we see in the useful *sashimi* and *shiokara* ⟦Tr. salted fish entrails⟧ for we Japanese not being useful for Westerners. As a result, despite saying concrete, useful labour is objectified and becomes use-value, the labour act in question is not only appropriate in terms of physics, if it isn't *zweckmäßig* [appropriate] socially – culturally as well, no matter how great the labour energy one pours into it it won't become the production of use-value. Only labour carried out in a way which is socially – culturally *zweckmäßig* [appropriate] is "objectified" and becomes use-value.

The subject of labour, when he or she produces a commodity, in other words when he or she produces not for self-consumption but for the purpose of exchange, he or she produces through a labouring which is a certain way of doing which becomes *zweckmäßig* both naturally-physically and culturally-socially, a product which is such that it fulfils a desire of, as it were, *das Man*, that is to say a product which is useful for *das Man*. And, when he or she goes to deal with an exchange carrying his or her produced goods, the rate of exchange is decided with no connection to the number of hours actually taken in its production but with regard to "how many hours in the case of its being produced under existing social – standard conditions of production and the social average of the intensity of labour proficiency", it being decided with the conversion based on the labour hours required by, as it were, *das Man*. When this happens, however, "people don't by reason of regarding their labour products as a mere thing-like being coating of homogenous human labour bring these thing-like beings into relation with one another as values. It is the opposite. Through equating in exchange different kinds of products as values, they equate their various labour as ⟨abstract⟩, human labour".

In the world of the commodity, people appear as equal possessors of commodities, but if commodity exchange is followed back it is an exchange of labour and labour, and it is the case that people in the world of the commodity appear through a surface position of being a "person able to carry out the socially necessary labour". That is to say, they appear as, as it were, *das Man*, as a person able to carry out "abstract, human labour", as the subject thereof. Concrete, real human beings *entgegenkommen* [encounter – face] each other *as das Man*.

It is this kind of twofold thing, where "the relation between person and person" appears "disguised as the social relation of thing-like being and thing-like being, of labour product and labour product", that is none other than value relation.

In the world of the commodity "all labour products are rendered hieroglyphs". People deal with *Gefragtes* "value" in *Befragtes*, and *erfragen* "labour". Precisely as Marx says, we can say that "determinativeness as the value of use objects [is], *in the same way as language*, a social product".

The existing of labour products as value things is in the subject of labour being *gelten* [Tr. valid] as *das Man*, and it is the case that use value things as value things, the subject of useful labour as the subject of abstract labour, exist precisely in a twofold structure (in all, a fourfold being-structure) identical to linguistic exchange.

In this, as we saw earlier, use value and useful labour which appear at a glance as if they exist in a natural being-structure-ness are also rendered social, and moreover—just as people carry out language activity in accordance with rules of grammar, and as it is only to that extent that they maintain the existence of the rules of grammar—the activity of people which appears reified is regulated historically-socially, and it is only to the extent that they submit to such that people maintain themselves, and that they proceed with continuously reproducing the world of the commodity as the world of the commodity.

It is in the scene of the establishment of the general equivalent value form that is currency[4] that this circumstance most directly appears, and it is well known that Marx, in his famous theory of value form, concretely describes and analyses the dialectical structure, with use value things as value things, with the concrete person as the abstract person, of the relation between the relative value-form and the equivalent value-form, the fourfold structure relation we speak of, which interact with each other in a twofold-ness. In particular, Marx's argument regarding the process of establishment of and the being-structure

---

4   Currency is not merely *Zuhandensein*, nor, again, is it something produced through the acting of individual subjects on objects—nor is it something produced through an algebraic sum of the subject – object relation of individual subjects and objects.—It is an essentially *intersubjektiv Gebilde* [Tr. intersubjective thing], a reified in-itself social *relation of co-operation*, something where it is in the end not possible to investigate its being-structure through the subject – object relation of modern times, and something where for the first time Marx was able to investigate it philosophically through positioning it in the fourfold structure relation mentioned above.

of currency as currency, of the general equivalent value form, contains points directly analogous to the process of establishment of language and the being-structure of linguistic communication, and when locating this in the analysis of the total process of capital which is dependent on the establishment of the market of labour power, when locating it in the structure of the scene where market price is established, we can perceive concretely the structure of the historical world.

Here, however, with it involving matters of time as well, I think I have been able to secure the minimum within at least the range of the above discussion required for the fundamental point of view and clues for the discussion to come, and so with this I would like to bring discussion regarding the "world of the commodity" to an end for the moment, and would like to expand my perspective to what I am calling the historical world.

2   The Being-Structure of the Historical World

When we speak of the world, representing a vast and boundless universe, we tend to think of the human world unfolding on the surface of the Earth, making up a corner of this world of Nature, as *vorhanden* [Tr. present-at-hand]. Viewed from a transcendent-*like* point of view it might, indeed, be possible to draw such a picture of the world. However, the world which opens out in actuality in our daily lives differs in feature entirely.

In the following, taking a direct look at the appearance with which the world appears to us, taking an as it were phenomenalistic viewpoint, I would like, invoking the mechanism of the world of the commodity, to take a look at the fundamental structural relations to be found there.

2.1   *The Twofold Nature of the Information World*
Our direct field of vision is extremely limited; what is detected there is a few "things",[5] a few people, the voices they produce, a certain kind of form appearing in the "things"[6] called television and the newspaper etc.—no more than roughly such an *Umfang* [extension – range].

However, that a war is being waged in Vietnam, that the Soviet army is stationed in Czechoslovakia, etc. etc.; we don't merely know a group of "facts", we are indignant about them, we form an attitude regarding them etc. In addition,

---

5   [Tr. The Japanese word here, 事物, covers "things" in the broad sense of both physical things and states of affairs].
6   [Tr. The word here for "things", 物, refers to physical things].

there are even cases where we take the same action we would on the occasion of being there ... watching the live television broadcast of the return of Apollo 8 from the moon or of Sumo in breathless excitement or spontaneously applauding. In this way, the world transmitted through information, in almost the same way as the "real" world opening out before our eyes, *has a direct effect on* our consciousness, or rather, *on psychological – physiological mechanisms*, stimulating an appropriate response. To this extent, we can say that the information world has an actuality which is the same as the so-called "physical world".

The world opening out for us in actuality, that is to say the world having a direct determining effect on our "psychological – physiological" activity, and the world where we are involved with it objectively – practically, is, in a sense, it seems to be no exaggeration to say, almost exclusively a world rendered into information—it seems, however, that even for the school of thought that purports to stand at a phenomenalistic standpoint this ends up being ignored—,and the "live" world is rather no more than the smallest part thereof.

What, then, is the information world? What kind of structural fact, then, is being involved with the information world? Although this may be *bekannt* [something we have great familiarity with] it is not in the final analysis *erkannt* [something which is completely known from a scientific point of view].

To begin with, what we are given directly is the "sensuous forms" of writing, linguistic sounds, images, gestures, and, what's more, only such. If these "sensuous givens" only register in consciousness as simply that thing *als solches* ⟦Tr. as such⟧, then, however, the information world doesn't open out, and it is only in this given registering in consciousness as *etwas Mehr, etwas Anderes* ⟦Tr. something more, something else⟧ that the information world for the first time appears.

What then is this *etwas Anderes* which is the information content? This information content, which is transmitted, despite it being possible that it is a delusion of the transmitter, is in general an "objective" phenomenon for the transmitter. The receiver doesn't respond to the transmitter's "representation" of, for example, the Vietnam War, he or she is indignant about or opposes the Vietnam War as an "objective" phenomenon, and to this extent, we can say that the transmitter and the receiver share the "objective phenomenon" as a "single sameness" as a common object. The information world is for the receiver none other than the "physical" world seen with, so to speak, other eyes.

In this case, however, it is not that, for the receiver, the "phenomenon" in question is given, of course, sensorily, nor even representationally. Indeed, occasions where scenes of the Vietnam War come before us vividly in images may be possible, but that these images are not in accord with, that is to say, "the fact of transmission", and that, in reality, the receiver's taking of an antiwar stance is not in regard to these images but is only in the end in regard to the war as an "objective phenomenon",—it isn't necessary to argue for the existence of transmission which isn't accompanied by some kind of representation—; as will be understood if we look at these facts, we cannot mix transmission content and representation. In the end, despite the information world being in reality given it is not the case that it is given for the receiver as a *real* form. What is given as *real* for the receiver are only "signs", and the information content is no more than given, in an as it were *irreal* way, as an *irreal* form.

In this regard, we can no doubt say that the mode of opening out of the information world is analogous to value being embodied in use value (archetypically in the physical currency object), with the use value object *gelten* [[Tr. holding]] as the value object—with *real* semiotic forms *gelten* as *irreal* information content.

Analogy with the world of the commodity or currency doesn't stop here. An analogy is seen regarding the aspect of the subject. I said earlier that the receiver sees the objective given with, as it were, the same eyes as the transmitter, but such is possible, that is to say, the receiver is able to "understand" signs dependent on the transmitter and the receiver being what might be called "*langue* subjects" in the semiotic system (*langue*) concerned,[7] and on signs embodying what, to use the language of Marx's theory of value, might be called the "congealment" (*Gallerte*) of general language activity. Although not the subject of abstract, general labour, analogously to the human being in the world of the commodity, as, as it were, the subject of abstract, general semiotic activity, only in the receiver being to this extent such a "person", does the information world for the first time exist.

I think that we can provisionally take note of the fact that in the information world *real* semiotic forms *gelten* [[Tr. hold]] as *irreal* information content, and that the information world opens out in the twofold-ness of the *real* receiver being a given only insofar as he or she exists as an *irreal langue* subject, that is to say, that it exists in a fourfold structural relation.

2.2   *The Problematics of Theories of Meaning*

If it isn't the case that information content, that is to say, transmitted "meaning", is given as a *real Gebilde* [form – composite form], in just what kind of way can we say that it is given? Also, what kind of thing is it in terms of its being-structure characteristic? I'd like now to consider these problems.

---

7   Marx-Engels write that language is the "actuality of consciousness" (*Deutsche Ideologie*), that "ideas do not exist apart from language" (*Grundrisse*), anticipating the so-called "Copernican revolution of Geiger".

To investigate the matter directly, if we firstly consider things in regard to a so-called concept word, for example that which is made meaning through the sign ⟨tree⟩ and which is transmitted, it possesses a functional characteristic wherein things can be, as it were, substituted through the numerous denotations of pine, cedar, cypress etc, and, what's more, it possesses a universal characteristic in expressing the essential homogeneity wherein in contrast to the individual denotations being special it itself is any of these, and further, conversely to the actual tree being referred to by it being in the form of the continual growth and change involved in growing and dying it itself neither grows nor dies and it has the immutable characteristic of maintaining a self-identity—so when one takes the thing itself and asks regarding its being-structure characteristic it has in the sense used by a certain kind of school of thought a "supra-spatiotemporal being-structure characteristic". Does such a *Wesen* ⟦Tr. essence⟧ in reality exist? Even if one uses the expression the third empire of meaning, if that's all there is then one can't escape the criticism of old from a position of nominalistic empiricism that such is Platonism. This is precisely none other than the point of contention between nominalism and realism.

Leaving until later a stating in regard to how for us we would deal with this point of contention, if for the time being we accept the fact of the above-mentioned "supra-spatiotemporal being-structure characteristic" = *ideal etwas* ⟦Tr. ideal something⟧ I can't deny that the problem of information – transmission—rejecting the invalid "black box theory of consciousness"—can provisionally be explained. A little earlier, I spoke of things in the manner of the transmitter and the receiver seeing the same "objective phenomenon" with, as it were, the same eyes, and if we assert that the two—with the one at the locality, and the other in signs—"intuit the essence" of the same thing (here, rather than conceptual meaning, it is the *ideal* thing of the same *Sachverhalt* (situation)), it is true that this is a provisional explanation. In order that transmission exists as transmission the demand is met that the transmitter and the receiver have to be "intentionally" conscious of the same objectivity, the same *Sachverhalt*, and it is the case that the information world is not given in a *real* way but is given in an *ideal* way.

As far as I'm concerned, I'm willing to grant provisional authority to such an "explanatory method". But, in the end, does an *ideal etwas* ⟦Tr. ideal something⟧ really *bestehen* [strictly exist – exist]? Is such a thing as essence intuition actually carried out? The answer, of course, is "No". Following Marx, we have to be, I think, for-itself to the secret of "reification".

Where lies the secret of the "*ideal Wesen* [ideal essence]" and *Wesensschau* [essence intuition]? Here, again, if we for the moment focus along the lines of "concept words", I consider things to be in the following way. We tend to

THE THEORY OF REIFICATION OF THE HISTORICAL WORLD

think that a group of objects expressed by the same word have the same property—because they have the same property (cause) they are expressed by the same word (result)—and we fall into the result of having to require the *irreal etwas* from an attempt to purely ascertain *das Identische* [the identical thing] in question, and we have to say that this is precisely the same "reific-atory" cognitive distortion as that where by reason of their having the same value objects are mutually exchanged. It's simply that the identical nature of meaning, the *ideal das Identische*, has been thought. Be that as it may, we can't overlook the fact of the intersubjectivity of the belief that "things called by the same word ought to have the same essential property", of the intersubjectiv-ity lying at the foundation of this belief. In language activity, although there is in principle no necessity whatsoever in what an object is named, in any case intersubjective unity historically and socially amongst individuals is to be seen, and with this intersubjectivity as the basis, although when, for example, persons say "a tomato is not a fruit", "a melon is a fruit", the facts are simply the difference of whether people call the object something or don't call the object something, the situation is regarded as if the essential attributes pos-sessed by the object itself reciprocally differ. It seems that (1) the thesis that "the individual is subjective" is transformed and regarded as "that which is not the individual is objective", and (2) through a combining of this with the "exper-ience" that the "objective" is intersubjective, before one knows it the schema of "the intersubjective is objective" has formed and so—based on this schema it ends up, does it not, being thought from the intersubjectivity of people alike expressing something with the same word that "the same, certain 'objective thing' ought to exist there?"

Even though the thinking that "that which is meaning", which possesses an ideal being-structure characteristic, exists in itself, but is based on the kind of distortion wherein the functional relation of language communication (exchange) appears reified, "meaning" is not necessarily *nichts* [nothingness], rather, in the same way as is the case with the objects of pure mathemat-ics, it is appropriate I think that its "being-structure" right be provisionally recognised. Even though "meaning" and the objects of pure mathematics are no more than thought (*vermeinen*) "existences", this *Vermeinung* [thinking] is something which exists only to the extent that people intersubjectively carry out a self-forming and an as it were homogenising, and we can't deny that their state of consciousness changes fundamentally in accord with whether they actually have this *Vermeinung* or not. What's more, although the inten-tional object of this *intersubjektive Vermeinung* [intersubjective thinking] is as a *realitas nichts* the *Vermeinung* in question itself is a *realitas* which is not *nichts*.

To this extent, whilst we render for-itself the reification of the *intersubjekt-ives Zusammenwirken* [intersubjective co-operation] which is "meaning", this "secret of reification", and we prohibit the *Fetischismus* of seeing as autonomous the objects of intersubjective thinking, following the insight of Marx's theory of value we want to deal with *ideal* objectivity or *Sachverhalt* [propositional states of affairs], or if one wants to put it that way *Satz an sich* [propositions themselves], as if they *bestehen* [exist], and as if they are *vernehmen* [received – cognized] intersubjectively.

2.3 *The Objectivity of Social Acts*

In our daily lives, we are "socially" regulated in the manner of behaving in a manner suitable to the for-human environment-scene of the occasion, and for the most part we act in accordance with such. At school like a teacher, at the alumni association acting "as if I have gone back to my student days", and then at home like a father ... in such a way, in the same way that an actor performs in a manner suitable to character and scene, I am continuously performing according to, to use the terminology of a certain school of sociologists, status and role.

In what I am calling character and performance, we have from the specialised – concrete of like a presenter when presenting at an academic conference, or like a moderator, to the general – abstract of like a Japanese person, or like a human being, and if we expand this concept, we can say that naturally the method of execution of business activities as a capitalist, the method of labour of a wage labourer, the method of activity of a judicial officer or a politician, but also the method of acting which is "social – customary" such as wearing a tie despite it being so humid, or not going into the house with shoes on, and in addition, the forming of facial expressions, the taking of a pose, etc. etc. through to and so on and so forth; that all human social behaviour is carried out as what might be called performance. (In putting things forward in this way I think that that I wish to declare that with determinations such as *besorgen* [concern] or *fürsorgen* [care] the actual form of *In-der-Welt-sein* [being-in-the-world] cannot be completely grasped; this, I think, can be understood. As I will touch on later, if I put forward my view, even the mode of being of the "existential" is already none other than a form of performance, to say nothing of the mode of being of *"Das-Man"*).

In this life theatre there is stage (curtain – place), stage sets and props, and plot. In this theatre, rather than director and writer being absent, they themselves appear as actors. And although performers are able to change to some degree stage, sets and props, and plot, these are for the most part pre-existing, and we can say that even character, rather than selected one's self, has a strong aspect of being something allotted to one. That is to say, we are compelled to perform in an almost fixed form, based on a pre-existing stage – sets and props – plot.

With this "life theatre" as a key I think that we can approach what it is that society in a so-called broad sense, that is to say society in the broad sense subsuming such things as family and state as well, to say nothing of the "small society" of such as school and company, is; that we can approach what is the being-structure of such.

Firstly, the thing which is likened to stage (curtain – place) and settings and props; it seems that we might be prone to think firstly of the "natural environment". However we mustn't forget that though we say "natural", it is a from-the-beginning *Zuhandensein* limited nature, and we cannot not acknowledge that the "natural environment" in reality opening out to us, be it fields or forest, is culturalised (*kultivieren*) nature, is, so to speak, manufactured "nature". Marx-Engels point out that the real sensuous natural world is certainly "not a Nature immutable and unified which has existed from the eternal past", and that it "is the product of industry and the state of society ... and what's more in the sense that it is an historical product it is the result (*Resultat*) of the activity of the complete line of generations. ... this activity, the sensuous labour and creation which progresses successively, this production is the very foundation (*Grundlage*) of the total sensuous world existing in reality"; this is, I think, precisely to the point. Roads, fields, and mines and fishing grounds are the products of an objectification of human activity over many years, and we can say that they are "nature" to the extent that they became, as it were, *use value objects*. To this extent, although the stage and sets and props as so-called "natural environment" are for the actor himself or herself existing material givens, we can say that they are objectifications and reifications of human social and co-operative activity.

We must take note too, incidentally, of the fact that in "stage – sets and props – plot" exists social environment in the narrow sense, and social forms. In particular with those things called "systems" it is the case that performance of the "plays" of for example elections and court cases are not possible without the system of representation and the judicial system, and these occupy an important position as stage in excess of that of "natural environment". "Systems", as well, are reflected at first glance as if they exist, as it were, in themselves, as if they exist independently of the individuals involved. At the least, the fact that they possess an, as it were, "external restricting force" towards the acts of individuals is certain. And on this point, social forms of the like of social customs and morals which have attained a particular fixity all possess in the same way "external restricting force". However, that these social forms are, originally, stereotypification of the forms of the acts (including thinking) of people, that they are the agglutination (*sichfestsetzen*) and reification of the for-others-for-one's-self way of being of human activity, that they are the *réification* [reification] of the *manières d'agir, de penser et de sentir* (forms of behaviour, of thought, and of sensitivity) of human beings—these things we can easily perceive. Considered from a different perspective, so-called "systems" too, once again, are a rendering fixed of the forms of human activity, of the forms of performance, and can be regarded as being reified things.—Considering things in this way, although those things which are called social forms, which are called the social environment, pre-exist to individuals as a given, we see that they are things established and existing through reification of forms of behaviour of other people preceding us (including we ourselves in the past), through reification of *Verhalten* [acts of relation] of this in-itself co-operation.

That the social—including culturalised nature – environment world is a reification of the acts and their forms of preceding others, that this is the given of stage and sets and props in regard to people's character performance, and, what's more, that such even controls plot, and, at the same time, "forces", as an externally restricting "objective" controlling force, performance of a certain "form";—we have seen above such objective aspects which form an analogy with economic rules, in particular the "rule of value", and we must at the same time recognise the aspect also that the acts of each person in his or her performing that form of role—indeed even though he or she brings a degree of change due to his or her individuality—functions as one scene in the reification process of social forms – the social "natural" environment world. In performing a certain character people transformingly reproduce the given as a new social form.

The actors of the human play which is social life, do not, however, strictly speaking, have an essential self. For the actor on the stage there is a differentiation between life on the stage and private life outside the theatre, and there is real meaning in the distinction between an essential self and the self on the stage. But in the life theatre which is society there is no life external to the stage. At school as a teacher, at the club as president, at home as a father; in this manner one is always performing a set role and so a distinction between the "self as self" and the "self as actor" doesn't come into being logically. My expression regarding performance etc. earlier was a way of speaking accommodated to the individual self-ism of modern times, and we have to say that for human beings there is no entity-like essence and that for human beings we are truly an "ensemble of social relations". Even so, to the extent that there are grounds for the fact of people on occasion being conscious of a split with character, being conscious of performance as performance, and to the extent that consciousness of *Ich als Ich* ⟦Tr. I as I⟧ is in reality individually thought, the expression, I performing a role as someone, *I as someone else* (I as someone separate to an essential self), will, I think, be permitted. (Regarding this problem of the "self", see Utsunomiya Yoshiaki's "Role and Self"—included in *Problems of Modern Philosophy* edited by the Philosophical Association of Japan). Regarding the "someone" here and status and role, there is a need to differentiate in detail such things as such occurring in the dimension of class, and such occurring too in the functional determinateness of it being one's turn, etc. etc. However, if for the moment we focus things along the lines of general structure, we can I think confirm that, in any case, people proceed as someone as someone to reify a given transformingly – reproducingly, and herein exists that which is called society [*Welt* (the world)] in the fourfoldly structuralised dynamism of such.

2.4   *The Historical Nature of the Natural World*
We have touched on above the fact that that which is called the natural environment world is not necessarily nature *als solche* ⟦Tr. as such⟧, that it is not only said to appear as *Zuhandensein* but is an as it were rendered, "historicised nature"; yet is it not the case, however, that we have to accept that that to which transformation through reification of human activity directly extends is limited to the surface of the Earth, with the nature of the so-called greater Universe or the interior of the Earth being Nature as such? Is it really possible to think of even these as "historicised nature?" I would like to touch on this issue, in order, in addition, to elucidate the denotation of "historical world" we are using.

To start with the conclusion, I have on another occasion (in the above-mentioned essay, "The Intersubjective Being-Structure of the World") considered as a main theme of discussion the sensually given, or rather the phenomenalistically unfolding, "natural world", and it is my conception that such is in-itself historically – socially intersubjectivised. Viewed from so-called forms of perception, this has, already, been what we might call rendered into signs, and is rendered in consciousness as an *etwas Mehr* intersubjectivised historically – socially.

To put things in the manner of Marx,

> "human sensuousness is not directly as it is, is not objectively as it is, human sensuousness, human objectivity". "The senses of other human beings and their spirit become my own ... and *social organs* are formed", and people view nature with these social sense organs, and from the given of the so-called high level perception faculty "through to emotions and sensations [all are] rendered ideology".

To come to the point, the sound of a clock only sounds as *kachi kachi* to we Japanese, but sounds as tick-tock, apparently, to English-language peoples, and thus the way sounds sound is determined historically – socially – through, for the time being, linguistic communication. Even if we have the same language "sound", something which to us only sounds like the call of a bird sounds to a given language peoples with appropriate segmentation, and so that even if the "same" sensory stimulus is given how that is segmented and perceived, and what kind of natural image arises, is restricted historically – socially; this today, through, in particular, cultural anthropology research, can be said to be the standard view.

> Figuratively speaking, 'simple existents' for human beings living in a certain history – society can be completely different to 'simple existents' for human beings living in another society. In the manner of our not being able to think of Oriental thought as an undeveloped stage of our thought, that is to say, of our not being able to think that through getting rid of some things from their thought and adding some things it becomes our thought ... they should be regarded as belonging to completely different, separate systems, ... and so in this way the world for a particular society and the world for another society form completely different systems. ... There is no more extreme error than supposing that by reason of the identical nature of the sense organs human beings all have the same perception, or, are able to have. We perceive things with, as it were, 'social sense organs'. In the manner that different species of animals likely perceive differently, different societies, different eras, have different perception ...[8]

Etc. etc. It may perhaps not be necessary to go so far as to quote this kind of argument again.

When it comes to nature as *Vorhandensein* [Being present-at-hand], distinguished from phenomenal nature, I will be able to have you understand I believe that such indeed is a part of the intersubjectivised "information world" transmitted through historical-social education, and is a system "embodying" that aforementioned ideal "meaning", and that through reificatory inversion this is regarded as nature as real existent itself, and the real, phenomenal world ends up being regarded as its phenomena, as, in the extreme case, illusion— I have gone into detail regarding this on another occasion and so I will avoid repetition here.

---

8 〚Tr. Hiromatsu provides no reference here〛.

The natural world unfolding in reality for us, this is not a simple *als sol-che* given; that it is, in-itself, and *fur üns*, rendered, as it were, a sign (symbol), rendered historically – socially intersubjectivised, is complementary to the fact that we encounter nature by means of in-themselves "socialised eyes" and an in-itself "socialised psyche". Here once again the previously discussed matter of the fourfold structure of "encountering as a particular person as someone a given as something" can be recognised.

From another angle, the way of being given which is so-called "nature as scientific existent", nature as *Vorhandensein,* is also, too, something which corresponds with a special form of the way of being which is "as someone", with an as it were *"Das Man"*-ized way of being, and is none other than a variant of the above-mentioned fourfold structural relation.

In addition, if we add some discussion in relation to these matters in relation to the laws of history, the laws of nature which are *vorhandenseiend* are, in reality, a part of the aforementioned *ideal* system of "meaning" and are not laws of "raw nature" itself, and the necessity of *ideal* laws of nature is the logical necessity possessed by the mathematical formula formularising them—going further back, the theological necessity which lies at the foundation of such or the vestiges of this—and in the same way that the sum of the interior angles of a triangle on the blackboard does not precisely speaking make a straight angle, the actual natural world is in no way subject to classical "necessity". That that which is a natural necessity is something posited through an idealisation (*idealisieren*) of actual phenomena relations, and that when abstracting the necessity itself and rendering it absolute it is no more than a fiction, and the fact that, nonetheless, such necessities are frequently reified and rendered absolute laws;—we can through a rendering for-itself of this "secret", caution ourselves against the foolishness of *fundamentally* distinguishing between natural laws and historical laws. In a dimension one step back from this we too ought perhaps to distinguish between natural laws and historical laws, but we reject, in focusing along the lines of the way of being of nature which we have just looked at, the doxa [conjecture] which renders nature and history a dualism, and, as a result, which distinguishes in absolute terms laws of nature and laws of history.

2.5   *The Fourfold Nature of the Historical World*

We have looked at in the discussion above the fact that that which is called the "world" is an almost entirely "information-ized" world, and the fact that even though being the so-called "immediate world of perception" a part of such is a "reification" of people's "performative" objective activity, and that to add to this the world is, as it were, "rendered a sign" and appears in an historically – socially intersubjectivised form.

Marx-Engels argue that "we know only one science [*wissenschaft*, system of knowledge], namely the science of history. History can be investigated from two sides, classifying into the history of nature and the history of human beings, but as long as human beings exist, however, the history of nature and the history of human beings will mutually restrict each other and these two sides cannot be separated off (*trennen*)", and, as we saw in the quotation before, they speak of "historicised nature" as a more detailed explanation of this. Certainly, we can confirm that the world we are being-in is in general an historically opened out world.

I took the expedient of discussing the way of being of this "historical world" through the comparison for me of it with the "world of the commodity" we have just looked at, and the grounds of existence making this analogy possible ought to lie in the fact that the world of the commodity is one scene of the historical world. Now, including points of discussion regarding the world of the commodity as well within my scope, I would like to render for-itself the grounds of the "philosophy of history", reconfirming as I do so the fundamental structure that is the reason the world can exist as an historical world.

It goes without confirming again that that the *Umwelt* [environmental world] is an "information-ized" world certainly doesn't mean that we have as it were constructed an idealist castle and are living therein. It is certainly not the case that that which is the information world exists *vorhandend* [[Tr. present-at-hand]] in space, and in this sense it is *irreal*, but, calling for a change for us in the way of looking at that which is the "world", we assert that that which is the infinite spatial universe is in fact a form of the information world, and, in this dimension, it's perhaps now necessary to retract the compromising description that the information world is *irreal*. The information world, in this dimension, is the very, truly, *wirklich* [[Tr. real]] world.

Viewed within this dimension phenomena too of the "physical" past are of the present (*gegenwärtig*), and cultural heritage of the past which has physically already disappeared, and also even the foreseen future, can also be said to be of the present. Further, the distinction between "base" and "superstructure" Marx refers to is also not a distinction in terms of substance. Though it "pre-exists", the social – cultural structure composition is the reification of people's objective activity, of *intersubjektiv*, or, rather *zusammensubjektiv* [[Tr. co-operative-subjective]] activity, existing as "performance" of a specific role, and what exists in actuality is the dynamic whole-as-process of the fourfold structural relations; what exists in actuality is fundamentally this whole.[9]

---

9 Although a living thing is an organic whole, and is a body of universal functional relations,

According to materialist history, it is in the reification of this structure com-position that history exists as history, and Marx-Engels express this in the fol-lowing way.

> This self-agglutination of social activity; that the products of we human beings ourselves coagulate and go beyond our control, frustrate our ex-pectations, and become a physical force which derails our plans ... this social force, ... that is to say, this force which is formed through the co-operation, determined by the division of labour, of various individuals, by reason of the fact that the co-operation itself is not of free will but is natural, appears to the individuals not as a combined force of their own (*eigene*) but as an estranged (*fremd*) force lying outside themselves. The individuals don't know how this force has been brought about nor its future, and for that reason, not only are the individuals not able to command this force, rather on the contrary it is this force which moves through a series of forms and development stages following a particular route, independent of human will and movement, nay, controlling human intention and movement etc. etc.

If the "philosophy of history" is able to construct a diachronic, law-propound-ing system, it is through the reification of this *intersubjektives Zusammenwirken* [[Tr. intersubjective co-operation]].

The following types of points can be put forward I believe regarding the syn-chronic fundamental structure supporting this historical reification—I have to restrict myself here to abstract, general statements, however.

People's objective activity, as provisionally a "natural phenomenon", brings about a certain change in position in existing natural relations, and this "nat-ural phenomenon" not only possesses in-itself equipment significance, it pos-sesses social significance. For example, let us say that a member of a group of primitive peoples pursuing some deer successfully shoots one. This "natural phenomenon", however, "compels" a change in people's "practical stance" and has an *etwas Mehr* [[Tr. something more]] social significance—putting aside

---

between such as the heart or the brain and the capillary blood vessels or the peripheral nerves the significance these have as determinants for the make-up of being of the living body as a whole differs, and so, analogously to this, the structural relations of the production – repro-duction of material life are for society—nay, are for the existence of the historical world and changes within it—a fundamental determinant, and the problem of the interaction between that which are called "base" and "superstructure" should, I believe, be understood in regard to this actuality.

here skill value and moral – aesthetic value etc.—, such that the members of the group no longer have to pursue the other deer, such that they have to deal with the shot deer in a manner different to that which they have had up until now, etc. etc. Incidentally, this "compulsion" is not a natural – physical compulsion, it is a social, customary compulsion, and it follows as it were a "grammar of social behaviour". Producing a language sound, treading out a path, enclosing a fertile field by tying up a rope, assassinating a king, occupying Yasuda Auditorium;[10] such "natural phenomena"—regardless of a change in position in the natural relations between the individuals and the things, in some cases, for example in such as the transfer of land ownership, being of a natural course *nichts*—, in-themselves, have a "social significance" which has gone beyond themselves, and they bring about a change in their social meaning, and bring about a change in the totality of social significance relations. It can be acknowledged that this "change", what's more, is not change appearing to a contemplating perspective, but is actual change. To come to the main point, people's objective activity doesn't only have simply an equipment significance as something simply bringing about a change in position in relations of equipment significance, it exists in a twofold nature as something having at the same time social significance—the objective twofold nature of the world of the commodity in which the production of use value is simultaneously inseparable from the production of value is simply a form of this.

Regarding, too, the "subjective" side of objective activity, this activity which can be regarded provisionally as a physiological – physical "natural phenomenon", fundamentally carries a social determinateness. The subject of the activity of shooting the deer performed the social part of archer, and what's more of "first archer", and in doing so he cuts off a performing of this role by another person. In general, the fulfilling of a certain role by someone means an excluding from that role of other people, and viewed from this aspect too the action of a person means the "compelling" of alteration of the subsequent form of action, of the "practical stance", of other people, and of oneself. That people's action exists as performance of a given role, that moreover, for example, the "at the risk of their existence" battle for the Yasuda Auditorium appears to a third party as the action of *Das Man*—the action, I need not go so far as to say, of a some one, of an anyone individually, a nameless certain *person*—, appears rendered double, in an exactly analogous structure to the subject of concrete,

---

10   [Tr. In January 1969 students occupying the Yasuda Auditorium at the University of Tokyo, after violently resisting, were violently removed by riot police. Widely broadcast on television, this battle between students and police has become the major symbol of the student protests, and the protests in general, in Japan in the late 1960s].

useful labour *gelten*ing ⟦Tr. holding⟧ socially as the subject of abstract, human labour. And, reification of this part-taking is simply something which becoming the objective two elements carries double significance.

In this way, people, already on each occasion (*immer schon*), in an historically – socially being-bound (*seinsverbunden*) manner, perform a role as someone, and whilst doing so, through a positing *zusammenwirkend* ⟦Tr. co-operatively⟧ and reifyingly of the given as *etwas Mehr*[11] ⟦Tr. something more⟧, reproduce the synchronic – diachronic, dynamic process relations and bring into being the historical world. In the historical world, in-itself *Zuhandensein* for-itself simultaneously *as Mit-gehalten-sein* ⟦Tr. with-participation-being⟧, and *persönlich* ⟦Tr. personal⟧ objective activity *as entpersönlich* ⟦Tr. impersonal⟧ reifying *co-operation*, appears in a twofold-ness, and in this, *Mit-gehalten-sein* exists not as a so-called "objectification of the subjective", but as the reified appearance of *zusammensubjektiv* ⟦Tr. intersubjective⟧ involvement (*Beziehung*)—to put it more appropriately the appearing *zuhandend* of *Mit-gehalten-sein* is in the part-taking of people in being-bound relations of co-operation.

Making the means of analysis Marx's perspective on "the world of the commodity", I have focused above on the way of being of "the historical world", and it seems to me that positioning oneself in this way of unfolding of the world we can, can we not, locate the so-called modern understanding of the world as a variant thereof? Here, however, extending the scope of discussion to this would be too premature—to proceed with this task it would be necessary on the one hand to carry out in advance appropriate analysis of the modern world picture, a picture having a close relationship with the map of epistemological thinking, and, on the other hand, in regard to the "historical world" too to grasp in advance the part-taking, *Zusammenwirken* ⟦Tr. in co-operation⟧ focusing along the lines of the actual form of *in-sein*. Accordingly, I set this task for a later opportunity, but, as far as it relates to what I said in the introductory remarks, and as far as it is possible to take into account that Heidegger's "Being-in-the-world" propounds an anti-thesis towards "the age of the world picture", I will add some superfluous remarks.[12]

---

11   It will seem repetitious but I will add once again that this twofold nature is a double nature containing the real twofold distinction of use value things as value things, of useful labour as abstract labour, and is certainly not the double nature of reflective tautology, of A as A, of B as B—in order, simply, to express that it is not an indeterminate thing.

12   ⟦Tr. The following two paragraphs operate as a quasi-footnote i.e. the discussion is parenthetical in nature. The text is indented, but it is not, however, marked off as a footnote proper⟧.

The determination which is *Zuhandensein*, to my eyes, has to be seen as a relation of individual self and object which still doesn't in the slightest leave the bounds of the modern relation of "subjective – objective", and *Besorgen* [[Tr. concern]] too in the end remains within the confines of an attitude of consciousness. *Zuhandendheit* [[Tr. Readiness-to-hand]] is certainly no doubt a form, but that in referring to equipmentality it is through the kind of role performed that a thing becomes equipment or becomes *nichts*, and that equipment existing in *its usefulness* is in regard to a person's *role*, that it unfolds as this kind of *Zuhandensein* only towards a specific historically-socially being-bound *Besorgen* and is not *an-sich-liegend* [[Tr. in-itself-being]], that the world appears as the objectivity of *zusammensubjektiv* [[Tr. co-subjective]] practical relations, and as the reification of people's *zusammenwirkend* [[Tr. co-operative]] relations which are not the simple subject-object relation, that through this the world exists in a social significance relations structure, (that despite it being possible to say that social significance, including *Sitte* [[Tr. customs]] and the like, is in the end a part of *Zuhandendheit*, that it is a reification of *zusammensubjektiv* relations, and that it differs in being-structure characteristics to *Zuhandensein* as far as this is so named by Heidegger); I believe that these matters ought to be understood for-themselves. Indeed, Heidegger points out that "human beings are essentially *Mitsein*", and he speaks of *Mitdasein*. But *Mitdasein* in his case is in the end no more than a relating of isomorphic, atomic other people and in what's more the attitude of *consciousness* which is *Fürsorge* [[Tr. care for]]—indeed not simply an intellectual attitude but not one which is a truly practical *Beziehen* [[Tr. relating]]—, for me I find this fact unsatisfactory. *Mitdasein* performs an always historically-socially *schicken* [[Tr. sent]] concrete character and in this already excludes other people from this character, and moreover it *mitdasein*s in the "practical" relation of tension where a person's way of being "restricts" the concrete way of being of other people. *Fürsorge* it seems to me is simply a flaccid variant of this. *Das Man*; this certainly exists as a form of "performance", but it certainly isn't a thing of the type that is a way of being which is a degenerated form of the existential; "the person exists" in the mode of being where the "at the risk of one's existence" battle for the Yasuda Auditorium or concrete useful labour simultaneously *gelten* [[Tr. holds]] as the act of someone, anyone, the act of the "occupying students" and the "riot policemen", as abstract human labour, and so the existential and *Man* are not to be sufficiently grasped as *alternativ*. In the case of *das Man* it is of course so, yet from the beginning even those things where the situation is called the way of being at the risk of one's existence or an "anticipatory resoluteness" are *historically-socially* being-bound, and they are not more than a form of the *zusammenwirkend* [[Tr. co-operative]] way of being of *Ich als Wir* [[Tr. I as we]].

To sum up, Heidegger's understanding of the world—even though it is of a stance which sublates the modern understanding of the world as a variation of thereof—is limited to one aspect of the historical world, to a projection brought forth from a plane which only contains twofold of the fourfold structure composite; for me, even if I put on hold my doubts regarding his philosophy of "being", I am still nonetheless led to have to say this.

In order to provide in addition my particular grounds for such "reckless remarks", I take it upon myself to re-form using direct terms things which I spoke of using figurative language such as status and role, stage, props, plot, the grammar of behaviour, performance etc., and moreover I take upon myself the task of a "philosophy of history" which discusses thematically the concrete way of being and the structure of relations of these, and with this I ask that I might be allowed for the moment to bring my meagre discussion to a close.

CHAPTER 4

The Historical Reification of the Natural World

When speaking of the view of nature of Marxism it would appear it seems that an unsaid understanding that "in the end, it is no more than a *mutatis mutandis* (with the addition of appropriate changes) ratification of the nineteenth century natural science view of the world" is held by one and all. It cannot be denied that the treatises of self-proclaimed – and proclaimed-by-others "Marxists" contribute to the circumstances of the spread of this kind of preconceived idea. The like of the officially licensed Marxist textbooks of so-and-so countries or the exegeses of such are certainly cut to fit a "dialectics" fallen into caricature—to fit a Procrustean bed—but in terms of the facts, there are things where it would perhaps be natural if the view of nature of Marxism gave an impression of a variant of the classical physics picture of nature.

To change direction, in the case of Marx-Engels, however, putting aside for the moment the relation with the dialectical natural philosophy of Hegel, theoretical construction occurs through strict opposition to precisely the so-called crude materialism (this is none other than the very archetype of natural science materialism) which swept the German reading world in the middle of the previous century.[1] Bearing this fact in mind, it ought to be difficult to regard Marx-Engels as having simply ratified the natural science world picture. In reality,

---

1 When I mention crude materialism (*Vulgärmaterialismus*) people are likely to think of Carl Vogt, Jakob Molleschott and Ludwig Büchner, and are likely to associate it with the confused saying that "the brain secretes thought, as the kidneys secrete urine ..." However, this notorious nonsense is a distortion made by somewhat irresponsible philosophers and critics, with Vogt, Molleschott and Büchner themselves having written in the following way.

Vogt: Ein jeder Naturforscher wird wohl, denke ich, bei einigermaßen folgerechtem Denken auf die Ansicht kommen, daß alle jene Fähigkeiten, die wir unter dem Namen der Seelentätigkeiten begreifen, nur Funktionen der Gehirnsubstanz sind, oder um mich einigermaßen grob hier auszudrücken, daß die Gedanken in demselben Verhältnis etwa zu dem Gehirn stehen, wie die Galle zu der Leber oder der Urin zu den Nieren. (*Physiologische Briefe für Gebildete aller Stände*, 1847, 2. Aufl., 1854, S. 323 f). [Every natural scientist with a reasonable degree of logical thinking will probably conclude that all those capabilities we see as activities of the soul, are mere functions of the brain's matter, or to put it more crudely, that thoughts relate to the brain in the same way as gall does to the liver or urine does to kidneys. (*Physiological Letters for Educated People of All Social Rankings*), 1847, second edition, 1854, p. 323 f.]

Molleschott: Der Vergleich ist unangreifbar, wenn man versteht, wohin Vogt den Vergleichspunkt verlege. Das Hirn ist zur Erzeugung des Gedankens ebenso unerläßlich wie die Leber zur Bereitung der Galle und die Niere zur Ausscheidung des Harns. Der Gedanke ist aber so wening eine Flüssigkeit, wie die Wärme oder der Schall. Der Gedanke ist eine Bewegung, eine Umsetzung der Hirnstoffs, die Gedankentätigkeit ist eine ebenso notwendige, ebenso

they accept the proposal of Feuerbach's which overtly advocated for an overcoming of the modern philosophy understanding of the world and a searching
towards a new philosophy world-view, and viewed, as well, from the position
of the details of the forming of their thought they existed under a problematics wherein they had to pioneeringly overcome the horizon of the scientistic
Objektivismus world picture (and the humanistic *Subjektivismus* which forms a
duality with it). The reason I wish to extol them is concerned with this matter,

---

unzertrennliche Eigenschaft der Gehirns, wie in allen Fällen die Kraft dem Stoff als inneres
unveräußerliches Merkmal innewohnt. (*Der Kreislauf des Lebens. Physiologische Antworten
auf Liebigs Chemische Briefe*, 1852, S. 284f.). ⟦When one comprehends where Vogt places his
point of comparison, the comparison becomes incontestable. For the production of thought,
the brain is just as essential as the liver is for the production of gall and the kidney is for
the excretion of urine. Yet thought is no more a liquid as are warmth or sound. Thought is
movement and the conversion of cerebral matter. Thought activity is as essential an attribute
of the brain and inseparable from the latter, as force is inherent in substance as an internal
inalienable attribute. (*The Cycle of Life. Physiological Answers to Liebig's Chemical Letters*, 1852,
p. 284f.).⟧

Büchner: Selbst bei genauester Betrachtung sind wir nicht im Stande, ein Analagon zwis-
chen der Gallen-und Urinsekretion und dem Vorgang, durch welchen der Gedanke im Gehirn
erzeugt wird, aufzufinden. ... der Gedanke, der Geist, die Seele dagegen ist nichts Materielles,
nicht selbst Stoff ... die Seelentätigkeit ist eine Funktion der Gehirnsubstanz. (Kraft und Stoff.
Empirisch-naturphilosophische Studien, 1855. *Schriften zum kleinbürgerlichen Materialismus
in Deutschland*, hrsg. v. D. Wittich, 2. Bd., S. 442f.). ⟦Even on very close inspection we are
unable to find an analogue between gall and urine secretion on the one hand and the process
by which a thought is created in the brain on the other ... the thought, the mind, the soul
by contrast are not matter, are not substances as such ... the activity of the soul is a function
of the brain's matter. (Force and Matter. Empirical and Natural-philosophical Studies, 1855.
Writing on Petty-bourgeois Materialism in Germany, published by D. Wittich, second volume,
p. 442f.).⟧

The assertions of crude materialism, as can be gathered from the matters of which we have
seen a part above, were in no way complete nonsense. After the German March Revolution
which ended in failure in 1848, the role which crude materialism performed in the enlight-
enment of the people, in the "German consciousness revolution", was certainly not minor,
and it was inseparable too from "petty bourgeois democratic" thought. For this reason, the
crude materialist trend of thought had a distorted relationship too with the German socialist
movement.

It isn't necessary, I imagine, to cite the series of letters and other texts concerning the situation of the confrontation with crude materialism being for Marx-Engels of great concern
both theoretically and practically. Here, however, it will, simply, be sufficient I think to call to
mind the fact that Marx wrote a thematic book, *Herr Vogt*, 1860—though this is not indeed
directly a critique of the philosophy of crude materialism—, and engaged in argument with
Carl Vogt, and the fact that one motivation for Engels undertaking to write the posthumous
Dialectics of Nature lay in a consciousness of the problem of the confrontation with crude
materialism. Marx-Engels do not deride crude materialism in the form of knowledge obtained
as second hand citation, they seriously confront the content and the matter under discussion.

but as long as we endeavour to keep to the original Marx-Engels, preconceived ideas slandering the schema of so-called scientific realism, I believe, have to be, in this case, radically revised.

It is from the outset difficult within the limited pages of this manuscript to expect an attempt at a systematic reconstruction of the Marxist view of nature, but for the moment I would like, whilst summarising the fundamental composition of Marx-Engels' understanding of nature, to put forward a pawn which ought to be given consideration.

1

Marx, as we can tell from his doctoral dissertation, *The Difference Between the Democritean and Epicurean Philosophy of Nature* (1841), had an unusual interest in the problem of nature. Engels, too, since his student days, showed, in a sense greater than Marx, interest in the natural sciences.

Here, however, omitting a tracing from the beginning of the paths of the two, let us begin from a focusing of our gaze upon the following passage from the first joint work of the two, *The Holy Family* (1845).

> There are three elements in Hegelian philosophy. That is to say, firstly, Spinoza's substance, secondly, Fichte's self-consciousness, thirdly, the Hegelian unity ... of the two, absolute spirit. The first element is nature separated off from human beings and disguised metaphysically, the second is spirit separated off from nature and disguised metaphysically, the third is the metaphysically disguised unity of the two, real human beings, the real human race.
> MEW, Bd. 2, S. 147

Marx-Engels relate the situation wherein the "metaphysically disguised unity" (*metaphysisch travestierte Einheit*) of nature and spirit in Hegel was, in the process of development of the Left Hegelians, in the process of development, that is to say, which is D. Strauss, B. Bauer and L. Feuerbach, first dissolved and then brought to a new unity, a situation which can locate their own philosophical activity and position.

> Strauss, from the position of Spinoza, and Bauer, from the position of Fichte, each consistently develops Hegel within the domain of theology ... With the appearance of Feuerbach, he, through a reduction of the metaphysical absolute spirit to 'the real human being standing on the founda-

tion of nature', for the first time completed, and critiqued Hegel standing in Hegel's position. (ibid., S. 147). The former opposition of spiritualism and materialism has been thoroughly fought out, and has been finally overcome by Feuerbach.

ibid., S. 99

Marx-Engels at this time, to the extent that they position Feuerbach in this way, and to the extent that they had attempted to take up his position, advocate "the truth that is different to both idealism and materialism, and which at the same time, moreover, unifies the two" (Marx *Economic and Philosophic Manuscripts* 1844), and "a position which sublates the opposition of idealism and realism" (Engels *On Carlyle* 1844). When it comes to the following year, however, they had, before others had done so, attained a perspective which overcomes Feuerbach, and had reached a point of constructing a unique materialism, and in this the motif of an in-itself-for-itself unity of human beings and nature is maintained.

Eighteenth century materialism, in place of the Christian God, simply absolutises nature and places it in opposition to human beings. In eighteenth century philosophy objectivity was opposed to subjectivity, nature to spirit, materialism to spiritualism. ... The eighteenth century didn't resolve the opposition of substance and subject, of nature and spirit, of necessity and freedom. The eighteenth century, however, put in opposition ... the two sides of these oppositions having developed them completely, and, as a result of this, it made necessary the sublation of these oppositions.

MEW, Bd. 1, S. 500, S. 551f.

Regarding the consciousness of the topic of a "unity of nature and human beings" set forth based on this understanding, it may receive the comment that "it is something which has existed since German romanticism and it does not warrant particularly special attention." However, in the case of the Left Hegelians, this motif is supported by the self-aware intention of overcoming the "horizon of modern knowledge", a horizon which takes as a precondition the schema of a dualistic separation between matter and spirit, between nature and human beings, and, I think, it conceals things which ought not to be looked at hostilely.

Entering this century,[2] in an age when the horizon itself of modern philosophy came to be critically investigated, that Martin Buber, who took up a

---

2 ⟦Tr. i.e. The twentieth century⟧.

unifying grasping of "I and thou", and of "I and it", as his focus, and Karl Löwith, who took up a unifying arrangement of the "with-world (*Mit Welt*)", the "environment world (*Umwelt*)", and "human beings", highly evaluate the pioneering work of Feuerbach is not without justification, and Feuerbach's theory of "I – thou" is backed by a consciousness of the issue of a "sublation of existing philosophy in general."

"The completion of modern philosophy is Hegelian philosophy. For that reason"—says Feuerbach—"the historical inevitability and justification of a new philosophy joins, for the most part, with critique of Hegel" (*Grundsätze der Philosophie der Zukunft* [[*Principles of the Philosophy of the Future*]], 1843, §19). At the same time as grasping that "the beginning of Cartesian philosophy, that is to say, the abstraction of sensuousness and matter, is the beginning of modern speculative philosophy" (ibid., §10), Feuerbach locates Hegelian philosophy as its completion, and he was the first to hold to the motif of an overcoming of this modern philosophy itself. In this regard, Bauer was the same (vgl. B. Bauer: Charakteristik Ludwig Feuerbachs. *Wigand's Vierteljahrsschrift*, 1845, 3. Bd).

Marx-Engels, whilst inheriting from Feuerbach and Bauer, their senior Left Hegelians, a consciousness of the issue of a true unity of nature and human beings, respond to it through a unique theoretical composition, and this was the reason why they open up a horizon of a new view of nature – view of human beings, and consequently of a new world-view. We see a rough sketch of this in *The German Ideology* (1845–1846), their second joint work.

"Feuerbach"—they write, critiquing the older thinker—"doesn't see at all the sensory world surrounding him as not a constantly self-identifying thing existing directly and unmediatedly from the eternal past but as being the product of industry and the situation of society." The natural world is certainly not a self-existing substance object world, of a type only given to a "higher philosophical insight which perceives the 'true essence' of things", or of a type "disclosed only to the eye of the physicist and the chemist", "even the objects of the simplest 'sense certainty,'" which Feuerbach favours, "are only given to him through social development, industry and commercial intercourse."

> In our view which grasps things focused along the lines of how things really are and how they occurred if profound philosophical problems dissolve into empirical facts. For example, the important problem (or, even, to put it in the manner of Bruno Bauer 'in the opposition between nature and history'—just as if these are two 'things' mutually separated, as if human beings don't necessarily always have before them an *historical nature* and a *natural history*) of the relation between human beings and

nature ... that which is the celebrated 'unity of human beings and nature', is something which existed in the place of industry from olden times, and if we have insight into the fact that it has existed from olden times in different forms in each age according to the degree of development of industry, the problem naturally melts away.[3]

What is being put forward here is not in any way simply that even the so-called natural world is a product changed through human activity.

No matter at what stage in history, a certain material result, the totality of the forces of production, and a relation created historically towards nature and mutually between individuals are to be seen. This is something which is passed on from the preceding generation to each generation, but although indeed it is in one aspect changed by the new generation, in another aspect it designates the particular life conditions of the generation in question, and endows a particular development on this generation and a special characteristic, and in this way in the same way that human beings make their environment, the environment makes human beings.

Fixing their gaze on such an "historical" way of being of human being, Marx-Engels re-grasp the world (Kawade Ausg., S. 16 ff., S. 50 ff.).

In this way of being, a way of being which ought to be called "being-in-history", the relation of human beings to the naturally given is not, primarily, the *theoretisch* ⟦Tr. theoretical⟧ relation of object perception, it is a *pragmatisch – praktisch* ⟦Tr. pragmatic – practical⟧ involvement rooted in interest in material life, and also as a result, relation with others, starting with the thou, is not the *static Anerkennung* ⟦Tr. recognition⟧ of primarily recognition as other selves, it is the *persona* relation arranged in terms of role, a division of labour co-operation in the place of material life.—This towards nature and between individuals act-of-relation (*Verhalten – Verhältnis*); although in-itself existing even in animals, "for an animal its relations with other things do not exist as relations", "an animal doesn't for-itself have a 'relation' with anything at all, having from the beginning no relation" (ibid., S. 28), with the existing for-itself of the towards-nature – intersubjective relations occurring only in human beings.—That materialist history, whilst positioning in its outlook the spiritual-cultural dimension as "superstructure", establishes, provisionally, its foundational perspective in the place of material production and exchange,

---

3 ⟦Italics by Hiromatsu⟧.

means simply that it views the foundations of the towards-nature – intersubjective relations of human beings from this angle.

Through taking a stance within this outlook Marx-Engels ascertain in a real – concrete (con-cret = together with – mutually, *konkret* = *zusammengewachsen* ⟦Tr. concrete = joined⟧) form towards-nature relations and interhuman relations, which in preceding philosophy had from the start been made items of discussion as abstracts, and without separating human beings and nature off dualistically, they re-grasp them precisely along the lines of their dynamic arrangement (*Gliederung* ⟦Tr. structuring, organisation, formation⟧) structure.[4]

Here, sublating the dualistic separation of matter and spirit since Descartes, the cutting off from each other of nature and human beings, both ontologically and epistemologically a horizon of new understanding opens out regarding "nature" as environment-world (*umweltlich*), environment-world to the extent that it can be objectified anew as a branch moment of the world arrangement, and the project of a "new view of nature" came to be able to be presented.

2

Before we take up the issue of the view of nature of Marx and of Engels, we need to briefly look at the stance which is the understanding of the "historicisation of nature" and also that which is the "naturalisation of history".

---

4 From the text of Marx-Engels from the section quoted in the body of this paper, it is clear I think that they attempt to grasp being-in-the-world in extremely concrete form, and that they place ontological significance on practical *Bezug* ⟦Tr. relation to; drawing to⟧ in the place of the activity of production.

   Incidentally, when compared to the foundational perspective of materialist history, even in the view of Karl Löwith, who argues that in Heidegger's "being-in-the-world" *Ansatz* ⟦Tr. approach⟧, both the environment-world and the with-world (*Mitwelt*) are at best only determined *privativ* ⟦Tr. individually⟧, who replaced them with the arrangement of *das Selbst-mit-Andern-in-der-Welt-sein* ⟦Tr. Being-with-others-in-the-world⟧, and who determined *Verhältnis* ⟦Tr. relations⟧ with a focus along the lines of a *personhaft Korreflexivität* ⟦Tr. personal co-reflexivity⟧ (vgl. *Das Individuum in der Rolle des Mitmenschen* ⟦Tr. ref. *The Individual in the Role of With-Humans*⟧, 1928, S.48, S.77, etc)., it has to be judged, I think, that Heidegger's being-in-the-world not only remains abstract, but that its ontological scope is limited.

   Marx-Engels determine the concepts of "human existence", "consciousness" and "personhood" in regard to "being-in-history", but in this paper I will omit the task of examining this. In regard to this matter, I would like to have you refer to the original text section of the Kawade Shobō Shinsha version of 『ドイツ・イデオロギー』 ⟦*The German ideology*⟧ S.25, S.28, S.120, S.128 ff. etc.

The real, sensual natural world

is the product of industry and the social conditions ... and in the sense that it is moreover an historical product it is the result (*Resultat*) of the activity of the complete succession of the generations. ... This activity, the sensual labour and creation (*shaffen*) proceeding one after the other, this production, is the very foundation (*Grundlage*) of the entire sensual world existing in reality. ... Of course, in this case, the priority (*Priorität*) of external nature remains, and it does not apply to the first human beings who appear for the first time in history. However, this distinguishing only has meaning to the extent that we consider human beings and nature as completely separate things, and this nature which precedes human history, ... although it may possibly exist on the two or three coral islands which have just appeared off the coast of Australia, is something which doesn't exist anywhere any more.

The thesis here, made in *The German Ideology*, might perhaps, to those captive to preconceived ideas, appear "non-materialist." In fact, such as a certain authority in East Germany, treats this passage as if to say that it is going too far. We have no intention of further emphasising the fact itself of change to the natural world through the activity of human beings, but we ought to verify the circumstances of the fact that the thesis here is certainly not a "momentary going too far", and the fact that this thesis carries an important significance for the logical composition of Marxism;[5] so let us with this in mind quote from texts from Marx and Engels' later period.

---

5 Although in the end it has been censured as "heresy" by the "orthodox school", and has recently been subjected to covert attack, in East Germany as well at a certain time in the late 1960s the following claim appeared:—on the occasion of the restoration of Marx-Engels' incomplete manuscript, *The German Ideology*, with the removal of the "forgery acts" of the Stalinist era it was openly declared, reliant on this incomplete manuscript—: "It can't be overlooked that most description (in particular starting from Plekhanov) in Marxist philosophy has been influenced by Spinozism. ... That Marx rejected making the Spinozian substance, that is to say 'nature separated off from human beings and re-formed metaphysically', the starting point for philosophy, is definite. ... In the same way that human beings without nature are 'non-being', nature too, in a form separated off from human beings, is for human beings no more than an abstraction. Human beings ... only know things to the extent that they become practical and theoretical objects for themselves. For example, atoms certainly existed in-themselves before they became the object of philosophical thought, from long before they became the object of chemistry, physics and industry. For human beings, however, in coming to be able to make atoms their own object atoms came to exist for the first time. Regarding the being-in-itself (*An-sich-sein*) of an object, in principle nothing can be said before the

Both the natural sciences and philosophy have previously completely ignored the influence the activity of human beings has on thought. They exclusively only know nature in the one case and thought in the other case. But, that which forms the most essential and most direct foundation of human thought, is not simply nature itself, it is the *changes to nature made by human beings*. And, in accordance with the extent to which human beings have acquired ways of changing nature, human intelligence has developed in proportion with this. For this reason, Draper-style[6] naturalistic historicism, that is to say regarding things as if nature exclusively has an effect on human beings, and that natural conditions have everywhere exclusively conditioned the historical development of human beings, is one-sided. It forgets the fact that human beings too exert a reaction on nature, and that they change nature ... and are making new life conditions. Amongst the 'nature' of Germany from the age of the migration of the Germanic tribes there is virtually none which

---

object in question becomes an object for us (*Gegenstand für uns*) through the practical and theoretical activity of we human beings". In existing dialectical materialism, the situation is such that an object is exclusively "grasped only in its object-thingness or its insight form and is not grasped as human activity – practice", in other words, they have ended up falling into the error which Marx seems to attack in *The Theses on Feuerbach*. And, for that reason, in dialectical materialism the epistemological structure of the historical – social restriction of cognition remains unknown. With their existing "systems", dialectical materialism and historical materialism cannot be truly unified. In such as existing dialectical materialism which is described as the fundamental relation between "matter and consciousness" and a universal law of nature in general, human practice doesn't occupy the position of a central category. However, only through making the practical involvement of human beings with the natural – social environment-world—through making this fundamental viewpoint of materialist history—a starting point is systemic integrity guaranteed for the first time, etc. (Helmut Seidel: Vom praktischen und theoretischen Verhältnis der Menschen zur Wirklichkeit *DZfPh*, Heft 10, 1966).

This argument of Seidel's was not necessarily one in isolation but was one which swam with the tide of what, at the time, might be called the "new wave of the East German philosophical world." In fact, in 1967, riding this "new wave", East Germany's own *Marxist Philosophy – a Course* was published, and the centrality of this position was such that for a time this publication occupied the position of the "mainstream" and "state-authorised course"— it was only in publication for a short period, until three years later under pressure from the Soviet camp (?) it was deemed "Use Ended" and a return was made to a "translated version" of a Soviet produced course. We will hold in reserve any criticism of Seidel's position, rather it is the case that as a piece of corroborating evidence I have deliberately cited a long section from this East German manuscript to corroborate that my argument in this essay is certainly not outlandish—that it is a gestalt which naturally floats in to view to the extent that one faithfully reads Marx-Engels' texts having relinquished the filter of "Russian Marxism".

6 [Tr. John William Draper]

remains today as it was. The land, climate, vegetation, fauna, and in addition human beings themselves have changed endlessly, and moreover, all these changes are changes through the activity of human beings, and during this time changes which have occurred in nature in Germany without the involvement of human beings are insignificant.

MEW, Bd. 20, S. 498 f.

Engels makes the same point regarding "Mesopotamia – Greece, and the countries of Asia Minor" (vgl. ibid., S. 453), and this kind of understanding is something which determines not only his view of nature – view of society, it also determines his theory of the future society (vgl. ibid., S. 276 ff.).

In this way of thinking, isn't it the case, however, that that which is "nature" ends up in the case of that on the Earth being limited to the surface of the Earth, and the nature of the Universe being omitted? If that is the case, doesn't the scope of the unity of human beings and nature fail to reach "true nature?" Putting aside for the moment these possible doubts, we can for us, I think, verify at least the point that the passage from *The German Ideology* quoted a moment ago is certainly not a "momentary going too far", and the point that it is at least a consistent assertion made by Engels.

Here, people might perhaps think of a certain passage from Heidegger's *Letter on Humanism*. "The essence of materialism isn't in the assertion that everything is no more than matter, rather it is in the metaphysical determination that all beings appear as the *Material* of labour" (*Über den Humanismus* 1947, S. 27) etc.—Certainly in the *Economic and Philosophic Manuscripts* the early Marx uses the form of expression of "nature, ... that is to say, the sensuous external world ... is the material (*Stoff*) on which his ⟦Tr. the worker's⟧ labour is realised" (MEW, Ergänzungsband, 1. Teil, S. 512); however, he considers at this time as well that "nature is the inorganic body of human beings (*der unorganische Leib des Menschen*)" (ibid., S. 516), and argues that "the practical production of the objective world, the very manufacturing of inorganic nature, is the displaying of them as the fruit of human beings as conscious, species beings. ... An animal produces only itself, whilst *human beings reproduce the whole of nature*" (ibid., S. 517). In Marx, nature is not simply the material of labour, external to the subject. Even in his early period, he deals with the unity of human beings and nature, in a form of in-itself-for-itself (*an und für sich*), of nature as the inorganic body of human beings, and so the Heideggerian understanding is in the end not appropriate.

From the above we need to place in mind again the *Grundverfassung*[7] that the above-mentioned thesis that though "nature", in its historical reality it is

---

7 ⟦Tr. *Grundverfassung* = foundational disposition; grounding disposition⟧

already "human-made", and the thinking that determines nature to be the inorganic body of human beings (incidentally, in *Outlines of the Critique of Political Economy* too, a later work, Marx speaks of nature as the inorganic subject of labour or its inorganic conditions),—leaving to a later stage whether or not these consider that which is the natural world only on the scale of the surface of the Earth—-, and that for Marx-Engels they are, first and foremost, attempting to grasp the "natural world" in the form of an in-itself-for-itself unity with the historical lives of the human race. When we do so, the mediating circle of the unity I speak of, as looked at in the previous item of discussion, is none other than the place of production of material life, the place of towards-nature – intersubjective practical co-operation.

Comparing things to this, we can understand Engels' "notorious" thesis involving natural things themselves existing in-themselves, involving the thing itself. Taking the criticism by Hegel of Kant's "thing-in-itself" into account—as is well known, this is symbolised by the phrase "an abstraction from all for-other existence" (*eine Abstraktion von allem Für-anders-sein*)—Engels too was aware that Kant's "thing-in-itself" involves *homo noumenon* (vgl. MEW, Bd. 20, S.508), but for the moment, in regard to the natural thing, he puts forward his view in the following way.

> Decisively important having rebutted this view is that to the degree possible from the position of idealism Hegel has already put forward his view. The materialist points Feuerbach added to this are clever rather than profound.' 'The most appropriate rebuttal to this kind of philosophical delusion is practice, is, that is to say, experiment and industry. We create a certain natural phenomenon ourselves, and if we are able to generate it from its conditions, then Kant's unknowable 'thing-in-itself' is finished. The various chemical substances made inside the bodies of fauna and flora (for example, pigment alizarin), were, until organic chemistry came to produce such, that kind of Kant's 'thing-in-itself'. When organic chemistry came to produce them this 'thing-in-itself' became *Ding für uns* etc etc..
>
>   MEW, Bd.21, S. 276

There is surely room for differences of opinion in regard to what extent this argument is valid as an epistemological critique of Kant's thing-in-itself, and it is surely not the case that Engels himself thought that in regard to the point that if a thing comes to be able to be produced artificially *Ding an sich* changes into *Ding für uns*, that matters are herein complete epistemologically. He thinks that "matter itself *als solche* [[Tr. as such]] is the creation of pure thought, a pure abstraction. ... Matter itself is not something which exists sensually. When the natural sciences intend to search for elemental matter itself, ... what the natural sciences are aiming at is the same as striving to discover ... fruit itself, rather than cherries or apples" (MEW, Bd. 20, S. 519), and for him, he says that "matter itself" in this way doesn't exist, locating it as simply *Ding für uns*. Here, "thing for us", however, is not in the dimension of simply "known thing", it means *Da-und Sosein*[8] discovered through the historical practice of human beings (fundamentally the "activity of production"), and discovering, what's more, does not mean material objective creation or alteration itself, it is the revealing of *an und für sich werden = bei sich sein*.[9]

For this reason, the doubt that isn't nature actually formed historically "limited to the environment world on the surface of the Earth?" is able to be dismissed, and "nature" in which human beings have "being-in" in intersubjective, co-operative objective activity (*zusammenwirkende gegenständliche Tätigkeit*), to the extent that it is shown historically, comes to be able to extend to the so-called scale of the Universe (see my 『世界の共同主観的存在構造』 [*The Intersubjective Being-Structure of the World*] Part I, Chapter 3).

Marx-Engels, to the extent that so-called social – cultural forms appear through reification (*versachlichen*), proceed to tackle the naturalisation of history together with the historicisation of nature, and as a whole this world is not indeed the Heideggerian style *Zuhandensein*, it is an historically mediated common lifeworld (*Mit-lebenswelt*). Marx-Engels, fundamentally, view "nature" in this form.

3

Marx-Engels haven't written down their view of nature for us in a systematic form. Promising a systematic exposition of the "dialectic of nature" Engels spent twenty years on such, but in the end such was not completed. Even so, based on their "notes" and incomplete manuscripts we can draw a rough sketch, and drawing on the gist of what they have to say a continuing and developing of what they say is not altogether out of the question.

In doing this, important texts for our enterprise are the chapters concerned with natural philosophy in *Anti-Dühring*, a serialised work written from 1876 into the following year, and the incomplete work *Dialectics of Nature*, written

---

8 [Tr. *Da-und Sosein* = Being there and as it is]
9 [Tr. *an und für sich werden* = becoming in-itself and for-itself; *bei sich sein* = being at home with oneself]

over the more than ten years between 1873 and 1886. Incidentally, even though the first of these was published several times during Engels' lifetime in a one volume form, because of the principle that "as this book is a book of debate, when my adversary is unable to make corrections, I too for my part am obliged to make no corrections whatsoever" (Preface to the Second Edition), the relevant chapters have not been revised and corrected. However, there are signs that a certain change occurred in the thinking of Engels himself regarding several important theses contained in this work with the famous "three laws of dialectics" first among these. For this reason, hasty conclusion that the propositions of this work of debate are Engels' final thought is not to be permitted. Here, what comes into focus is the parts of the incomplete *Dialectics of Nature* written after *Anti-Dühring*. However, this incomplete work is not originally a unified sequence, with striking differences being recognised between older layers and newer layers in, naturally, structure, but also in intellectual level. Regrettably, however, the existing edition, which follows the *re-edited* form of the Stalin era, takes, in a form which ignores differences between older and newer layers in the handwritten manuscript, a form of forcibly re-composing parts which are notes and "systematising" the text, and as a result it is highly problematic textually speaking. This being the case, in order to consider it carefully textual criticism of the unfinished manuscript *Dialectics of Nature* is first required. Fortunately, the fundamental materials for doing that have already been provided, with a "Restored Original Edition" expected to be put together in our country in the near future, but here it should be sufficient to separate out the *Grundverfassung*[10] coming from the edges.

To put it simply, Engels—and in this regard Marx is of course the same— places a "dialectical" view of nature in opposition to the view of nature of *mechanistic* materialism. It goes without saying that, as far as the knowledge content which was their material, they didn't leave the bounds of the natural science of the mid-nineteenth century, but Engels reads a shift "from mechanism to dialectics" in the changing of these natural sciences. That is to say, he perceives – points out the fact that pressured by a deepening in the research of the natural sciences themselves, they are, whilst sublating the mechanistic conceptual composition, moving in the direction of accepting dialectics in-itself (*an sich*). He illustratively picks out dialectical structure in nature as it appeared, in this kind of context, in the knowledge of the natural sciences. However, for us, and firstly, we can seek the basic composition of his view of nature in the gaze of contrast of "mechanistic vs dialectical".

---

10   ⟦Tr. *Grundverfassung* = basic constitution; basic disposition⟧

It goes without saying that in critiquing the mechanistic view of nature, and in placing the dialectic in opposition to it, Engels has the precedent of Hegel. However, it's not such that the matter is settled by converting Hegel's philosophy of nature in terms of materialism. By the second half of the nineteenth century the philosophy of nature, regarded as a particularly "weak loop" in Hegel's system of philosophy, was too out of date in terms of material, and also, in another regard, it was necessary to respond to the critique directed towards Hegel's dialectic itself by crude materialists. For Engels, the manipulation of borrowing natural science *materialism* to critique Hegel's idealism, and borrowing Hegel's *dialectic* to critique the mechanism of the natural sciences, couldn't possibly suffice. This is why, for him, researching the natural sciences of the time from within, he critiqued the philosophical world-view and the conceptual composition which the natural sciences took in-itself as precondition, and this is why through this he set himself the task of constructing his own system of a theory of science and also the task of describing systematically his own view of nature. This enterprise of systematisation, rather than having ended without being finished, met with inevitable failure, but the viewpoint and arguments of critique directed towards the mechanistic world-understanding of the natural sciences are left for us in considerably vivid form.

Engels, following the usage of Hegel, calls non-dialectical thinking of the type which includes mechanism, as well, "metaphysical", and, for example, he writes in the following way.

The natural sciences start at the earliest in the second half of the fifteenth century. ... Separating nature into its individual parts, dividing the various natural processes and natural objects into particular groups, investigating the internal structure of living things in regard to the multifarious anatomical forms; these are the fundamental conditions for the great progress made, with nature in mind, during the recent 400 years. However, this has also left us the habit of grasping natural things and natural processes as disconnected individual parts, separated off from greater holistic connections, and consequently, the habit of grasping things as stationary things rather than moving things, as essentially fixed, constant things rather than essentially changing things, as dead things rather than living things. Then, carried out by Bacon and Locke and others, this way of thinking was transferred from the natural sciences into philosophy, where it produced in the recent several centuries a peculiar narrowness i.e. a metaphysical way of thought.

MEW, Bd. 20, S. 20

—Engels also directs critique at empirical positivism, but our issue for the time being concerns the removal of "the narrow way of thought the natural sciences inherited from English empiricism and which was peculiar to such" (ibid., S. 14), "the metaphysics of the seventeenth, eighteenth century—in England Bacon and Locke, in Germany Wolff" (ibid., S. 333), of this "metaphysical" world-view, view of being, and form of thinking.

"The metaphysical way of thinking captured by individual things forgets the connections between them, captured by their being forgets their generation – extinguishment, captured by stillness forgets movement, doesn't see the wood for the trees". Metaphysics determines in its wisdom things and the concepts which correspond to them in the aspect of being "individual and disconnected", "unrelated to other things", "fixed and immovable".

> The metaphysician thinks of things in the aspect of unmediated oppositions. His language is 'yea yea; nay nay: for whatsoever is more than these cometh of evil' [Mathew 5:37]. For him, it is whether a thing exists or doesn't exist. Similarly, a thing cannot be itself and simultaneously another thing. Affirmative = positive things and negative things mutually exclude each other absolutely. For the metaphysician, cause and effect, once again, are immovable terms. This way of thinking is the so-called commonsense way of thinking and seems at first glance to be plausible, but ... beyond certain limits it falls into insoluble self-contradiction.
>
> ibid. S. 21

It is the case that here dialectics is placed in opposition to metaphysics, but within simply the quoted material above Engels own view of being should indirectly come into view. He sees all things synchronically in the form of interpenetration and diachronically in the form of generation and flux. This, from the first, cannot be a simple return to an ancient view of nature. For him, he critiques the modern science style of a view of being, that is to say, the view which grasps the natural world as a mechanistic composite of the immutable elements of things fixed as substances, and, according to him, the natural world is "not a composite of *things* but a composite of *processes*" (MEW, Bd. 21, S. 293), nature "does not *exist* it *becomes*" (vgl. MEW, Bd. 20, S. 317). "What gave a narrow, metaphysical characteristic to the modern theoretical natural sciences" is the conceptual composition of "exclusive, bipolar oppositions, fixed divisions, [and] fixed classifications". "Such oppositions and distinctions, however, only have relative validity, and, on the contrary, it is the awareness that the immovability and absolute validity such oppositions and distinctions are regarded as having are things which have been brought into nature for the first time through our reflection, it is this awareness which forms the very core of the dialectical view of nature" (ibid., S. 14).—As is seen in this sentence Engels certainly hasn't adopted a simple copy theory, rather he points out that for him the conceptual composition which thinks that science is a copy conceptualisation of the reality of objective objects is in fact "something brought into nature through the reflection of we the aware side", and he puts in place of it the dialectical understanding of being.

Engels' view of nature presented here sees, without rendering space-time – matter autonomous as absolute existents, the unity which is moving matter or matter movement as fundamental (*archē* [[Tr. foundational]]) existent, and puts, at its core, in place of the sequence schema of cause – effect, the category of interaction, and, though it is an unfinished rough sketch, it has dazzling elements, with his dismissal of deterministic views of laws and re-grasping of unfolding based on a new concept of laws the first among these—I no longer have space for exposition of his views, so I would be obliged if I could have you view the appropriate parts of my 『マルクス主義の地平』 [[*The Horizon of Marxism*]] and 『マルクス主義の理路』 [[*The Logic of Marxism*]].[11]

I, from the outset, am not one to firmly believe uncritically – unconditionally the explanations of Marx-Engels. And, what's more, I have no intention of insisting that Engels earns first runs in regard to knowledge of this century[12] of the like brought about by relativity theory and quantum mechanics. But, I think the composition of the dialectical view of nature he placed in opposition to the modern science view of nature, in the present day when the bottleneck of the modern science conceptual configuration has been exposed to all, merits being re-composed in a way supplementary to that whole picture.

I will, however, leave this task, together with ontological – epistemological investigation of the understanding which sees a "co-operatively historicised nature, and, an intersubjectively naturalised history", to another, due and proper place, and here I must for the time being put down this pen of these

---

11   In Russian Marxism, that "Marxism although indeed not a fatalism is a type of determinism", has been the "fixed opinion" since Plekhanov and Bukharin. However, Engels severely criticises the "determinism (*Determinismus*) which was transferred from French materialism into the natural sciences, and which attempts to decide matters by simply denying contingency"; he severely criticises, in other words, this "scientific determinism".—Engels aims at dialectically re-determining the concepts of contingency – necessity, and he plans to go beyond the horizon itself of a similar opposition between determinism and nondeterminism, and for him, he had in mind a new concept of laws corresponding to this. (Please refer to pp. 34–35 and following of this book). This is without a doubt none other than something inseparable as well from the composition of the theory of reification.

12   [[Tr. The twentieth century]].

Vorbemerkungen,[13] rather than of an "Introduction", having attempted giving a jolt to existing ideas of a "crude Marxist" bent and having verified the location of the points of discussion.

---

13   ⟦Tr. *Vorbemerkungen* = introductory remarks⟧

CHAPTER 5

Philosophy in Marx

Today I'm presenting my views under the title of "What was 'philosophy' for Marx"? But, of course, it's not that the definition of "philosophy" is at issue. Re-grasping in a self-aware manner the grounding disposition of thought itself of Marxism at what might be called a meta-level; this is the topic.

I have emphasised for some time that Marxism is essentially something which goes beyond the horizon of the modern ideology, and, from that stand-point, at the same time as critiquing the so-called Russian-Marxist style "scientistic Marxism", I have critiqued as well the so-called Western Marxist style "humanist Marxism". Both scientistic *Objektivismus* and humanist *Subjektivismus* are things which precisely stand within the horizon of the modern ideology, and this is because subjectivism and objectivism are none other than a complementary polarity within the horizon of modern philosophy. However, it's not my intention to rehash this discussion itself today.

Incidentally, it's said that, in recent times, in the accelerating movement away from Marx amongst the young – students, yourselves, that that is not simply that you shut yourselves away inside a conservative shell within the system, but rather that people who are convinced they have gone beyond Marxism, saying, "Marxism is out of date", are on the increase. If you have really overcome Marxism then I am more than willing to give you my deep admiration, and I'd like *you* to instruct *me* (laughter). However, as far as I see it, there is, somehow, far too much superficial discussion.

Marxism is, of course, not a completed system, and, what's more, amongst the theses put forward by Marx or by Engels there are indeed bound to be not a few which require re-examination. Marxism is not a rigidified system of dogma, and so we have to carry out, with re-examination, a constant creative unfolding of it.—Yet, in the existing state of self-called – called-by-others "Marxism" there are elements which make one avert one's eyes, and the progression too of the phenomenon of what is called the movement away from Marx is not without cause. I'm not saying, in any way, that any and everything should be seen as the result of existing Marxism being in deviation from the thought of Marx himself. Nor, again, do I say the like of that it is sufficient if we adhere dogmatically to the words left to us by Marx-Engels. Nevertheless, however, when it comes to the level of the principles of thought of Marx himself, I don't think that we are yet in a situation where, in our present-day historical stage, we can all that easily and straightforwardly say "it's out of date" or "it's become an object for overcoming" (applause).

My preamble has become a little long. Today, however, I would like to talk about why I understand things in this manner, with a focusing along the lines of the dimension of Marx's "philosophy", wherein his stance of thought ought to be revealed directly.

The stance of Marx's philosophy: in response to my saying this the hasty may attempt to bring matters to a close with the dialectic or materialism. However, today's talk is about what might be called the *Grundverfassung*,[1] a more fundamental stance.

Amongst philosophers, whilst there are those who discuss thematically what to begin with philosophy is, in the manner of Aristotle, Hegel, or Husserl, in the case of Marx, unfortunately, he doesn't discuss directly what philosophy is. However, you who have read Marx's texts are likely to think here of those famous words in *Introduction to a Contribution to the Critique of Hegel's Philosophy of Right*.

Namely: "The head [*Kopf*] of human emancipation is philosophy, the heart [*Herz*] of human emancipation is the proletariat". After these words Marx continues with: "Without sublating (*Aufheben*) the proletariat philosophy cannot make itself a reality, and without making philosophy a reality the proletariat cannot *Aufheben* itself".

From this we can see that Marx thought that the self-realisation of philosophy and the self-sublation of the proletariat are inseparable. With this way of putting things alone things are too abstract; preceding this conclusion Marx unfolds his discussion in the following way. Such is a two-edged criticism of on the one hand the practical party, that is to say, the party which turns its back on philosophy and solely asserts the "negation of philosophy" (*Negation der Philosophie*), and the philosophy party on the other hand, that is to say, the party which solely engages in philosophical critique of the current situation. Marx's critique of these two parties is, if we take the first of the two first, that even if one attempts to negate philosophy "philosophy cannot be *Aufheben*-ed without realising philosophy", and, if we take the second of the two, even if we attempt to realise philosophy "we cannot realise philosophy without *Aufheben*-ing it". What is asserted then is that, in Marx's thought at the time, the realisation of philosophy and the *Aufheben* of philosophy have to be carried out inseparably.

Marx wrote this *Introduction to a Contribution to the Critique of Hegel's Philosophy of Right* in his younger years, when he was twenty-five, and after this his thought underwent dramatic development. In addition, what is being called "philosophy" here carries a particular nuance, and so it is true that if one takes

---

1 ⟦Tr. grounding base; fundament⟧

the discussion as discussion of philosophy proper there will be something of a mismatch. Nonetheless, the attitude of Marx towards philosophy we have just had a glance at can be said to have the same frame as his attitude and stance towards philosophy thereafter. In terms of the frame his stance at this time continues through thereafter.

There is probably a tendency amongst you to pay particular attention to the fact that in this *Introduction* Marx asserts that philosophy has to be *Aufheben*-ed. And I think there would be a tendency to emphasise that Marx eventually "*Aufheben*-ed his being a *philosoph*er and became an *economi*st" (laughter). But is it the case that Marx really became, straightforwardly, an economist? In *Theories of Surplus-Value* he repeatedly states to the effect that economics has already been completed in Ricardo. What he wrote was *A Contribution to the Critique of Political Economy*, and the subtitle too to *Capital*, is, as you would know, "A Critique of Political Economy". Amongst Marx researchers are those who point out that "Marx didn't attempt to establish a system of economics, he *critiqued* economics", and that "Marx attempted to *Aufheben* economics". If this is the case, then this is likely to give rise to the issue of whether it is really permitted to speak of "Marxian economics"—speaking of modern economics vs Marxian economics—, but, in any case, the issue of whether Marx aimed, in the same way that he aimed at an *Aufheben* of philosophy, at an *Aufheben* of economics is no doubt an issue which can be considered head-on. Be that as it may, it is worth remembering the fact that Marx didn't label it a system of economics but only advocated a critique of economics. And, in fact, this concept of "critique" is an important concept in understanding Marx's philosophy, and especially in understanding his stance of thought.

I imagine that amongst you [there is a tendency] to recall here a famous sentence from once again *Introduction to a Contribution to the Critique of Hegel's Philosophy of Right*.

Namely, Marx's sentence: "The weapon of criticism cannot take the place of the criticism of weapons. Material *Gewalt* [[Tr. force]] must be overthrown by material *Gewalt* (a voice saying, "That's right!") But, as soon as it grips the masses theory too becomes a material *Gewalt*".

The concept of "critique": this is, from his earliest stages, an important concept for Marx, and, in actuality, it is none other than an important concept in the Hegelian camp, not only for the early Marx. This is so much so that one would even be permitted to say that in putting a unique content into the concept of "critique" Marx established a unique stance of thought. So, what is the unique content Marx gave to "critique", and what is the reason that that endows Marx's position "philosophically" with what kind of particular characteristics, and, further, how does that connect with his "critique of economics"?

To look at this, we need to consider the details of how Marx went beyond Hegel's philosophy, and in addition how he went beyond the philosophy of the Left Hegelians.

I won't go in to all that detailed a discussion here, in any event, but it goes without saying that, led by the *Critique of Pure Reason*, it is Kant's three critiques which brought forward "critique" as an important concept in philosophy, and in Hegel too "critique" is inherited as an important concept. I can have you understand this, I think, from the fact that the name of the bulletin of the Hegelians, published directly under the direction of Hegel, was *Jahrbücher für wissenschaftliche Kritik* (*Yearbook for Scientific Critique*). Of course, though the same "critique", the meaning is already different between Kant and Hegel, and when it comes to such as the Bruno Bauer faction of the Left Hegelians the meaning finally becomes different again. But, before we look at how Marx took it on, and how he forged it anew, let us first proceed from the prior matter of how "philosophy" was self-determined in Hegel himself.

Hegel determines "philosophy" from several vantage points but here I'll focus on just three.

Firstly, the fact that philosophy really shouldn't be philosophy/*Philosophie*, it should be *Wissenschaft*. Philos + sophia, as you know, is Greek and it means "wisdom-love", "love" of "wisdom", and according to Hegel it's no good just loving wisdom, wisdom has to be systematically established. It has to be *Wissenschaft* (i.e. systematic knowledge). The word *Wissenschaft* is a Germanic word equivalent to the Latin *scientia*. *Scientia* has a different nuance to "science" in the modern period, being, looked at in terms of its content, a theological system, and the *Wissenschaft* Hegel speaks of is not simply systematic knowledge, it is, as we might expect, also fundamentally connected to theology.

Secondly and accordingly, in terms of content – object philosophy is the same thing as religion. In other words, it takes the absolute = God as its object. However, according to Hegel, they differ in terms of religion grasping God in the form of a representation in contrast to philosophy understanding the absolute in concepts. To put things succinctly, Hegel determines that philosophy is something which has understood in the form of concepts the same content as religion.

Thirdly, the philosophical system is, essentially speaking, unable to subsume the future—because it is something which has confirmed the self-revelation – self-unfolding of the absolute. This is the reason Hegel likens philosophy to Minerva's owl, that is to say, Minerva's owl which finally takes flight having completely made sure of the proceeding of things.

This third point is greatly related to my later discussion and so I'll quote to a certain degree the words of Hegel himself.

"The task of philosophy lies in grasping conceptually things as they actually are. ... Philosophy is something which has captured the age in the form of thought. If philosophy thinks that it has gone beyond the present world it is as foolish as the individual who dreams of jumping beyond his or her own age". "To add a further comment regarding teaching us how the world should be, philosophy, in any case, arrives always too late to teach us such. Philosophy, insofar as it is thought about the world, appears for the first time after reality has completed its formative process and has finished completing itself, etc.".

Hegel states thus, saying, in short, that philosophy cannot anticipate the future, and cannot tell us how the world should be.

You will have more or less guessed, I think, what kind of dissatisfaction the members of the Left Hegelians had towards such a view of philosophy of Hegel's (Hegel's view regarding that which is philosophy), and in what kind of direction they critiqued it. I will omit a detailed introduction of such, but will provide here two points to the extent that they are connected to the *Aufheben* of philosophy spoken of by Marx.

The first point I would like to provide is that, and this is something asserted by Cieszkowski and Moses Hess, amongst the Left Hegelians, a move towards a philosophy of praxis, a philosophy of action, appeared. According to them, the fact that the scope of philosophy doesn't reach into the future is a limitation of philosophy itself, and we now have to *Aufheben* the philosophy itself which carried such a limitation. Just how then does that become possible? According to them, it is possible through a move from the position of *theoria* to praxis, to the position of practice. Practice: this is something which in its essence contains the future as well, and is something which mediates the past and the future. According to them, to Cieszkowski and Hess, in practice we have to *Aufheben* philosophy itself, philosophy which is a study of the past. In "practice" they are thinking of a particular type of socialist practice; practice is not simply a matter of moving the body. Accordingly, it now becomes necessary to theoretically ground this practice. In such a scene, they had come to fall into the somewhat strange situation of on the one hand speaking of the *Aufheben* of philosophy itself whilst on the other hand speaking of, as the *Wissenschaft* of practice, a philosophy of practice, a philosophy of action.

As I'm sure you have already realised, whilst inheriting their motif of the *Aufheben* of philosophy itself, Marx aims at breaking free of the type of dilemma-like situation into which they had fallen. However, there is one more point I would like to introduce in connection with Hegel's view of philosophy before I move my discussion on to this point.

The second point I would like to make reference to: it relates to Hegel's think-ing that "philosophy and religion are, in terms of content, the same thing", and it was the reason that in response to this Feuerbach and Bruno Bauer critique Hegel's philosophy simultaneously and inseparably with their critique of reli-gion. Feuerbach and Bauer re-grasped the determining in Hegel of philosophy as something which describes observationally the self-unfolding of absolute spirit = God, re-grasped this in the sense of God being in fact human being, in the sense of absolute spirit being in fact none other than the self-consciousness of human beings. Now, this means, in the case of Bauer, that that which Hegel presented as the self-unfolding process of absolute spirit is none other than the historical process of self-realisation of the self-consciousness of human beings. And, this self-realisation of self-consciousness is closely connected to and indi-visible with the concept of what Bauer calls "critique".

The situation is such that Bauer's concept of "critical criticism" ends up recast as Marx's concept of "critique", so I will insert a certain amount of com-ment on this here.

It is frequently said that Bruno Bauer re-formed Hegel's philosophy in close alignment to Fichte's philosophy, and this is likely to be because he re-grasped Hegel's absolute spirit as self-consciousness and persisted in the practical self-proposition of this self-consciousness. Incidentally, although he speaks of the unfolding of self-consciousness, it's not the case that everything is a self-aware process. In Hegelian terms, there is an in-itself process of unfolding, and this, in a certain kind of situation, becomes a for-itself – self-aware process. However, fundamentally, what drives this historical progression is what Bauer calls "criti-cism". At the ontological level, in Bauer's case, "critique" is none other than that which provides the power for the historical self-realisation, the self-unfolding, of self-consciousness. And, it's the case that that which makes critique, cri-tique, lies in its being self-aware – conscious activity, and according to Bauer, in this critique which is the movement of self-consciousness, the side of the considering subject and the side of the considered object are therein unified as one. The task of the unity of the subjective and the objective: this in Bauer is realised in the way of being of "critique". What's more, that critique is a for-itself re-grasping of an in-itself situation, and, in addition, this self-aware re-grasping is not simply a confirmation of an in-itself situation, it is a critiquing re-postulation, and so, if we focus along the lines of the structure of cognition critique, it is also a critiquing analysis which links to a type of ideology cri-tique. Well then,—how does Bauer link such "critique" and practice? Amongst Bauer's well-known phrases is "the terrorism of pure theory" (*Terrorismus der wahren Theorie*), and he is in this regard quite idealist, maintaining a viewpoint that it is philosophical critique which is the most superlatively practical.

For Marx, he *Aufheben*-s the two routes presented by his Left Hegelian seniors attempting to internally overcome the philosophy of their master Hegel, that is to say, the Hessian "philosophy of action" on the one hand, and the Bauerian "philosophy of critique" on the other. With, for the moment, internal critique of Hegel's philosophy of right as his axis, he *Aufheben*-ed these two routes in a unique and particular way, and established a unique stance.

When, in this way, I introduce the two routes which arose inside the Left Hegelians, you are likely to bring to mind once again here the double-edged critique Marx carries out in *Introduction to a Contribution to the Critique of Hegel's Philosophy of Right*, that is to say, the double-edged critique in regard to the two parties, in regard to, on the one hand, the practice school which emphasises the *negation* of philosophy, the *Aufheben* of philosophy, and, on the other hand, the critique school which emphasises the realisation of philosophy, the *Verwirklichung* [[Tr. realisation]] of philosophy. In fact, seen too from the fact that in regard to the parties Marx critiques in *Introduction to a Contribution to the Critique of Hegel's Philosophy of Right* the words "political parties in Germany today (*politische Partei im heutigen Deutschland*)" are used, he had a broader range in mind, with this expression not simply referring in any way to an opposition of internal strife which arose within the Left Hegelians. We mustn't forget this fact, but that Marx has in mind the two parties within the Left Hegelians is in the first place certain, and there is no mistake that his double-edged critique applies most directly to these two parties internal to the Left Hegelians.

As we saw earlier, Marx says: "The weapon of criticism cannot take the place of the criticism of weapons. Material *Gewalt* must be overthrown by material *Gewalt*. But, as soon as it grips the masses theory too becomes a material force (*Gewalt*)". Through joining in a mutually mediating way the revolutionary *practice* of the proletariat and theoretical *critique* in philosophy, he appropriately unified the demand on the one hand for an *Aufheben* of philosophy and the demand on the other hand for a realisation of philosophy. Although, whether the issue is finally resolved with Marx's statement of things at this time can't so easily be said. At the least, it is clear that points requiring theoretical arrangement, and points requiring concretisation, remained.

If we consider things further back, Marx writes in his dissertation, *The Difference Between the Democritean and Epicurean Philosophy of Nature*, under the strong influence of Bruno Bauer, in the following way.

"The practice of philosophy is in itself theoretical. Measuring in *ideas*, individual existences in their essence, the various particular realities; this is critique". Marx, in the period of the *Rhenish Newspaper*[2] too, at least at the begin-

---

2 [[Tr. *Rheinische Zeitung*]]

ning of such, developed, as one might expect, from a position close to Bauer like this, "critique" in the manner of: "without being misled by the judgement of experience ... provide the yardstick of the essence of internal ideas to the actual existence of things".

There's something here in terms of logical composition which requires attention. It concerns from where and how the criteria of "critique" are introduced. If a person is totally immersed, from head to toe, in experiential reality, even if she or he is able to confirm given reality she or he is not readily able to critique such. It would appear that there is no alternative to bringing in the measure of critique, what might be called the criteria of critique, from the "outside", as it were, in regard to the present situation. That Marx speaks of "ideas", and says that we mustn't be misled by the "judgement of experience", is to that extent understandable. However, just where are these ideas which are the criteria of critique to be obtained from? Completely unrelated to experiential reality, from where is it said that they arise, a priori as it were? Even though the ideas which ought to be the criteria of critique are not things obtained through a simple confirmation of the current situation but are things which have to be relatively independent of the current situation, they ought not, however, be things which completely transcend the current situation. In this regard, Hegel's saying that philosophy cannot go beyond its age, and that philosophy's arrival to be able to teach us how the world should be is always too late, is extremely important. It's not that in shouting that this is how the world should be there is no effect, but that, according to Hegel, the ideal – idea of how the world should be, or, again, oughtness, already remains within the bounds of a confirmation of reality. Of course, the confirmation of reality isn't confirmation of experiential reality as it is. To the extent that the rational is real, and the real is rational, does this mean that real = immediately the rational?

For Marx, although up until the period of the *Rhenish Newspaper* indications are to be seen that for the most part he understood matters in line with this position of Hegel's, he reached a point where he was placed in a position where it was no longer possible to leave things with such abstract language. Here, from where and how are the ideas which are the criteria of critique to be obtained? He has reached the point where a concrete propounding is now required of how the ideas obtained in this way are to be authorised.

For Marx, he heads in the direction of solving this major problem by locating matters in the real tendency of history. In this, if things had remained within the area of grasping that which is the direction of the unfolding of history as the process of realisation of the idea of "freedom" in the manner of Hegel, at best matters would only have become a kind of "historical idealism". In addition, if he had remained in the area of regarding "critical criticism" as the drive of history, he would have fallen into an idealist view of history which seeks the principle of history in self-consciousness. However, Marx went beyond such an Hegelian frame and came to finding the drive of the real unfolding of history, to finding the law-like nature of history, in a different direction.—That this process was not in any way a logically necessary straight path within the bounds of Hegelian thought and was a quite complicated process has been revealed through "positivistic" research regarding the process of thought formation of Marx. Here, however, I will omit discussion of this process of thought formation and will make do with presenting just the schema of the conclusion.

In *The German Ideology* Marx writes: "Communism is not a *situation* which ought to be created, and it is not an *ideal* in accordance with which reality ought to be rectified. What we call communism is real movement, real movement which *Aufheben*-s the current situation". In *The Communist Manifesto* he writes in the following way: "In understanding, *in theory*, the conditions of the proletarian movement, its path, its general results, the communist is in terms of ⟨consciousness – theory⟩ in advance of the remainder of the proletarian masses" [emphasis by Hiromatsu]. However, in the place of practice "the communist is not someone who advocates a special principle and who attempts to fit the proletarian movement into its mold, etc".—Here, consistently, a maintaining of a stance of *Engagement* ⟦Tr. French – engagement⟧ with the real proletarian movement can, I think, be easily recognised.

In relation to these propositions quoted just now from *The German Ideology* and *The Communist Manifesto* it can be seen that there was a slight difference in opinion from that time between Marx and Engels, and even if we put that aside, as Marx establishes after this a theory of *society* of communism – a theory of the *movement* of communism, and further, a theory of the *organisation* of the communist movement, these propositions would no longer be maintained in the form they were in. In that sense, this can't be said to be Marx's final thought.

These propositions, however, are permitted to be located as attempts at a specific answer from a position one step forward of *Introduction to a Contribution to the Critique of Hegel's Philosophy of Right* in regard to the double-sided problem of the type of dilemma the two parties which had arisen within the Left Hegelian movement had respectively fallen into, that is to say, on the one hand the problem of how to guarantee in reality the practice in question faced by the practice party i.e. the party which asserts the *Aufheben* of philosophy, and on the other hand the problem of how to guarantee the criteria of critique and make the weapon of critique a material force, faced by the critique party i.e. the party which asserts the realisation of philosophy.

Critically reacting to the "view of philosophy" or the "theory of philosophy" posed in order to attempt to overcome that of Hegel by the two parties, the practice party which aims at the *Aufheben* of philosophy and the critique party which aims at the realisation of philosophy, which had arisen within the Left Hegelians, Marx, in the end, can be said to have established the foundation for a stance of a sublating realisation = realising sublation of philosophy, positioning the "view of philosophy" or the "theory of philosophy" in the practical critique = critiquing practice of the proletariat which is the communist movement.

This way of putting things, however, is a matter of things being seen by a third person observer. It isn't known in detail how strongly conscious Marx was of it at the point in time *after Introduction to a Contribution to the Critique of Hegel's Philosophy of Right*. The motif of the *Aufheben* of philosophy of Marx himself seems, when looking at things focused along the lines of *The Holy Family*, published one year after *Introduction to a Contribution to the Critique of Hegel's Philosophy of Right*, to be something which is of a wider range.

In my talk today, things are such that my discussion is of the narrow frame of how Cieszkowski, Hess, Feuerbach and Bauer attempted to go beyond Hegel's view of philosophy or Hegel's theory of philosophy, and how Marx's dealing with such is related to this. However, Marx has an aspect which directly confronts Hegel's philosophy, without the middle term of their mediation. In addition, in my discussion of a little while ago things have taken the form of emphasising only the aspect where Hess and Bauer responded negatively to Hegel, but they are Hegelians to the end, and so they strive to carry on the positive side of Hegel. In this regard, Marx too is the same.

So, what points of Hegel's philosophy did Marx attempt to positively inherit, and where lies the reason that that critiquing inheritance was able to open up a unique, new dimension?

This is a large question, which can't easily be answered. At the same time, and on the other hand, I myself have attempted an answer, in my own way, poor though it may be, in several books ranging from 『マルクス主義の地平』 [*The Horizon of Marxism*] to 『弁証法の論理』 [*The Logic of the Dialectic*], and I will discuss things here focusing on one point.

Hegel, as Marx points out in *The Holy Family*, can be said to have unified in a unique way Spinozist substance-ism and Fichtean subject-ism.

The young Hegel from early on, stating that "Cartesian philosophy was something which expressed in the form of philosophy the universal and comprehensive dualism which had appeared in the modern culture of our northwestern Europe", pursued the *Aufheben* of this Cartesian, modern dualism. He aimed at an *Aufheben* of "the dichotomies of spirit and matter, mind and body, faith and wisdom, freedom and necessity ... and of reason and sensuousness, intellect and nature ... absolute subjectivity and absolute objectivity"; of these kinds of dichotomies. And, in the grotesque form of his absolute idealism, he, in his own words, believed himself to have *Aufheben*-ed both "dogmatic idealism" and "materialist dogmatism".

The Hegelian polemicists, first and foremost without exception, inherit this motif of Hegel's philosophy, especially the motif of the *Aufheben* of the dichotomy of subjectivity and objectivity. The young Marx too, of course, was no exception to this. In Hess's philosophy of action it was so, and, as is clear from the statement "critique is the union of the considered object and the considering subject" I introduced a little while ago, Bauer's philosophy of critique also precisely inherits this motif.

The problem, however, lies in the fact that no matter how much one shouts of the union of subjectivity and objectivity, to the extent that it remains in the form of theory, which is philosophy, in the end one doesn't leave the area of a subject-object union within the bounds of subjectivity. Thereupon, practice – action was brought out and a union of subjectivity and objectivity in the place of practice was proposed. This is certainly an argument worthy of attention. But, regardless of saying in short "practice" and "action", various dimensions exist within such. So then what kind of dimension practice is practice which truly unifies subjectivity and objectivity, humankind and nature? Marx-Engels' answer to this problematic, that it is "productive activity", especially the activity of material production—now a more fundamental practice than simply the political practice of the revolutionary movement—, is then the thesis of practice in this dimension.

Incidentally, though we may speak of a union of subjectivity and objectivity, of subject and object, a union of human beings and nature, in the place of production, if one remains in a position of having assumed dualistically, in a substance-istic conceptualisation, human beings as subjects on the one hand and Nature as object on the other hand, though one may call it a "union" in the place of production, at most it would remain in the area of an interactive joining of two substances standing at two poles. For the establishing of a true dialectical union of the two it is necessary to radically revise the ontological understanding of each of these two, of human beings on the one hand, and Nature on the other. Accordingly, assuming a dynamic place where, rather than a conceptualisation of subject and exterior environment, the term of subject and the term of environment are secondarily formed in its segmentation is the sine qua non.

When we speak of a dynamic place of this kind, of the secondary segmentation of subject and environment therein, we, today, immediately think of ecosystems and call to mind ecology. Incidentally, it was around about the time that *Capital* was published that the word *Ökologie* ⟦Tr. ecology⟧ was coined by Haeckel, and so at the time that Marx-Engels established materialist history the word *Ökologie* still did not exist. So, Marx-Engels could not have used the word *ökologisch* 〔Tr. ecological〕 as a word. It's now well known, however, that their thinking is extremely *ökologisch*.

In the case of the human ecosystem, by the way, differing to the case of plant ecosystems and general animal ecosystems, a certain striking characteristic is observed in the way of being of the interrelation between subject and environment. Such lies in the point of, to put things symbolically, a working on the environment, through a goal-oriented consciousness, using the intermediary means of tools. And, this productive activity, which is objective activity, is carried out as a co-operation (*Zusammenwirkung*), and in this the relations of production are socially arranged.

This *ökologisch* arrangement, and its positioning, what's more, in the way of being of "productive activity", which ought to be called the nodal circle of the *Ökologie* characteristic of human beings—herein lies the standpoint of materialist history. Re-grasping, positioned in this standpoint, the unity of subject and object, the practical unity of human beings and Nature; here can be said to be, I think, a major feature of Marx's "philosophy".

I've just said Marx's "philosophy". But Marx aimed at the *Aufheben* of philosophy, and so shouldn't it be the case that it wasn't the case that he attempted to establish a philosophy as philosophy? That's certainly true. But, simply referring to the sublation of philosophy or from theory to practice, even if acceptable as an in principle stance, it's not the case that matters end there.

Here the concept of "critique" comes into focus once again. It connects at a fundamental level with the fact that Marx, who planned an *Aufheben* of economics, attempted to construct, in the domain of theory, a system of a "critique of economics".

In 1858, the year he had written *A Contribution to the Critique of Political Economy*, he states in a letter to Lassalle in the following way: "The work I am focused on at the moment is a critique of economic categories (*Kritik der ökonomischen Kategorien*). If I might be permitted to say so, it is a critiquing describing of bourgeois economic [studies]. It is a describing of this *System* 〔Tr. system〕 and at the same time a critique of the *System* carried out through that description".

As we see here, Marx aims, in the field of the theory of economics, at a *kritische Darstellung* 〔Tr. critical description〕 wherein such is a description of the system and simultaneously a critique of the system. That critical description is not a comprehensive description of a specific phenomenon, but rather it is a critical description of categories, of, in other words, fundamental concepts.

Well then, in what sense of critique is the "critique" we speak of when we speak of category critique? The combination of the use of a category and the critique of a category is a matter which is a motif in the Hegelian dialectic too, so it can't be so easily dealt with, but it's certain, I think, for a start, that it involves the moment of a for-itself re-grasping of an in-itself state of affairs.

In *Capital*, Marx states in regard to the categories of bourgeois economics that they are "socially valid in regard to the relations of production of the historically determined social form of production that is commodity production, and for this reason they are objective forms of thought". "Socially valid" (*gesellschaftlich gültige*) under the present historical-cultural system and "for that reason objective" (*also objektive*) forms of thought; critical description (*kritische Darstellung*) of these is the task.—"Socially valid, and for that reason objective" forms of thought are none other than things exactly regarded as true from a standpoint internal to a given society, things regarded as true *für es*, and systematically describing these forms a crucial task, although we mustn't stop at simply ratifying them. They are things valid only in regard to "historically determined", specific relations of production, not unconditional, eternal truths. Things regarded as truths for the consciousnesses involved (*für es*) are certainly not straightforward truths for us (*für uns*). Having said that, it won't do for "we" in the position of science to just dismiss things regarded as true for the subjects involved as being things which are simply untrue. We have to elucidate the mechanisms of being which are regarded as completely natural, apodictic truths, and investigate and show the mediated existential structure of in-themselves "true existences". In order to do this, it becomes our necessary task to describe systematically from their fundamental categories things which are regarded as truths in-themselves, and, in conjunction with this, to proceed to, again, systematically carry out their "critique"—a "cognitive critique", in the form of a kind of theory of ideology critique, an epistemological – ontological critique.—Incidentally, the quotation of a moment ago from *Capital* is a quotation from the famous section, "The Fetishism of Commodities and the Secret Thereof", and in the current context it means, I think, that "critique" in the later Marx is, provisionally, analysing the mediated structure of being of in-itself states of affairs, exposing *für uns* their historical – social relativity and their origins, and rendering for-themselves in the manner of the theory of an epistemological critique, and, appropriately, in the manner of the *theory* of an ideological critique, *in-themselves* "objective" states of affairs for the consciousnesses involved within the order of things.

Whether or not it is immediately permitted to infer the composition of "critiquing description" – "systematic description = systematic critique", Marx speaks of focusing along the lines of "economics"—correctly, the "critique of economics", to his "philosophy"; herein lies a moment requiring careful examination. Because, in the mid-1840s Marx, according to the Preface of *A Con-*

tribution to the Critique of Political Economy (published in 1859), carried out a "self-settling of accounts with [his] existing philosophical *Gewissen* [[Tr. conscience]]" ... Further—this is a statement from Engels in his final years—it is predicted that philosophy in the future, excepting formal logic and dialectics, will disappear as an independent field of knowledge. When taking such facts into consideration, it is not that Marx didn't leave behind a systematic work of philosophy; rather, a hypothesis, no less, that didn't he from the beginning regard systematic description of philosophy itself to be out of the question?, can arise.

For me, whilst acknowledging that Marx didn't write a so-called philosophical system in the form of a work, I believe, however, that it is possible, nevertheless, to speak of Marx's philosophical system. In Engels' prediction of the future disappearance of philosophy there is, as well,—as what might be called a proviso—a condition attached. He makes the following statement:

> Modern materialism is essentially dialectical, and it no longer needs a philosophy standing above the sciences. As soon as the demand that, in regard to each of the individual sciences, the position each occupies within the total connections of things and the knowledge of things be clearly understood, a special field of knowledge dealing with the total connections becomes unnecessary. *When that happens* [[Tr. italics by Hiromatsu]], that which still survives independently within former philosophy is the science relating to thought and its laws – formal logic and dialectics. Everything else reduces into the positive science relating to nature and history (*Anti-Duhring*).

Under the current situation, however, to the extent that the sciences haven't gone that far, even Engels, I think, would acknowledge that the "special science" of philosophy is still necessary. In this quotation, the point of "the total connections" is emphasised, but it's the case that treatment of a *theory* of epistemological critique type—a process of the same kind as Hegel's dialectical combining of the "use" and the "critique" of categories—is also and at the same time crucial, and for Engels, he must have written in the aforementioned way foreseeing that in the future the sciences themselves would be not only descriptions of in-themselves "objective" "truth existences", they would be things which internalise within their systems the relevant critical process. If this is the case, in the future, philosophy and the sciences will not exist side by side separately, they will once again be unified, and the totality of the sciences will become a type of philosophical system. But, "the science relating to thought and its laws", not directly involved with objective knowledge—this doesn't simply stop at the area of formal logic, it includes a dialectics which takes as its structural moment an epistemological dimension as well—will, further, form an "independent" field separate to the systems of objective knowledge. The quoted material is understood as implying things in this way.

For Marx himself, he didn't have time to complete even his critique of economics, *Capital*, and so he didn't establish a specific plan to write himself either a total system of objective knowledge or an independent work of philosophy of epistemological critique. However, it shouldn't be a gross error to say that from their orientation Marx-Engels naturally desired the future realisation of a description of a total system of knowledge, a critiquing – systematic description, and, from the beginning, dialectics and above all a theory of epistemological critique "science relating to thought and its laws". Accordingly, it will be permitted, I think, to speak of "Marx's philosophy", not in the sense of a philosophy left behind in the form of a work, but in the sense of the "philosophy" which ought to have existed in-itself as his invention. The "philosophy for Marx" I am speaking of here is philosophy as such philosophy.

Philosophy for Marx in this sense, setting aside for the moment the "science of thought and its general laws", we can infer—can we not?—in regard to a system of objective knowledge, is the invention and composition he conceived in his "critique of economics", that is to say, it is a "simultaneously systematic description and a critique of this *System* ⟦Tr. system⟧ through that description" of an in-itself, "objective" state of affairs.

This is the reason, I think, that in the same sense that Marx's economics is not an economics in the usual sense but rather is a "critique of economics", this "philosophy" has the characteristic of being not philosophy in the usual sense but a "critique of philosophy"—a critique of the in-itself picture of the world, a systematic critique dialectically unified with a *theory* of ideology critique of the existing world-view, a critiquing system. It should be something which exists as a critique of everyday – real consciousness, and a "critique" of the existing sciences forming a "system of knowledge" within the horizon of this consciousness which is historically – socially relative; it should be something which exists as this kind of systematic critique = critiquing system.

For Marx, just why does this critiquing description = describing critique have to be something which is "systematic"? If the critique is finely focused, wouldn't it be sufficient for it to be one-pointed? Such might be questions in response to what I have just said. This matter is related to the fact that whether it be theoretical critique or whether it be the system of critiquing description, such is positioned for Marx as a moment of his revolutionary practice, rather, of the revolutionary practice of the proletariat, of this historical – social practice.

Although this is not limited to Marx, when aiming at a total transformation rather than aiming at a partial improvement of the human world, and when scientifically explicating the conditions – plans of this total transformation, and the post-transformation vision, partial research won't do; it is precisely necessary to research systematically the totality of the human world and to grasp it systematically. In the case of Marx, this was in actuality so, and, moreover, systematicity, systematic unity, becomes necessary as a matter of course to the extent that such is indivisible, as a condition of such, and also as a consequence likely to be accompanying such, with a total change in world-view, where the transformation doesn't stop in the domain of simple transformation of the social order.

I spoke, a moment ago, of the union of subjectivity and objectivity, the union of human beings and nature, as a motif Marx had inherited from Hegel and the Hegelians, and I stated that such in Marx bore fruit in the method of his locating it—not in the Bauerian place of "critical criticism", and not stopping at the temporary, intermediary step of substituting the critiquing subject = self-consciousness of the human race for the proletariat – in the scene of production, and what's more in the scene of "production" as the human ecological key, and I hinted at the significance this fundamental vantage point of materialist history has for "philosophy".

Incidentally, if one stops, substituting the proletariat or its class consciousness for Hegel's "absolute spirit" or Bauer's "self-consciousness", at speaking, thereupon, in the logic of the theory of Fichtean – Hegelian alienation – externalisation, of the self-externalisation and self-acquisition of the "large subject" in question, and if one remains with the *schema* in which Bauer spoke of the practical unity of subjectivity and objectivity through "criticism", then we will have to judge the composition of this theory of alienation as being still *prior* to materialist history. Brought down, as well, by an incomplete distinction between the theory of alienation and the theory of reification, Lukács was only able to grasp the scope of Marx's theory of labour and theory of objective activity in a phase which "reduces" such to those of the young Hegel (and, what's more, to those to the extent that he, Lukács, had one-sidedly diminished them), and because he was thus unable to fully grasp the horizon of materialist history, he, to put it bluntly, ended up pushing Marxism into a Bauer*ian* dimension.

Here is not, however, the place to critique Lukács, nor is it the place to discuss again my opinion regarding the move from the theory of alienation to the theory of reification, so I will leave things here at adding two or three comments regarding the relation between the systematicity of Marx's thought and the standpoint of materialist history.

As I said earlier, Hegel stated that it should not simply be *Philosophia* as love of knowledge, rather it has to be systematic knowledge = *Wissenschaft*. I've also already said that for Hegel himself this systematic knowledge coincides in terms of content with religion or a theological system.

When we speak of a system, there is a tendency to dislike systems in present times, and it seems that there is a tendency to associate them with theological systems, and it seems too that there is a tendency to dislike Marx's thought precisely because of its systematicity. However, the association of system and theology is, is it not, rather, as the matter goes, a coincidental situation? Although such as Euclidean geometry or classical mechanics (Newtonian physics) also boast of systematicity, such are, in the end, not systems which have grasped the totality of the world, but rather are simply partial systematic knowledge. In that regard, thought which aimed at a total system can be said to have been most strongly seen historically after all in theology. Or rather, I should perhaps say ... in theological philosophy. But, systematicity, and, what's more, the aim for a total world systematicity, is not, as a matter of historical fact, in any way a monopoly of theology. If we focus in along the lines of the matter, in the case of the theologian it is logical, to a great extent, that he or she would abandon systems, commenting that absolute systematicity will be left to God, with at best only fragmentary revelation being carried out by limited human beings, and that with limited human beings, grasping systematically the totality of the world is absolutely impossible. There ought not be a necessary reason for theology being associated with it because we have spoken of systematicity.

It seems, however, that, apart from historical accident, people associate systematicity and theology in all likelihood because of the mediation of the situation of the doubling over of the desire for systematicity and the desire for the absoluteness of theory. In this regard, systematicity is certainly not doubled over with absoluteness in the case of Marxism, or rather, provisionally, Marx's thought. This, no doubt, is the reason that Marx's thought, beginning with materialist history, is duly self-aware of the historical relativity of theory.

That Marx aims at systematic description, at the systematicity of a critiquing description, despite being aware of historical relativism—even though the composition of the "system" differs to the case of the *Encyclopédistes*—is none other than because he takes as his task the total transformation of the world, the total transformation of the real world and the world of thought. I would like to particularly emphasise this point.

Incidentally, when focusing along the lines of "production", the key to the human ecosystem, in which materialist history places its fundamental vantage point, it is hardly necessary, I think, to discuss in detail again that it is the transformation of the relations of production which forms the axis. The total understanding of the world is carried out positioned on this axis. And the "praxis" of "production", and the unity of human beings and nature which had its standpoint located there, the unifying understanding of subjectivity and objectivity, particularity and universality, freedom and necessity, etc., are concerned with the whole of the world-view and are not concerned with simply the hemisphere—in opposition to the "natural world"—of the like of "history" and "society" in modern thought. And, this is also the reason that the *Historisophie* revealed by this view of history sublates – realises in actuality precisely a philosophy of practice, a philosophy of action, in other words, that which the Left Hegelians Cieszkowski and Moses Hess had conceived imperfectly. In this sense, materialist history is certainly not an historical materialist "hemisphere" to be lined up with such as the dialectics of nature, and "practical materialism" is not such as a practical textbook of practical philosophy.

If in this way I state along the lines that "materialist history, indeed, is the central axis of Marx's philosophy", there is likely to be, I think, a tendency amongst people to point out that: "That's wrong"; "Marx's philosophy is firstly a materialist dialectics = dialectical materialism, and the dialectics of nature is established with the application – extension of this to the natural world, and historical materialism is established with the application – extension of it (dialectical materialism) to the world of history, etc".

For me, it's not that I don't "understand" the circumstance wherein such a commonly held idea came into being, from about the time of Kautsky at the Second International, or that it was brought into the creed of Russian Marxism by Plekhanov and Lenin, and it's not that I don't acknowledge the definite "effectiveness" and "convenience" of pushing things into such a schema when organising things in a textbook manner, but in principle, one can only conclude that such is a fallacy which completely fails to understand what philosophy was for Marx. I won't go over this circumstance again here, as I have discussed it in detail in 『マルクス主義の理路』〚*The Logic of Marxism*〛 (a new edition was published in the summer of this year (1980) from Keisō shobō), or, again, in my jointly-written 『現代哲学を考える』〚*Examining Contemporary Philosophy*〛 (Yūhikaku).

To tell the truth, I would really like, here, to attempt, whilst clarifying in regard to the relation between materialist history and ecology, the differences (*differentia*) between the logical composition taken in-itself by ecology and structuralism and Luhmannian functionalism, the task of reflecting it in contrast to a dialectical *view of being* (not simply the logic of such), but I will leave this to another occasion, and will, in the time remaining, touch on just one more necessary point.

You are probably going to make the point the gist of which is that as long as philosophy is philosophy, in the end practical self-sublation will not—will it not?—be completed within philosophy, despite talk of practical self-sublation through the practical realisation of philosophy. This is a task which the early Marx entrusted to the proletariat. The composition here, I believe, is maintained in more concrete form in the later Marx as well. However, people, even in regard to economics, or rather *Capital*, propound that even if theory is able to investigate *Sein*, it is unable from there to pronounce, in a logically necessary way, of the necessity of revolution, to say nothing of not being able to prove the *sollen* of revolutionary practice. Commentators separate things off, saying theory is theory and practice is practice. When this happens, it won't do to simply say as the young Marx did that theory, though theory, is a type of practice, nor will we get anywhere stating that practice, though practice, takes theoretical cognition as its moment. "Theory" and "practice" need to be united in an area beyond such a dimension. And it can be seen that Marx formulated at least partly consciously the deployment of this.

In the book 『弁証法の論理 – 弁証法における体系構成法 – 』〚*The Logic of the Dialectic – The Method of System Composition in the Dialectic*〛 published this spring (published by Seido sha), I argued that we must go a step further from the *für es*, *für uns* composition, and in the dialectic, originally a logic of dialogue, locate a method of system composition which has, in a self-aware manner, taken into account the dialogic composition between "author" and "reader". I'm sure there's no fear of misunderstanding here, but this, of course, is certainly not a matter of saying carry out discussion in the form of a dialogue between characters labelled "author" and "reader". Neither is it a matter of saying include the self and the other in one's object of description. Having incorporated the two moments of one and the other into one's descriptive content, this certainly doesn't equate to dialogue between the "self" and the "other" in the essential meaning of the words. It's not that for the described system, the self of the author and the other of the reader are likely to end up being incorporated into it. If one were to call a system of description into which one had incorporated the one and the other a "dialogue" between author and reader it is unlikely that this would even be an absurd swindle. I believe that you will be able to guess that it's not the case that I wrote 〚Tr. in the above-mentioned book〛 such a low trick.

My deliberately referring to what is likely to be regarded as a digression into matters concerning myself is as a condition for touching on the circumstances of what is the relation between Marx's theoretical system and his practical "appeal", of how through the medium of the descriptive system Marx the author and his readers, these two who stand "outside" the descriptive system,

are involved with each other, of with what kind of consideration a composition of dialogue (appeal and positive response) is dealt with in Marx's method
of system composition (not the content of description).

In the case of Marx, and the truth is no one is able to expect more than this
in description itself, he is unable to derive – determine in terms of formal logic
an imperative proposition from an existential proposition, and even if union
between *es* and *wir*[3] in theoretical cognition (even if this includes propositions
of a practical kind, including imperative propositions), and further, a union
between author and reader in terms of viewpoint, is established, this doesn't
mean that imperative practice is *logically* derived from that.

If people think that it is possible, rendering independent a theoretical system, a described literary content, to carry out, within such and self-completingly, so-called "proof of the *necessity* of revolution", and think that it is possible to
prove – derive in a logically necessary way a particular imperative, then that is
an expression of the fact that they have fallen into a form of "fetishism" regarding "writing".

A system of theory, a systematic description of thought, is the medium
between "author" and "reader", who stand "outside" the content of the
writing—and because this frequently brings about an expected *Resultat*[4] from
the perspective of the author people forget its composition of intermediar-
ity, this being the reason they are prone to "fetishise" writing, but, it is not
something which, self-completingly, "brings about logically" "understanding"
through proofs, to say nothing of imperative practice.

Consequently, rejecting fetishism of description itself, we take into consideration, in the form of "incorporating" it in a self-aware manner into the method
of system composition, the actual involvement between author and reader (in
such, the moments of the "understanding" of the "presentation", the positive –
negative "decision of attitude" to a "statement", and the "reception" towards an
"appeal" already exist in the scene of the meaning construction of representation theories, but I won't go into that here), but the expected practice arises
for the first time through the "resolved response" on the side of the reader in
regard to a "declarative appeal". The circumstance is such that the description
of a system of theory is in itself, in general, "one particular" appeal—indeed,
even though the process of unfolding of description (understanding) has the
composition of continuous appeal – response between author and reader,
that a holistic response comes back in regard to the author is because such

---

3 〚Tr. *es* = she/he; *wir* = we〛.
4 〚Tr. *Resultat* = result〛.

occurs in a scene where the reader goes beyond the zone of "understanding" and reacts in a real way, and so it's the case that the manifestation of a "dialogical" interrelationship between the person of the author and the person of the reader only proceeds (going beyond the zone of a "dialogical progression" in the scene of sequential "understanding" of an argument) in the form of a piece of writing, the response of the reader, and expressing one's views through further writing—and it is only in the reader accepting in a particular way and responding to a given piece of writing (only in this kind of actual "dialogical" involvement with each other between author and reader through the medium of a piece of writing) that the expected practice manifests in the reader.

In this case, in Marxian terms, "being determines consciousness" and "being even determines unconsciousness", and so we are able to predict the form of response in a particular reader. That is to say, for such and such a social being, if such and such a theoretical understanding is established, we can predict in all probability, to the extent that such and such practical conditions present themselves, that the social being in question is likely to carry out such and such a practice. Marx's theoretical description is a critiquing description of the present world, and owing, amongst other things, to the fact that this description itself was positioned in terms of existentiality in an historical-practical reality, it brings about in regard to the specific social being of the proletariat its class for-itself, and in this, it self-determines as something which exhibits the content of an "appeal" bringing about an expected response. To the extent that this self-determination is appropriate, and not self-righteous, the activity of theoretical presentation of Marx the author gives rise in reality to an expected social – historical practice.

Through this condition being fulfilled, then, the conception of a real sublation – sublating realisation of philosophy becomes something real.

That which is philosophy for Marx is, to the extent that it is a theoretical system of critiquing description = describing critique, indeed a "systematic description which is at the same time a critique" of the present world, a *begreifen*[5] rendered for-itself of the mediated being-structure of the world, but this is in itself an "appeal" to the "reader", and it can be said to be of such a composition that it is able, in arousing, in all probability, the class practice of the proletariat, the proper social being, to be a "philosophy of practice", and is something which, in the actual "critique" which is the practice in question, self-sublates = self-realises.

---

5 〚Tr. *begreifen* = understanding; grasping〛.

The second half, in particular, of my talk today ended up being rushed, but I hope that I have been able to have you understand in general the gist, the outline, of what I have been talking about. Regarding any sections which were difficult to follow due to the haste with which I spoke, the journal *Inpakuto* is—if the consent of the organiser is able to be obtained—providing a space for publication of a record of this talk, so, having supplemented your understanding with the printed text, I would be pleased to receive your critique.

I thank you for your quiet attention. (Applause)

Expanding the Theory of Reification

As indicated in the Prologue, whilst this book carries the general title of *The Schema of The Theory of Reification*, at best it only discusses "the composition of the theory of reification in Marx" and does not contain a complete description of my own conception of a schema of "the theory of reification".—The theory of reification also involves an ontology and an epistemology and, in addition, it is of a composition also involving the method of constituting a system, and so of course it is difficult to expect an exposition of one's complete conception in the limited space of an epilogue. Nonetheless, in this book, which is being published ahead of the publication of 『存在と意味 – 事的世界観の定礎 – 第二巻 – 実践世界の存在構造』 [[*Being and Meaning – The Foundations of A Koto-centred*[1] *World-view – Volume II – The Being-Structure of the World of Praxis*]], I would like to give at least a partial foreshadowing of the methodological aspect of the mechanism of the reifying of phenomena in the world of praxis, and at the same time I wish to bring into focus the fact that a certain phase of what I am specifying as my understanding of reification has already been critically dealt with in the already published 『存在と意味 – 事的世界観の定礎 – 第一巻 – 認識的世界の存在構造』 [[*Being and Meaning – The Foundations of A Koto-centred World-view – Volume I – The Being-Structure of the World of Cognition*]] as well, and to make clear the underlying foundation of the theory of reification common to both volumes and also to 『存在と意味 – 事的世界観の定礎 – 第三巻 – 文化的世界の存在構造』 [[*Being and Meaning – The Foundations of A Koto-centred World-view – Volume III – The Being-Structure of the Cultural World*]].

Here, however, I'd like to forego a proper outlining exposition, and, as a general frame, to put together my discussion in a form in accordance with the parameters of the kind of direction in and deployment on which I hope to continue and expand the theory of reification of Marx and Engels investigated in this book.

Reification, following the everyday sense of the word, would mean "some sort of thing" "changes" into a "thing-like being". In the concept of "reification" as a technical term, however, though, and as was also true in the case of Marx and Engels, there is a need to make clear the differences and connections

---

1 [[Tr. *Koto* translates as something like "state of affairs", as "thing", in the sense of "event"]].

between it and the everyday, established image. Otherwise, we are likely to fall into tragicomic confusion.

In the everyday, established concept, when we speak of reification, because of the fact that the particular "some sort of thing" which changes into a thing-like being is assumed in itself to not yet be a thing-like being—and through an exclusive dichotomisation of thing-like being and the mental[2]—there is a tendency to regard it as a "mental some thing". Or, again, there is a tendency to regard it as a "subjective thing", accompanying the fact that thing-like being is taken as referring to an objective thing, and, accompanying the rendering of subjective things and objective things into an exclusive dichotomy (the matter is considered in this way, in fact, within the schema of reification of a "subjective thing" in M. Weber and Lukács). However, Marx and Engels, and I myself, reject at a fundamental level the straightforward dualism of "material things" and "mental things", of "objective things" and "subjective things", in modern philosophy, and in the modern common sense understanding, and, consequently, for us, "the thing which transforms into a thing-like being" is neither a so-called "mental thing" nor simply a "subjective thing". So what, then, is it? Answering for the moment formally and in general, it is a particular kind of "relation". When I say "relation", however, it is not possible to separate such, in the manner, captive to the modern dichotomy, into simply "subjective relations" and simply "objective relations", and, going further back, it is not possible for one to "thing"-ify what is a "relation", and represent it in the form of relation as a *thing*. (Marx, incidentally, uses on occasion the expression "reification of the person", but "person" here means "a unity of social relations" and so working backwards it settles to a determination of "relation").—In order, too, to positively determine what I am calling here "relation" let us move the discussion one stage further.

Regarding the "change" involved when we speak of reification in the everyday conception, once again, this is represented in the sense of the so-called objective change occurring in such things as the changing of water into ice, the changing of a caterpillar into a butterfly, the combining and changing of oxygen and hydrogen into water; occurring in other words, in an objective process developing independent of knowing cognition. Reification used by Marx and Engels, however, and my use of reification, is not this kind of "purely objective change". For us it refers to the process by which something, which is, to the person of scientific reflection (*für uns*), determined by a specific relation, appears

---

2   〖Tr. The Japanese word here, 心象, covers the emotional as well as the mental (as intellectual activity). As a translation "psychological" is, perhaps, a possibility. I have chosen to translate it as "mental" as this seems to fit best with its dichotomous pairing with "thing-like being"〗.

as a thing-like being for the consciousness of those immediately involved (*für es*).—"Appearance" (*scheinen*), however, holds here only from the perspective of scientific reflection, whilst for the person involved it can be said that it directly "exists in the form of a thing-like being". "Existing in the form of a thing-like being" is not simply a matter of cognition, it means "existing", for the person involved, in a form wherein it determines not only his emotion and will but his action as well.—It describes, then, the situation in which what exists as a relation to we in the position of scientific reflection [*Verhältnis für uns*] "changes" into a thing-like being for the persons involved [*Sache für es*].

It becomes necessary now to determine just what kind of existence this "thing-like being" is. Let me establish this to the extent necessary for the current discussion.

"Thing-like being" can be broadly divided into the two kinds of "existent states" and "significant states". Existent states separate into two types, the "material" and the "mental",[3] and the significant separates into two types, "meaning" and "value".—Among existent states those which are "embodied" significant states are called "the ready-to-hand" and corresponding to the two types of the significant i.e. meaning and value, "the ready-to-hand" divides into those which are "symbol forms" and those which are "propertive forms".[4]

As the distinguishing marks of thing-like being: (a) existing independently of cognizing knowing, so-called "objectivity"; (b) existing in itself, independent of a human subject—that it is a so-called "objective entity"; and (c) internal "regularity" (*Gesetzmäßigkeit* i.e. structural connections or rule-like connections possessed in themselves self-sufficiently) can be given as being possessed in common. In addition to these three things, however, (i) the existent are con-

---

3 [Tr. The Japanese word here, 心的, covers the emotional as well as the mental. See note 1 above].

4 The two types of the existent differentiate respectively into the subtypes of "material substances", "material qualities" and "material relations", and "mental substances", "mental qualities" and "mental relations". (In this case, "qualities" includes so-called "function", and "relations" includes so-called "structure". Further, "relation" here is constituted based on the prior existence of "substances" and is understood as secondary).

The two types of the significant differentiate respectively into the subtypes of "meaning essence", "meaning form" and "meaning linkage", and "value essence", "value form", and "value linkage".

The two types of the ready-to-hand differentiate respectively into the subtypes of "symbol form substance", "symbol form characteristics" and "symbol form relations", and "propertive substance", "propertive characteristics", and "propertive relations".

If we present the above diagrammatically we get:

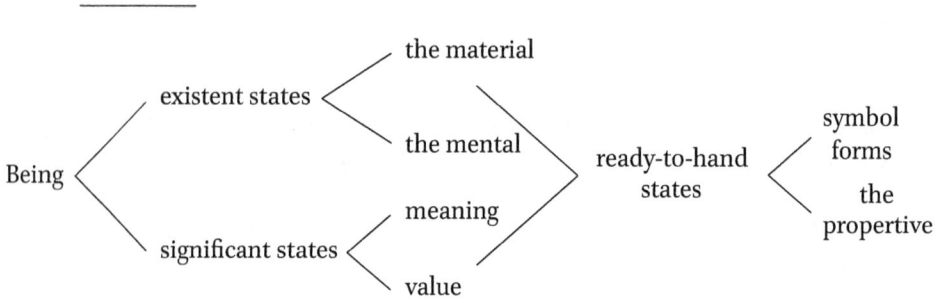

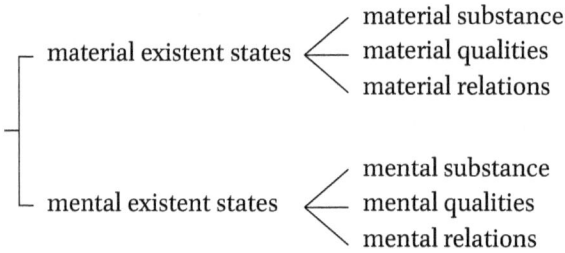

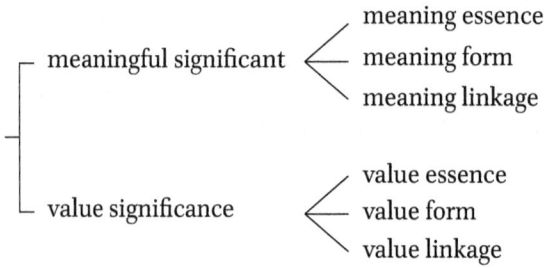

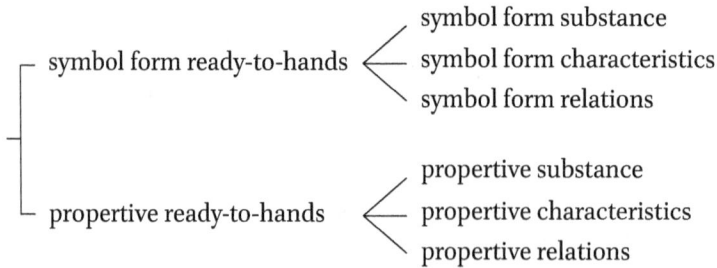

sidered as things which are (d) spatio-temporal, and (e) non-significant, (ii) significants are considered as things which are (d)' supra spatio-temporal and (e)' significant, and (iii) the ready-to-hand are considered as things which are spatio-temporal and significant.

"Reification" means, in the final analysis, simply "changing", in the afore-mentioned sense, into a "thing"-like existence of the type determined above, that is to say into an existent state $((a)(b)(c)+(d)(e))$ or a significant state $((a)(b)(c)+(d)'(e)')$ or a ready-to-hand state $((a)(b)(c)+(d)(e)')$.

The phenomenon of reification itself, by the way, to the extent that it is able to contain current day concepts such as self-existing "objectivity", internal "regularity", or so-called "spatio-temporality", is as old as human cognition and is not in any way particular to modern thinking.—If we look at just modern science, scientific knowledge of an object doesn't want to recognise the exist-ence of "the significant state" (if we regard these as existing independently they present as *irreal* = *ideal*, presenting "supra spatio-temporal", that is to say what Marx calls supra-sensible (*übersinnlich*), supra-natural (*übernatürlich*) charac-teristics of being) striving to reduce such as much as possible to the existent state. (In this regard, philosophy isn't necessarily averse to positively pursuing the reificatory self-existence of "the significant state", with traditional meta-physics being typical in this regard). To the extent that it is unable to completely ignore the significant state, despite being modern science, it takes as its object here symbol forms or "propertive" being "embodied" in the existent state, and it is usual on such occasions that it aims at fixing the existent as much as pos-sible in the material existent, striving to reduce even the mental existent into the material existent. Modern science is carried out according to this kind of approach and it has attempted to explain all phenomena by reducing them as much as possible to the material existent. From our perspective, this becomes the reason for this attitude of modern science being held strongly captive to a reification into "the material existent".

When we put forward this idea in this way, we may perhaps cause a tend-ency amongst readers to respond, "accepting" that reducing so-called mental phenomena or valuative phenomena into the material existent is "reification" and an "error", that nevertheless is it not the case that treating objects which are from the beginning material being as material existents the natural sci-ences truly know the phenomenon as it really is and that this is in no way a *reification*?; and that surely in no way should the concept of reification be applied to "the natural world" or to "object cognition in the natural sciences"?—However, from our perspective (*für uns*) so-called material existents them-selves are products of reification. That is to say, objectively, independently exist-ing entities, the material characteristics of such entities, the material relations forming between such entities, and these material existents themselves which the natural sciences take as their objects, are already none other than products of reification. For the purposes of the current discussion there would be no problem, here, accepting for the moment such a thing as the "pure objectivity" of the Kantian "thing in itself" (*Ding an sich*), but the reality is that a material existent actually known in any degree is provisionally a thing where the composition of the "phenomenal given – meaningful cognized" has been made self-existent. To state things clearly and concisely, so-called existents thought of as having a self-existing objective state are in reality the mediated product of the reification of the "knowing – known" relation (fully, the fourfold relation "knowing – cognizing – the given – the cognized" as explained in detail in *Being and Meaning Volume I*).

To provide support for this conclusion let us continue our discussion a little further. We have for some little while now been distinguishing in conducting our discussion between "the existent state" and "the ready-to-hand state", in a partial accommodation of the modern understanding; but, the truth is, that which people think of as non-significant existents, are already, in actual fact, a type of ready-to-hand state. This is because unless one actively propounds something which is in principle not cognizable such as the Kantian "thing in itself" or the Aristotelian "primary substance", generally, cognizable object states are at a minimum "phenomenally given – meaningfully cognized" states (regarding this matter see the Introduction to *Being and Meaning Volume I* and Part 1, Chapter 3, Section 1, and also Part 2, Chapter 2, Section 2, and Part 3, Chapter 3, Section 1 etc), and therein the meaningfully cognized type of the significant state is already "embodied".—When people think of "the existent state" separate to "the ready-to-hand state", the truth there is it is in a form where "valuative meaning" has been *abstracted* from the ready-to-hand state, but here as well "the meaningful significant" is operating as an intra-structural moment. For us, *to the extent* that we might *provisionally* approve this particular "abstraction", we can for the moment accept that such existents conceived by theorists are *non*-valuative. Yet even so, however, it needs to be pointed out that an object state actually appearing before persons is a pre-such this particular abstraction phenomenon and therefore it "carries" valuative meaning, and it is, in reality, in the broad sense of the term a "propertive ready-to-hand". (When speaking of valuative meaning, that is to say, "value" in the broad sense, I distinguish between and among values which are (a) desire based, (b) evaluative, (c) practical, (d) assessing, (e) aesthetic, and (f) faith based. (a) includes from pleasant – unpleasant-like good-bad affective value to so-called utility-based use value, (b) concerns *Wertung* [Tr. assessing], and includes "economic" income-expenditure value and ecological value in their broad sense, (c) is goal – means based, oughtness – normative based, right – duty based ... etc, (d) is *beurteilen*-ed ⟦Tr. judged⟧ true or false, good or bad, right or wrong etc, (e) is beauty – ugliness, sublimity – coarseness etc., and (f) is the sacred – the profane, the absolute – the relative ... etc). Things which are non-significant existent states (pure existent states which are not ready-to-hand states) are, as Heidegger points out in regard to a distinguishing between Being ready-to-hand (*Zuhandensein*) and Being present-at-hand (*Vorhandensein*), simply secondary states posited and constructed "in a scientific manner" accompanying abstraction of moments of significance.

In this way, when, having put aside established ideas, we reflect on the true state of things, the phenomenal state manifesting as a reality in a direct form, is, including the "natural thing" which is a division of the so-called "natural world", in fact a "significance" (meaning – value) "carrying" "ready-to-hand state". Considering this, those things which are "naked natural things" or "material existents" and which are regarded as if they are things of primary being are mediated, posited things, and, moreover, by reason of the above described set-up, they are products of reification. (In order that there be no misunderstanding I might add that, when positioning it as a reified picture of the world, it is not that we deny that existents, and in particular material existents, are treated as primary – foundational being, and that the ready-to-hand are treated as secondary – superstructural being. We have no intention at all of ending up excluding from the very beginning the type of scientific process which constructs a system based on a view of "naked natural things" and "material existence" as primary – foundational being. From the perspective of a particular way of dealing with the ontic (*ontisch*), the pursuit of the notion of a foundational nature – primacy in "material existence" is, indeed, permissible. However, when considering matters ontologically (*ontologisch*) the fact that a thing is a mediated reified product has to be rendered for-itself.—When doing this, I would like it to be borne in mind once again that reification is in no way simply a way of saying "objectification" of "the subjective").

The reader will no doubt call to mind here that well-known passage from *The German Ideology* which I have come to quote repeatedly in the main text of this book. Marx and Engels state that:

> Feuerbach speaks in particular of insight in the natural sciences and refers to the secrets revealed only to the eyes of the physicist and the chemist [i.e. the true form of a matter unable to be seen by the eyes of the everyday person], but if we didn't have industry or commerce just where would the natural sciences be able to be? Despite reference to the 'pure' natural sciences, not just the material but even the purpose of such are obtained

for the first time through the sensuous activity of human beings, through industry and commerce.[5]

And they declare that, "even the objects of the most simple 'sensuous perception' are given through social development, industry and commercial intercourse" and even go so far as to declare that "it is so to such an extent that this activity, this ceaseless sensuous labour and creation, this production is, indeed, the very foundation of the entire sensuous world actually existing today."—Positioning, in accordance with this understanding, that "history can be considered from two sides and can be divided into natural history and human history with neither side, however, being able to be separated off, and, for as long as human beings live, the history of nature and the history of human beings will mutually condition each other", they conceived "the science of history" as "the single science".

When the above quoted series of sentences is read superficially, I fear that an impression particularly comes to the fore of the point being made of the fact of the "altering of nature" through the objective activity of humankind.[6] Of course, the pointing out of this fact is in itself important.—In the later years of his life, as well, Engels frequently pointed out the historical fact of this "altering of nature", with him commenting that that which is nature in Europe in the present day is certainly not natural nature, that it is entirely different compared to the period of mass migration of the German race, and that, moreover, almost all of the change has arisen due to human activity (with the portion due to the "purely changes in natural history" of weather erosion being minute). He makes the same point regarding the Orient and elsewhere using the knowledge of the time, and he repeatedly emphasises, to use the language of today, ecological transformation of the natural environment.—It needs always to be borne in mind that nature as environment which people are involved with in actuality in their daily lives is in no way a natural nature eternally unchanged but is a "culturated nature", and an "historicized nature", transformed by the historical activity of humankind. However, this "altering of nature", that is to say the change in appearance of the natural world arising in practice through the sensuous – objective activity of human beings is only one part of the matter.

---

5 ⟦Tr. Parenthetical material by Hiromatsu⟧.

6 ⟦Tr. This paragraph begins a parenthetical discussion which runs through to the paragraph on page 211 which begins "In summation ...". In the Japanese original it is distinguished from the main body of the text by a reduction in font size. Strictly speaking, however, it is not indicated as being a footnote. It has been included here as part of the main text because it flows naturally inserted into such, and discussion in the main text assumes that it has been read. It needs to be kept in mind, however, that in the original it is a quasi-footnote⟧.

EXPANDING THE THEORY OF REIFICATION

To render all parts of the matter for-themselves (*für sich*), it will be convenient to lend ourselves to possible imagined questioning of the following kind:
In *The German Ideology*, the productive activity of humankind is stated to be
"the foundation (*Grundlage*) of the whole sensuous world [i.e. the actual world
which forms the object of perceptive cognition, which we see, hear, touch etc.]",
and "the sensuous world" is even concluded to be "the product of industry and
of the state of society" and "an historical product", yet is it not the case, however,
that it is only the limited area of the surface of the Earth that the activity of
human beings, activity which changes the appearance of its objects, reaches
in practice, with the natural world of the universe existing independently with
almost no connection to the existence or activity of human beings? In addition,
is it not the case that even though the "altering of nature" by humans occurs at
the Earth's surface this is no more than superficial change and if we look at
things at the level of "atoms", the level of "truly existing" things, they exist independently with no relation to industry or the state of society? If this is so, is it
not then inappropriate, from the beginning, to proclaim that "natural history
and human history cannot be separated" and conceive as a result of "the single
science", "the science of history"?

To respond to these conceivable questions requires considering things
within the areas of ontology and epistemology, but neither Marx nor Engels
has left discussion where the subject matter deals with these areas. Nonetheless, using the fragmentary material which they have left it is possible for us to
conjecture as to what kind of approach, generally speaking, they would have
replied with if they had been confronted with the above retorts. This is not, of
course, the place to make a thorough attempt at this task, but let me give an
abbreviated statement of the main points.

The reader will recall that in the previous, quoted material appeared "secrets
which were disclosed to the eye of the physicist and chemist" etc. If we follow
Marx and Engels' interpretation of things, when Feuerbach spoke of "insight"
he was thinking of things in a twofold form. One of these is the ordinary every
day insight which apprehends natural things in the form "clear to the naked
eye", whilst the other is a higher-order scientific insight which apprehends
things in the form of their "true essence". The latter corresponds to the aforementioned "eye of the physicist and chemist", and for Feuerbach this scientific
insight is placed at a higher level than everyday insight.—This needs to be kept
in mind as background knowledge.

So then, in the "questions" under consideration, it is exactly nature in the
form disclosed to the "higher-order scientific insight" which apprehends things
in the form of their "true essence", disclosed to the "eye of the physicist and
chemist", that is in focus. In the common understanding it is this very nature

in this form as well as things in general which are the objective existent form itself, and it is usual to treat nature in the form clear to the naked eye as simply "appearance". In contrast, Marx and Engels, though certainly not simply reversing the relationship of importance of the two, point out in effect that what is being called the "scientific eye" itself is an historical – social formation, and that, consequently, "objective existent forms" "apprehended" by this "eye" are also historically – socially relative.

People may respond with further questions here. Is it not the case that that which are historically – socially relative "objective" existent forms, and that which is "nature" disclosed to "scientific insight" in a particular age and society, are not nature itself but only an image of a perception of nature? Is it not the case that although a view of nature as an image of a perception might well be able to be said to be historically – socially relative and "the product of industry and the state of society", natural existence itself exists independently with no connection to human existence and activity? Etc.

The existing epistemology distinguished between "nature itself" and "a picture of nature". There is in fact a natural reason for this and a simple conflating of the two is unacceptable. But what is the reality of the thing which is being called here "nature itself"? It is, indeed, not "nature in the form clear to the naked eye". Yet, in the final analysis, isn't it simply "nature in the form revealed to scientific insight" today? Doesn't it, in other words, reduce to the "scientific picture of nature" disclosed to "the insight of the physicist and the chemist" today? Indeed, it is logically possible to posit an "objective nature itself" separate to this scientific picture of nature. And, in fact, positing this is a hackneyed convention of modern epistemology. But nonetheless, once we leave a specific "scientific picture of nature", isn't it the case that this concept of an "objective nature itself" is in effect empty? As a matter of fact, it is, is it not, a "scientific picture of nature" which continues to be "recognised" within a particular age – society – cultural sphere as the "true form of reality"?; it is this, is it not, which is in fact the very objective "nature itself"? When speaking of such things as a picture of nature or picture of the world things end up being treated as if, under the triad in modern epistemology of "object – content – effect", we are speaking of a mental picture internal to the subject, but what is being called here the scientific picture of nature is certainly not something which is literally "inside the head", but is truly one and the same thing as nature itself external to human beings. Although "Nature" in this sense, i.e. "[nature] disclosed [only] to the eyes of the physicist and the chemist", is not the very thing which changes directly and in practice through the activity of humankind, it is, in the end, an historically – socially relative historical product.—Marx and Engels, because they grasped this, at least in-itself, made the position of "grasping the sensuous world as the combined, total, living sensuous activity of the individuals who form it" their own, and went so far as to use, in addition, the expression, "the history of nature, that is to say, of the so-called natural sciences", and, stating that "the history of nature and human history cannot be separated", are surmised to have been able to conceive of "the science of history" as "the single science".

Amongst readers might arise here instead the tendency to conjecture in the following way: the conjecture that Marx and Engels thought, did they not, that that which is nature revealed to so-called "scientific insight" is an ideological secondary construct, and that "nature in the form clear to the naked eye" is indeed the true existent?—To get straight to the point, this conjecture is off the mark. "Nature in the form clear to the naked eye", that is to say, "the form of actual cognition of the sensuous", is also already, in Marx's view, not exempt from being ideological. If reference to *The Eighteenth Brumaire* is permitted, Marx includes such things as "perception, imagination and modes of thought" in the "superstructure" which is "formed in a particular way, based on the existing social conditions", and he certainly doesn't take the view of taking, in the manner of the positivists, "perception" alone as a complete given equating to being neutral and meta-historical.—"Nature in the form clear to the naked eye", direct, environmental nature which people are involved with in their everyday lives, is not only historicised in practice through the object altering activity of humans, it is also historicised indirectly as well through "the way it is disclosed".

In summation, that which is the natural world which manifests in an independent form, whether it is "the form revealed to scientific insight" or "the form clear to the naked eye", is in fact an "historicised nature" formed dependent on a reification of the "⟨combined,⟩ total living sensuous *activity* of the individuals".

Although Marx and Engels, however, to quote once again, declared "we know only a single science, the science of history. One can look at history from two sides and divide it into the history of nature and the history of human beings. The two sides are, however, inseparable; the history of nature and the history of human beings mutually condition each other so long as human beings exist", and declared the conception of the science (*Wissenschaft* = "system of knowledge") of "history" the unifying of nature and society, they were not able to realise this proposal. Of the two sides – moments of a "naturalised history" and an "historicised nature", concerning the former they did leave a particular systematic discussion of the "natural reification of history", but they have not left a detailed discussion concerning the latter, of the "historical reification of nature".

My planning to "expand" – "develop" the schema of the theory of reification into and across the dimension of "natural existent states" can be regarded – viewed from a third-party observer point of view, separate to the process by which I myself came to an awareness of the matter—as a desire to fulfil a proposal which Marx and Engels conceived but "left undone".

It seems to me that the reason Marx and Engels didn't get as far as fleshing out this proposal can't simply be said to be just a matter of a lack of time. Whilst they, (if we treat matters in keeping with the two "forms" of historical nature they themselves "distinguish" in the context of their criticism of Feuerbach), possessed in a clear form a schema for discussing the practical historicisation of "nature in the form clear to the naked eye" (the world of everyday life), positioning it in the place of the objective activity – praxis which is the activity of production, conversely, though, regarding the *epistemological* conceptual mechanism for explaining the matter of the historical relativity of "nature in the 'secret' form disclosed to the eye of the physicist and the chemist" (the so-called world of the "scientific existent"), they appear to have stopped short of formulating it concretely in a sufficient form. (Although Engels did leave a valuable consideration of this area in his later years. Nonetheless, he has to be seen to have not been able to get as far as a final formula. To discuss this matter, textual criticism of the posthumous work he composed over ten or more years, *Dialectics of Nature*, would be required, so I will not go into this matter here—incidentally, written over many years, this work, if read following the chronology of its writing, has several areas where discussion appearing in older layers is self-critiqued – retracted in newer layers, and has in newer layers "retraction" of "infamous" discussion from *Anti-Dühring*, but in the current edition,[7] re-edited in the Stalin era, the difference between newer and older in the hand-written manuscript and the notes has been ignored and a systematisation has been forced through a "cut-and-paste process", making it impossible, if reference is made to the current edition, for the *Verfassung*[8] of Engels in his later years to emerge).

In my view, a difficulty that Marx and Engels faced in preparing a conceptual apparatus to *epistemologically* explain the historical relativity of the view of nature as "scientific existent" lay in particular at the place where they assume in general a twofold configuration for the sensuous phenomenal world. And this difficulty is not difficult to understand. If we are speaking simply of a schema of a twofoldness in the phenomenal world there are the precedents of the Aris-

---

7   ⟦Tr. i.e. the current edition at the time Hiromatsu was writing, 1983⟧
8   ⟦Tr. *Verfassung* = make-up; constitution; state⟧

totelian theory of "substance – appearance", the Kantian theory of "substance – form", and the Hegelian deployment which "sublated" both of these. But in overcoming Hegelian *idealismus* and making the configuration in question one's own, it is first necessary, even if we put the moment of *materia* aside for the moment, to grasp anew the reason that Aristotle misconceived "appearance" as a metaphysical entity, and, again, the reason that Kant mistakenly positioned "form" to be an a priori subjective form, to lay bare these reasons from within and grasp anew the matter ontologically – epistemologically from the ground up. We in the present day can formulate relatively easily a twofoldness of the phenomenal world through a comparison of positive and negative legacies developed and left to us by several schools of thought since the later years of Marx and Engels, but at the time of Marx and Engels it was necessary to begin this task anew from the beginning, and so naturally considerable difficulty in this area was unavoidable.

From a different perspective, however, Marx, for his time, was in the vanguard of solving this problem, and we can see the work which marks this in *Capital. Capital* is not a work which takes ontology or epistemology as direct topics, and so, naturally, it is not the case that the phenomenal world as a whole is dealt with there. Nonetheless, the insight Marx gains when focusing on the "world of the commodity" and revealing its twofoldness (and consequently its fourfold structure of relation), and investigating the being-structure and mechanism of existence of the world of the commodity, reveals a schema which can act as a model for us when we come to investigate the being-structure and mechanism of existence of the world as a whole.—As we have seen in the body of this book, especially in Chapter 3, Marx in comprehending objects in the world of the commodity in the dichotomous unity of use value and value, understands the "commodity" as "sensuous and supra-sensuous thing" (*ein sinnlich übersinnliches Ding*), determining and describing thus a twofoldness of "real – irreal". That when we attempt to objectively determine the "commodity value" itself in a form of being where it is an autonomous *thing* it is "supra-natural (*übernatürlich*)", and to that extent "metaphysical", and that, however, seeing it as autonomous is a "reificatory" error, and that, with it being in reality a reflective determined of a particular social relation; that, precisely, is what Marx identified.

What Marx shows through analysis of the value-embodying commodity is, from the perspective of discussing, as I do, the "significant state" divided into "meaningful significance" and "valuative significance", in the final analysis, the schema of establishment of the valuative-significance-embodying "propertive ready-to-hand state".—Even referring to use value, Marx was of course aware that this is not simply a natural attribute but that it is in itself a type of valuative significance. Yet in the style employed in *Capital* he develops his argument in a manner showing no reluctance at treating use value as if it were a mere natural attribute, to say nothing of the fact that concerning "natural things", he does not go into their twofoldness. However, even without the introduction of argumentation of the style I am using, though "natural things", they are certainly not straightforwardly non-meaningful – non-significant. Even if it is the case that "natural things" do not carry propretive significance – valuative significance, indeed, they already carry symbolic significance – meaningful significance, however, and they are at least a twofoldness state having "meaningful significance" as its structural moment.—In the form of extending the schema of being of the twofoldness of the propretive ready-to-hand state made clear by Marx we can render for-itself the twofoldness of the symbolic-form ready-to-hand, that is to say, the twofoldness taking "meaningful significance" as its structurally internal moment. In doing this, it should be permissible, what's more, to locate this in the configuration of "appear as (*als et. erscheinen*)" and "appropriate as (*als et. gelten*)" revealed by Marx. Moreover, in a following of Marx's revealing the reification of the intersubjective mediation and social relations of *valuative* significance, we can begin the task of locating the reification of the intersubjective mediation and social relations of *meaningful* significance.

It is, then, that I am aiming precisely at an expanding along these inherited lines, that is to say at a broadening deployment which extends what Marx determined through focusing on "valuative significance" to "meaningful significance" in general, and through this, I believe that, in addition, in fact, we will be able to secure the conceptual apparatus to explain epistemologically – ontologically the mechanism of the historical relativity of the view of nature in general, and, consequently, of the "historical reification of nature", which were left to us as unresolved problems.—To put it in an abstractly schematized form, I hope in this context to expand – develop along the lines inherited from him the configuration of "the Marxian theory of reification".

This statement is an extreme abstraction – schematisation, and it hardly needs explaining in detail that I am one who plans to continue Marx's theory of reification across the concrete areas involved.

That in exposing – critiquing reification at the level of "the state of the existent", (as an actual problem the level of the "symbolic ready-to-hand"), a level described above, I am aiming at locating the configuration of the twofoldness of "*real* – *irreal*" (to the point relevant for us here, the "fourfold structure of relations" which includes the moment which inseparably supports the establishment of the "*irreal*" moment) which Marx revealed focusing on the world of the commodity, through a temporary "abstraction" "downwardly" into an ontologically – epistemologically "generalised" formula:—I think that I have been able to gain a general understanding of at least this schematic line of reasoning through my discussion above.—It is true, however, that as regards the path leading to this conceptualisation in my own surface level consciousness a separate line of reasoning internal to epistemology was the basis of my thinking, but I hope that there will be no objection if I restrict discussion here to the connection here to the line of argument inherited from Marx, which was rendered for-itself after the fact.

Perspicacious readers will have already, I fear, sensed along which lines I plan to treat reification of the "significant" (which includes so-called ideal "meaning" in general, together with transcendent "value" in general in the broad sense used in the philosophy of value).—I will not attempt to nullify from the very beginning the phenomenon of reification by labelling it mere illusion, rather, following Marx, I will first and foremost "confirm" the fact that it manifests in an immutable objective form, and that it not only controls people's cognitive consciousness, and that, in actuality, it controls their actions, to say nothing of their emotions and their intentions. If we limit our discussion to this context, significant states are sensed in consciousness by persons (the persons involved, and, in "scientific knowledge" internal to the system insofar as it shares a hypodigm with the persons involved) as a clear "object-ive objectivity", and, then, when we investigate the characteristics of being of these "significant states" they present a strange characteristic of being, where philosophers, at a loss for words, call them "*meta*-spatiotemporal" or "*irreal*" or "ideal (i.e. as in the manner of Plato's "ideas")" or "transcendent" etc. If we think of the *things* called "significant (meaning or value) states" as having an irrefutably objective existence, that they are a "strange existence" having characteristics of being different to usual real existence is undeniable. As Marx indicates in regard to economic "value", it can only be said that it is of a "supra-sensible", "supra-natural" objectivity. It can't in any way be "reduced" to being simply such things as a "subjective emotion" or a "subjective function of meaning" or a "subjective function of evaluation". This being the reason that philosophers of the ancient world and the mediaeval world positively asserted the various kinds of "significant states", clearly differing in characteristics of being to real existence, as being metaphysical existents, and the reason that they even went so far as to proclaim that these, indeed, were the actual true existents. Within the positivistic intellectual horizon of the modern period, however, metaphysical existence and the like have a poor reputation and the majority of thinkers attempt to forestall the matter by declaring that such substitutes do not, from the very beginning, exist at all. Nevertheless, unable to ignore the fact that, when considering the matter properly, *in thought* irreal – ideal significant states do indubitably exist, a considerable number of philosophers came to confirm the indubitable existence of ideal – irreal significant states, but even the majority of them attempt to avoid rash statements of a metaphysical kind by insisting that "significant states are not real existents, yet, having said that, they are also not a metaphysical existence, they are a third type of existence". These philosophers, however, have been unable to positively show where significant states are different in terms of characteristics of being compared to traditional metaphysical existence, and they have been unable to positively determine the existentiality of significant states. Upon reflection, what particularly stands out here is Marx's insight. Because he was able to reveal the secret of the reification of the significant state (or rather in his case, as an initial step, of "value" in economics), he was "content" for the moment, to also point out, indeed, in a form relating to the everyday thinking of persons, that they are "supra-sensible", "supra-natural", and "metaphysical". In reality, that "value"— which not only determines value evaluation consciousness for persons in the world of the commodity, but objectively rules the economic activity of persons and is the objective determining factor in the arrangement of economics in society and in the laws of economics—is something which indubitably exists has to be provisionally accepted. To see, however, "value", or to put it more generally that *thing* which is the "significant state", as existing independently and autonomously is a reificatory misapprehension; it is, precisely, a distorted reflection of given social relations (and is *not* the "subjective evaluation – projection of subjective emotion" which some thinkers regard it to be). It is something which has its grounds in the actuality which is these social relations, and it is certainly not a mere illusory conviction, but to see that which is supra-sensible – supra-natural value, that which is the significant, as being objectively autonomous is a reificatory error.—Marx exposes for us that the significant state, ideal from the standpoint of *für es*, is, *für uns*, a reificatory reflection of "the relations of people to nature and mutually between themselves". It is my intention to re-grasp not only value in terms of economics, which Marx took as his direct, main focus, but what, in the so-called philosophy of value, is called transcendent "value in general", and, consequently, also to re-grasp ideal "meaning in general", which takes linguistic – semiotic meaning as its archetype; to re-grasp these as reificatory products of the same type as that which Marx revealed, taking this upon myself as a direct expansion and continuation of Marx's theory of reification of value.

Needless to say, in extending the configuration of Marx's theory of reification, as seen in *Capital*, to the "significant state" in general, and, in addition and consequently, to "the ready-to-hand state" (and as a result, to the various

kinds of so-called "cultural properties"), it will be necessary to concretely spe-
cify what we are calling "social relations" in regard to each of the phenomena
of reification across the various levels and types.—Although it is, of course, not
my intention to proceed into the various discussions involved here and now, I
will next give a number of my thoughts as far as they concern the general proposal for the extending expansion.

Regarding the particular "something" which gives rise to "reification", I have
up until now stopped at making a simple statement to the effect that it is a type
of "relation", and we are now at the stage where it is time to take the configuration of that "relation" itself as our main focus. I believe that through this we
should be able to also make convenient reference to my proposal to expand and
continue Marx's theory of reification.

Readers may already have questioned the fact that in my discussion I have
used the expression, the state of fourfold relation of "given – cognized – knowing – cognizing" in regard to the state of "relation" which "changes" into a
"material thing". Even though "knowing" and "cognized" are each rendered twofold in this expression, it would be natural, indeed, if I have invited the criticism
that in the end isn't it the case that I remain within the schema, in the style of
modern philosophy, of "subjective – objective"? In fact, the fourfold state of
relation of "given – cognized – knowing – cognizing" I propose is a provisional
formula I deliberately chose in order to bring forth a connection point with this
schema representative of modern philosophy, and we certainly cannot leave
things as they are here. In fact, "cognized", "knowing" and "cognizing" which
appear in this model are all reflective nodes of the relation determination of
"for-others – for-itself", and the model itself is not closed within an internally
existing four term relation.

From another perspective, Marx, as we have seen repeatedly in the main text
of this book, whilst determining the essence of human beings as the totality of
social relations, determines society as being none other than the relations –
connections themselves between people, and what he calls social relations
can, if we express things as a model, be expressed by the phrase from *The German Ideology*, "the relations of human beings to nature and mutually between
themselves (*Verhältnis der Menschen zur Natur und zueinander*)". And, it surely
hardly needs noting again that it is none other than the "relations of production" which form the fundamental stratum – key structure of this "relations of
human beings to nature and mutually between themselves".—It is not because
I have the intention of stating a difference of opinion in regard to this model
but to make things easier when extending the reification of Marx's "social relations" into various phenomena that I bring several conceptual devices into the
model itself and attempt to concretise it. This attempt is also at the same time

an anticipation of a formularisation of the "for-others – for-itself" "intersubject-ive and to-the-given" state of relation, a rendering which renders the model of the aforementioned fourfold state of connection into a projecting form.

Schematically speaking, it seems to me that through adding in here the con-figuration of "role-theory"—that is to say, not that of the so-called American sociology style of such, but the type introduced by Karl Löwith in his critique and continuation of Feuerbach—into Marx's model of "to-nature and inter-human relations" we can complete the matter at hand.

I assert that even so-called cognition has to be located as a structural moment of practical relations-in-the-world, and proclaim that the mechanism which establishes intersubjective homogenization as the cognizing subjective and the intersubjective homogeneity of significant cognizeds has its ground-ing in the "for-others – for-itself" relation in a role-theory type of configuration, but this is probably not the appropriate time to go into these matters, matters which belong to an epistemological situation.

It is also not necessary, I think, to go on at length and in detail here and now about what kind of configuration a "role-theory type of configuration" is. It is necessary, I think, however, to state for the moment at least the point of reading the concepts of role-theory into what Marx calls "the relations of human beings towards nature and mutually between themselves".—The rela-tions Marx calls "towards nature and mutually between" is something which does not allow separation between human beings' "relations towards nature" and their "mutual relations", with both being mutually mediating – mutually penetrative – mutually determining; but for convenience of discussion, let us establish both moments separately as a topic for the time being.

Firstly "the relations of human beings towards nature"; this is not simply a cognitive "subject – object" relation, it is a *practical* relation which takes this cognitive relation as an intra-structural moment, with "nature" unfolding there in a form "carrying" a degree of valuative significance. Nature as it unfolds in the setting of our lives not only manifests to consciousness in a desire based – evaluative ... aesthetic – faith based value form, but confronts us in the form of "generative value", (not only an inducing of action as a positive or negat-ive goal, a signalling significance inducing a specific act, but such value in a broad sense including valuative significance at the level of bringing forth an attitude of interest in good or bad), "instrumental value", and also "limiting value" (all bindingness which controls forms of action, including both such which form positive, enabling conditions and those which form obstructing conditions for action"). As a concrete image, what I am talking about here is probably, I think, communicated most easily if we have in our minds relations toward nature in the situations of gathering – hunting – agricultural cultivation, but in conceptualising it it might be useful to have in mind the "stage" (in its broad sense, including, as well, scenes – backdrops – large props – small props etc) in the theatre. In our life-world, which can be likened to a world theatre (*Welt Theater*), divisions in nature not only appear before us as objects inducing an attitude of interest in human beings or action towards positives – negatives, they also become instrumental means for specific action, form the limitations making appropriate goal-oriented action possible or not possible, and also form the conditions aiding or obstructing anticipated action.—In *Capital*, Marx, due to the limitation of what is being discussed, undertakes his discussion with the accent on nature as the object of labour and the means of labour, but we will be permitted, I think, to bring our view to nature as object – means – condition in our practical involvement with it in general, and as a whole as the "stage"-like place of limitation in our practical involvement with it. "Relations towards nature" is a being-in nature as environment, in the sense of an involved connection with this nature as "stage".

What we are calling nature as stage, incidentally, is not the eternal, unchanging, self-unified natural nature. Although it is for the most part a fixed limitation in regard to an act on its occasion, it constantly changes through the activity of human beings. That nature as stage is an established given is a matter of it being so in regard to an act on its occasion, whilst *für uns* nature as stage is "historicised nature", and a product of the activity of human beings. Taking this moment into consideration, we would have to say that the "relations towards nature of human beings" are in addition "stage-reconstructing relations", and, in general, that they are "bound-by-limitations and reconstructing 'toward-stage' relations".

Further, in rendering for-itself the fact that nature as stage is "historicised nature" – "culturalised nature", we face the need to sublate the traditional distinction between the natural world and the world of human beings.—For example, that human flesh cannot become the object of eating, that a sacred tree cannot be used as firewood, ... and, in addition, that one cannot enter a Japanese tatami room with one's shoes on: these kinds of limitation are clearly a type of "stage" limitation. One type of theorist expounds that this is a limitation by human agency (*nomos*) and that such has to be clearly differentiated from natural (*physis*) limitations. We too, in a certain type of context, naturally distinguish between nature and human act. But whilst when making the distinction between natural limitations and artificial limitations in the manner of these theorists a conceptual differentiation at the level of theory is possible, as an actual problem "natural limitations" in the everyday lives of human beings are to a greater or lesser extent "permeated" with "artificial limitations" and it has to be said that such a thing as *pure* natural limitations *in actuality* hardly exist at all. In addition, it is usual that the people involved do not consciously distinguish between natural limitations and artificial limitations in everyday life. Even if on intellectual reflection something is an artificial limitation, in the everyday consciousness of the persons involved it is reified into the appearance of a "natural limitation". (The theorists will say perhaps that such things as not being able to enter a Japanese tatami room with one's shoes on, or not being able to be in the streets naked, that these are simply mental limitations. However, as a test one should have a try at actually doing these things. One's legs and arms are bound to come to a standstill and be paralysed, just as if they were physically constrained. These things are it seems built in to operations of cerebral physiology (subconscious physiological operations) through deep hypnosis-like workings i.e. through what condition response theory calls "conditioning", and as a result, and to that extent, they are probably acts which are physiological = "natural" limitations). Though normative – systemic "artificial limitations", when they are reified environmentally they are different from simple rule – code limitations, and they are, therefore, a group of conditions for stage-like limitations.

Given this, we should *begreifen*[9] the moment of "the relations towards nature of human beings" as towards "stage-"like relations involved with an historically reified nature, as a "bound-by-limitations and reconstructing" being-in.

Next is the moment of "the mutual relations between human beings", and that in the life-world this is more than simply a cognitive relation, and that, what's more, in reality it ought not to exist as a pure "person – person" relation separated off from towards-"nature" relations; these matters hardly need mentioning before we begin. Persons who appear on the life-world stage = world-theatre stage, in the stage-place of each particular occasion, mutually "carry" value, and have the "action" (action in a broad sense which includes attitude – facial expression – utterance) of the "self" triggered (*auslösen*) through the manifestation of "the other" in the "generative value" form of appearance – attitude – facial expression – utterance etc. When expressing its fundamental configuration as a formula, the mutual relations of persons can be said to exist in this kind of way.

I focus on this way of existing of the mutual relations, and, first and foremost, in cases where it can be recognised (at least *für uns*) as pattern action "expected" by the involved other or an observing third person, I include action put into operation in response to the manifesting of the generative value of an "other" within the concept of "role-playing" towards the involved other.

---

9   〚Tr. *begreifen* = understand; grasp〛.

Determining things further back, I call, then, "response-performing of action expected by an other – response-performing of action towards the involved other who is manifesting (*vorkommen*) in a triggered way (*auslösen*)—", this praxis in intersubjectively co-linked relationality, (at least *für uns*, this generally is code-following), "role action".

In doing so, I wish note to be taken of the fact that in contrast to some sociologists who determine role based on status or position I determine the concept of "role" in regard to the direct – basic self-other relation. That which we call "status" and "position" are things which come into existence for the first time through the configuration of role action being reified and its undergoing a kind of "systematisation", and making these pre-existent to "role" has to be called a reifying misconception confirming the "reified" state of consciousness of those involved.—Although, in the everyday consciousness of those involved, this reified inversion is absolutely real, and it is on the basis of the existence of "status" or "position" that people fulfil the expectation of or carry out appropriate action. With this in mind, I specifically call role performance at the level corresponding to the pre-existence of status or position "character-role" taking, and when necessary I distinguish in terms of level "character-role" from "role" in general.

On reflection, rather than Marx, it is in the case of primarily Engels that "the relations towards nature and mutually between human beings" are grasped as relations of "the division of labour", and even class relations are treated as a particular existing form of relations of the division of labour. This is an excellent deployment, placing its focus on the activity of "production", and I certainly have no intention of announcing any difference of opinion here. My aim is only, having for the moment moved "downwardly" from "the division of labour", to move "upwardly" from a more abstract determination, and through this, having for the moment brought together under, by dint of its being abstract, a universal formula, such things as married-couple, parent-child, and sibling relations, and, also, such things as human relations in situations which appear as if they are *seemingly* isolated from productive activity, I hope to begin the task of determining through the process of "upward" movement "type-difference" distinctions. Moving "downward" for the moment to the co-linked self-other relation of "role" theory is not something which is likely to be inconsistent with the intent of the deployment of the theory of "the division of labour" of Marx and Engels.—Incidentally, Marx in the Preface to *Capital* expresses the purport to treat the subjects involved in economic activity as "the personifications of economic categories", and this can be said to be, I think, if we determine it in the manner I am using, a treating of the subjects involved as "*character-role existents*".

222 EPILOGUE

I have in the above provided an outline of the proposal to grasp "relations" as the entities which are "reified", that is to say, Marx's "towards nature and between human beings" relations, in the form "co-linked role relations being-in the stage-world", but this is simply a shorthand statement of my view within the limited space of the "Epilogue" to this book, and a different form of exposition would be required in order to provide a full exposition of what I am calling the "role theory configuration". Now, however, I will forego using up any more pages regarding the "role theory configuration" itself, and, with scant regard for rough and ready haste, we are now at the stage of moving the topic to in what direction, with the "role theory configuration" as the base, I intend to aim at laying bare phenomena of reification.

Though stating it in the one word of "reification", reification in the "cognitive" dimension and reification in the "practical" dimension need to be distinguished.—Naturally, a distinction between "cognitive" and "practical" is not an absolute distinction. I don't intend here to repeat the obvious fact that "cognition" is a type of "practice", yet the truth is what we are calling "cognitive dimension reification" is strictly speaking not something which is self-contained simply in a situation of cognition but is only a structurally internal moment or a register in projection of "practical dimension reification". (In addition, if the cognitive process is left out, even if physical change is able to occur "reification" is not possible, and so even reification in the dimension of practice is not possible as completely independent of the cognitive process). Yet even so, if we change the arrangement of the cognizing moment in the cognitive dimension (even if for this alteration to happen a change in the arrangement in the dimension of practice is a necessary condition), "cognizing reification" of the type which recognises "resolution" as being provisionally possible in this reification itself, and "reification of the given" in which resolution is impossible by arrangement change in the cognitive dimension alone, reification one might say of a kind which takes "there-appropriate limitations"[10] (see 『存在と意味』第一巻 [Being and Meaning Volume I] p. 366) through the relation-form given as its primary factor, that is to say, reification of the type in which actual change through praxis reaches as far as the "lowest level" of the "given", can be distinguished relative to each other, and in actuality must be distinguished. The distinguishing between "nature in the form disclosed to the physicist and the chemist" (to speak more generally, objects in the form disclosed to "scientific" reflection even if it is the non-scientist, ordinary person), propounded by Marx

10   〚Tr. It is unclear whether the expression translated as "there-appropriate limitations" (向妥当の制約) is a phrase coined by Hiromatsu or whether it is a borrowing from elsewhere. There is a possibility, for example, that it may be a borrowing from Lask or Lotze〛.

and Engels in the context of their critique of Feuerbach, and "nature in the form clear to the naked eye", considered as a quasi-level of the argument being put forward here at the moment, is now no longer an absolute distinction, but can only have a relative meaning. However, acknowledging this, if we venture to imagine things metaphorically, despite describing them both in the same way as "historical reification of nature", that involved with the former can be called "reification of the cognized" in the "cognitive" dimension, whilst that involved with the latter can be called "reification of the given" in the "practical" dimension. (However, that even though we call it a reification state in the "cognitive" dimension, it is certainly not simply a mental image located "inside the subject" but as a fact is none other than a so-called "objective existent" opening strictly on the "outside" of human beings, that it is not simply a cognized but is a "given – cognized" formation, that the sending of space rockets into flight or the conducting of physical or chemical experiments is *in regard to* "nature" in the form of a "cognitive object-form"; these facts always need to be borne in mind).

So, if, in the situation of pointing out reification in the "cognitive" dimension, we lay bare the circumstance that the fourfold state of connection of "given – cognized – knowing – cognizing" appears in reified object-form in the consciousness involved we have provisionally completed our task. (Of course, this fourfold state of connection is not something which is internally self-completing but is, indeed, none other than a projected form in a "role theory composition", in an "intersubjective co-operation connection state to-the-other – to-the-self being-in the stage-world", but for the moment it isn't necessary to retrace things in detail back to that point). Reification as I examined it in 『存在と意味』第一巻 〚*Being and Meaning Volume I*〛 is contained for the moment in this dimension.—In exposing reification in the "practical" dimension, however, which is indeed that which 『存在と意味』第二巻 〚*Being and Meaning Volume II*〛 takes as its topic, we must rely directly on the "role theory composition".

On reflection, even though in Marx's case reification in the "practical" dimension was a matter of investigation, for the moment he remained within the area dealing thematically with reification of the sort seen in reification in commodity value, reification in economic laws, reification in the process of history. To that extent, when Marx focuses on the issue of the state of being of the practice of human beings he discusses such in regard to the determining state such as "the personification of the categories of economics", or "the division of labour" and "class", or when he considers things generally he discusses things at the sub level of "the activity of individuals and its combined power", and in doing so he was able to meet the requirements of the discussion at hand.

For myself, however, I am aiming at bringing into focus, based on a continuing expansion of the work of Marx, reification of "systems", reification of "norms", reification of "power", and, consequently, reification of "technology", "art", "religion" etc.—Moreover, in doing so, in referring to *systems* it is not only systems in the narrow sense of the arrangement of position – status – social status, nor is it only in the dimensions of family – society – nation, but systems in the broadest sense encompassing what Durkheim calls institutions i.e. "language" etc. that I have in mind. In addition, in referring to *norms*, I have in mind all regulative significant states, from customs and cultural practices through morals to the law etc.—That is to say, it is my intention to investigate the reification of all economic – social – political – cultural – historical forms (*Gebilde*) from a unifying standpoint, a unifying principle, a unifying method. Because of this intention, for me, the introduction of a "role theory configuration" becomes an indispensable strategic requirement.

Here and now I will omit going into discussion of how each type of "reification in the dimension of practice" can be explicated focusing on role theory configuration, but I'm sure that the discerning reader will understand the fact that "reification in the dimension of practice" can be approached from the perspective of the reification of the various value forms of the stage-given, from the systemic reification of role relations, from the normative reification of codes in role action, from the power reification of sanctions which accompany the execution of role action, from the historical reification of the diachronic dynamic of the organisation of roles ..., etc. etc.; that it can be approached from the perspective of the reification of the structural – functional factors of role theory configuration.

In addition, in continuing the methodological composition of the Marxian theory of reification, and his dialectic, I am one who places particular importance on the configuration of *für es* and *für uns*, and I wish to take the path of examining matters in the form of elucidating disjunction in the places in Marx where the *für es* dimension appears to have the dichotomous nature of "the actual consciousness of those involved" and "'scientific knowledge' internal to the system sharing in common the perspective of those involved" (formulas from the standpoint of preceding theory which remain within the horizon of paradigms internal to the system, or, the reflective self-formularisation which *can be expected* in those involved themselves).

Embarrassed though I am by the weak points I have made, especially my speculations in the latter half of this epilogue, I believe that provisionally through the above I have been able to sketch the "schema of the theory of reification" I hold to, showing under what kind of a deployment of Marx's theory of reification and in what kind of direction I am aiming at expanding it, and so I would like to bring my present writing to a close.

Index

www.ingramcontent.com/pod-product-compliance
Lightning Source LLC
Chambersburg PA
CBHW070922030426

42336CB00014BA/2504